COLD WAR AT SEA

COLD WAR AT SEA

*High-Seas Confrontation
between the United States
and the Soviet Union*

DAVID F. WINKLER

Naval Institute Press

Annapolis, Maryland

Naval Institute Press
291 Wood Road
Annapolis, MD 21402
© 2000 by David F. Winkler

Library of Congress Cataloging-in-Publication Data
Winkler, David F. (David Frank), 1958-
    Cold war at sea : high seas confrontation between the United States and the Soviet Union/ David F. Winkler.
        p. cm.
    Includes bibliographical references and index.
    ISBN 1-55750-955-7 (alk. paper)
    1. United States. Navy—History—20th century. 2. Soviet Union. Voenno-Morskoæ Flot—History. 3. United States. Navy—Operations other than war. 4. Soviet Union. Voenno-Morskoæ Flot—Operations other than war. 5. Cold War. 6. Collisions at sea—Prevention. I. Title
VA58.4. W55 2000
359'.00973'09045—dc21   99-052849

Printed in the United States of America on acid-free paper ∞
00 01 02 03 04 05 06 07   9 8 7 6 5 4 3 2
First printing

Contents

Acknowledgments

The impetus for this came in November 1984 in the Sea of Japan. I was the officer in charge of a military detachment assigned to provide communications support to the Military Sealift Command oiler USNS *Navasota*. In those waters off Siberia, the *Navasota* participated in a fleet exercise involving three carrier battle groups. Naturally, our presence provoked a Soviet response, yet I was impressed by how the two sides interacted. With the Incidents at Sea Agreement (INCSEA) communications mechanism in place, I noted that the two sides acted with great professionalism and avoided the potential for danger. I remember wondering to myself how the INCSEA regime came into place. As I embarked to answer that question, many assisted in my research or provided inspiration.

As a student at Washington University in St. Louis from January 1988 to May 1991, I conducted my initial research on the subject. Dr. James W. Davis served as my advisor and helped refine a directed research project that explored the negotiation of the INCSEA accord. Sean Lynn-Jones of Harvard University's Center for Science and International Affairs provided background materials he had used for an INCSEA article published in 1985 in *International Security*. Lynn-Jones's assistance was important, as I received *no* support from the Office of the Chief of Naval Operations (OP 616). My research was not welcomed because the Navy had no interest in publicizing the accord. Fortunately, I received assistance from retired Rear Adm. Ronald J. Kurth, a veteran INCSEA delegation member, and from Bernard Cavalcante of the Naval Historical Center, who provided some declassified documents from the 1970s.

Upon graduating from Washington University in May 1991 with a master's degree in international affairs, I received my first shipment of documents I had requested from the State Department through the Freedom of Information Act (FOIA). As the shipments kept arriving, I realized I had the core materials for a dissertation covering more than the negotiation of an accord. Should I pursue a doctorate? Professor Emeritus J. H. Hexter of Washington University urged me to further my education. Dr. Hexter was one of the most inspirational men I have had the privilege to meet, and I still mourn his passing in December 1996.

As to where to further my education, Capt. Jim Bryant made me an offer I couldn't refuse. As the new OP 616 on the Navy staff, Captain Bryant came across my directed research project and invited me to come to Washington to explore how INCSEA could apply to the Middle East peace process. Together we drafted a presentation that was given by Vice Adm. Leighton Smith to visiting Arab and Israeli delegations on 12 May 1992. After the success of the presentation, Captain Bryant asked if I could work for him as a naval reservist. Assured of part-time income, I accepted an offer to study at American University.

Relocated to Washington, I began to refine a rough dissertation draft I had written in St. Louis. Norman Polmar persuaded me to focus on incidents on and over the high seas as documents discussing submarine operations would not be available for decades. Dr. Charles McLoughlin and Dr. Michael Kazin helped me polish seminar papers that formed the basis for two chapters. At the Pentagon, Captain Bryant introduced me to numerous individuals interested in the topic. Helpful contacts included Dr. Stan Weeks, Science Applications International Corporation; Dr. Charles Meconis, Institute for Global Security Studies; Dr. James Tritten, Naval Doctrine Command; Michael Krepon, Henry Stimson Center; Rear Adm. Robert P. Hilton Sr., Institute for Defense Analysis; Comdr. Howard Sidman, Department of State; George Fedoroff, National Maritime Intelligence Center; Comdr. Sam Tangredi, Office of the Secretary of the Navy; Lauren Van Metre, Office of the Secretary of Defense; Rear Adm. William H. Wright IV, who served on the Navy staff and in the Office of the Secretary of Defense; and Lt. Comdr. David N. Griffiths, formerly of the Canadian Maritime Command. With the

1992 Navy reorganization, OP 616 became N312Q. Other officers within N312Q who reviewed various INCSEA articles and point papers I wrote included Jim Bryant's successors: James Voter and Louis Hughes, as well as Capt. Jon Barker, Capt. Louis Boink, Capt. Larry Brennan, Comdr. Richard Massey, Lt. Comdr. Tim Meier, Lt. Comdr. Eric Anderson, Lt. Comdr. Wayne Noble, Lt. Comdr. Brian Eidson, and Nancy Shimp.

Naval Reserve pay can stretch only so far in the Washington, D.C. region. I want to thank the U.S. Air Force Historical Research Agency at Maxwell Air Force Base, Alabama, for a research grant and the Naval Historical Center for awarding me their 1995 Rear Adm. John D. Hayes Fellowship. At the Naval Historical Center, Senior Historian Dr. Edward J. Marolda took a personal interest in my research, as did Richard Russell of the Contemporary History Branch. Within the Operational Archives Branch, the aforementioned Bernard Cavalcante, Kathy Lloyd, and Judy Short helped identify relevant record groups. Legalman Chief Timothy Ayoub had the unenviable task of declassifying hundreds of documents, and I will be always appreciative.

I am in debt to Senator John W. Warner who made his personal papers available and provided photographs of the 1972 negotiations. He was one of dozens of individuals whom I interviewed and corresponded with on *Cold War at Sea*. Those individuals are listed in the bibliography and I thank all again for spending time with me.

Paul Stillwell at the U.S. Naval Institute alerted me to relevant interviews in his oral history collection. I also appreciate his assistance with the publication of my article, "When Russia Invaded Disneyland," in the U.S. Naval Institute *Proceedings*.

Mark Flanigan, a retired naval intelligence officer, provided me an artifact in the form of one of many ties given to the Russians in 1972 by Macy's. More significantly, he proofread the manuscript and caught my misspellings of Russian ship names. Fellow graduate students Kurt Hanson and Meredith Hindley also reviewed portions of the text and contributed invaluable recommendations. I also thank my brother Thomas for proofreading and retyping a section of this work.

Finally, I thank my dissertation panel of Dr. Robert L. Beisner, Dr. Anna K. Nelson, and Dr. David A. Rosenberg for their time, consideration, comments, and constructive suggestions.

« **1** »

PLAYING WITH
THE BEAR

In the early summer of 1972, a Soviet submarine squadron entered the Mediterranean Sea to relieve a squadron that had been on patrol for several months. As the Soviet squadron, composed of a Juliett and seven Foxtrot-class submarines, cruised on the surface in a column, they were escorted by a multinational force of American, French, and British destroyers and frigates, with each allied warship assigned to track a designated sub. From his flagship, Rear Adm. (Select) Robert P. Hilton Sr. kept an eye on the lead Juliett-class boat. At 2200 all eight submarines "went sinker." However, throughout the night, the allied warships maintained sonar contact, or at least thought they did. In the morning the Soviet submarines resurfaced. Hilton felt gleeful and transmitted a sitrep (situation report) to Commander, Sixth Fleet, that concluded with the statement: "HAPPINESS IS GOING TO BED WITH JULIETT AND WAKING UP IN THE MORNING TO FIND SHE'S STILL THERE." He soon regretted having written that. Upon closer inspection of the Juliett, he noticed that there were different markings as well as dents that had not been there the previous day. The other escorts also realized that they were now following different prey. Hilton's force was tailing the departing Soviet submarine squadron! The eight relieving submarines were now on patrol in the Mediterranean undetected. Hilton had his come-uppance.[1]

On deployment in the Mediterranean, Hilton performed several functions within the Navy command hierarchy. As DESRON (Destroyer

Squadron) FOURTEEN commander, he had administrative command over many of the American frigates and destroyers that were deployed to the Mediterranean. As an administrative commander, Hilton kept track of the condition of his ships and crews, and forwarded routine matters up his chain of command back in the States. In contrast, as Commander, Antisubmarine Forces Sixth Fleet (COMASWFORSIXTHFLT), Hilton had operational command of forces dedicated to tracking Soviet submarine activities in the region. Depending on the mission, Hilton reported to Commander, Task Force Sixty-Seven (CTF-67), Rear Adm. Pierre N. Charbonnet, and Commander, Task Force Sixty (CTF-60), Rear Adm. Donald D. Engen, both of whom in turn reported to Commander, Sixth Fleet, Vice Adm. Gerald "Jerry" E. Miller. Due to his various responsibilities and assigned missions, Hilton found the tempo of his deployment fast-paced, especially during March and April of 1972, when he took two of his ships down to the Gulf of Hammamet anchorage off Tunisia to conduct "Bystander Ops," an ongoing series of surveillance missions of Soviet naval activities by Sixth Fleet ships.[2]

Dispatched from Naples early on 26 March, the guided-missile destroyer uss *William V. Pratt* and the frigate uss *W. S. Sims* headed south. Hilton, embarked on board the *Sims,* issued specific instructions to his two ship commanders to avoid harassment of the Soviets. The two warships were to approach no closer than 2,000 yards to the surfaced Foxtrot and no closer than 1,000 yards if it went sinker. Hilton expected that Soviet surface ships might attempt shouldering tactics to block the American surveillance and that good seamanship would be required. In the event the Soviets were to conduct an antisubmarine warfare (ASW) exercise, the Americans were to avoid mixing it up with Soviet surface units. Finally, Hilton emphasized that if prudence resulted in a lost sub contact, "SO BE IT. OUR JOB IS TO LOCATE AND TRAIL THE FOXTROT — NOT TO HARASS SOVIETS OR CREATE AN INCIDENT AT SEA — AND TO GAIN MAX INTELL. YOUR PROFESSIONAL COMPETENCE AND JUDGEMENT WILL BE OUR GREATEST ASSETS."[3]

Upon arrival at the Gulf of Hammamet early on 27 March, the *Sims* deployed to the east of the Soviets and began a north-south racetrack patrol to block any Soviet movements out of the gulf. A P-3 Orion patrol plane had earlier identified three Soviet ships present as an Ugra-class sub tender (AS 938), a Kotlin-class destroyer (DD 388), and a Chilikin-class oiler. From his perch on the bridge wing of the *Sims,* Hilton observed the Soviets at morning muster in blue uniforms on AS 938 and white uniforms on DD 388, leading him to report, "SOVIETS HAVE THEIR OWN PROBLEMS WITH STANDARD-IZATION."[4] Meanwhile the *Pratt* closed in and slowly circled the Soviet formation and noted the presence of the Soviet Foxtrot. After completing the maneuver, *Pratt* joined with the *Sims* on the north-south patrol east of the Soviet formation.[5]

For the next three and a half days, the Americans observed a variety of Soviet Navy activities: refueling, painting and maintenance, restocking of supplies, inspections, gunnery drills, clothes washing, and recreational activities such as swimming. The Soviet oiler departed on the first day. American lookouts paid close attention to the Foxtrot. Observing the sub's poor appearance, the Americans dubbed her "Old Rust Bucket." Occasionally, ships of the two navies exchanged pleasantries via flashing light.[6] At 1335 on the third day, the Foxtrot broke the tranquil pattern and departed on an easterly heading, submerging to periscope depth. Within minutes both American ships were in pursuit, and soon the submarine was under sonar surveillance. At 1407 the Foxtrot surfaced and reversed course to return to the anchorage. In his sixteenth sitrep, Hilton observed, "CREW AT QUARTERS FOXTROT WITH OFFICER CONDUCTING APPARENT LECTURE ENDING WITH ADMINISTRATION OF CORPORAL PUNISHMENT TO SEVERAL CREWMEMBERS IN A WAY OF VICIOUS SLAPS AND KICKS. INDICATIONS THAT ADM GORSHKOV HAS NOT INSTITUTED G-GRAM PROGRAM FOR SOVIET NAVY," a reference to American Chief of Naval Operations Adm. Elmo R. Zumwalt's Z-gram program. Hilton went on: "MORALE ON U.S. SHIPS IMPROVED MARKEDLY WHILE VIEWING SOVIETS ROCKS AND SHOALS IN ACTION. ESTIMATE FOXTROT BILGED HIS ORI [Operational Readiness Inspection]."[7]

Finally, at midday on 30 March the Soviet submarine, sub tender, and destroyer proceeded slowly in a column on an easterly heading with the Foxtrot in the lead. With the two American ships assuming positions on the Foxtrot's beams, the joint formation continued eastward into the night.[8] Nothing dramatic occurred during the following day as the formation plodded on a course of 102 degrees true at eleven knots. During the morning the Kotlin occasionally billowed black smoke from her stacks and slowed to correct the propulsion problem.[9]

That evening, the Foxtrot closed to 1,000 yards of the sub tender and then dove at 1925. Although the Soviet diesel boat disappeared from the surface, she remained quite "visible" to the sonarmen on both the *Pratt* and the *Sims*. To throw off the trackers, the Kotlin charged at the American ships, cutting fifty yards ahead of the *Sims* and broadcasting in Russian, "BE CAREFUL, VERY DANGEROUS BUSINESS."[10] The Kotlin finally backed away from the *Sims* after Hilton grabbed a microphone and warned the Kotlin in Russian that she was too close and conducting dangerous maneuvers.[11] Beneath the surface, "Old Rust Bucket" desperately attempted to shake off her pursuers by zig-zagging, increasing speed and stopping, making tight turns, reversing course, running under the Soviet surface ships, running under knuckles left by the Soviet surface ships, and putting noise in the water.[12] The two American warships maintained contact and were soon joined in the hunt by a P-3 Orion patrol plane with the call sign Argentina 30. In his thirtieth situation report Hilton wrote:

> MAINTAINING CONTACT AS BEFORE WITH FULLY EVASIVE FOXTROT, AGGRESSIVE KOTLIN AND LARGE BLOCKING BACK OTHERWISE KNOWN AS 938. ARGENTINA 30 CONDUCTING MADVECS WITH ONE CONFIRMATION AT 2130Z. CONTACT WENT UNDER AS AT 2138Z. AS AND CONTACT BOTH WEAVING. CONTACT BROKE TO SOUTH CUS 180, SPD 10. PRATT NAILED HIM AT 2147Z, RANGE 4250 YDS. SIMS REGAINED CONTACT AT 2150Z, RANGE 5000 YDS. KOTLIN CLOSING FROM STBD QTR SIMS WITH CONTACT ON PORT BOW. CONTACT CUS 180T SPEED 05. MY 312200Z POSIT 34-57N9, 17-15.5E9.[13]

After midnight the Foxtrot surfaced and resumed on an easterly heading, and by daybreak the Soviet ships were again proceeding in a column. After observing the morning personnel inspection on the Kotlin, Hilton flashed to the Soviet destroyer, "GOOD MORNING." The Kotlin responded, "GOOD MORNING. WHERE ARE YOU GOING?" Hilton answered, "WE ARE GOING WITH YOU. WHERE ARE YOU GOING?" The Kotlin replied, "WE ARE GOING HOME."[14] After midday Hilton received a message from his boss, Rear Admiral Charbonnet, complimenting Hilton for the previous night's work. In addition, Charbonnet warned that recently the Soviets had failed to shake a Foxtrot loose and subsequently they had mustered a sizable surface force to deal with the pursuing Americans.[15]

Charbonnet's warning proved correct, as throughout the evening more Soviet warships joined up. At 0420, early on Easter morning, this new larger

Soviet formation began heading westward. With the sub tender, Foxtrot, and Kotlin again forming a column, the *Sims* found herself being shouldered by two Kashin escorts with a Petya II and other Kashins chasing after the *Pratt*.[16] In sitrep 39 Hilton wrote:

> SHOULDERED AS BEFORE. KASHIN 184 AND 182 UNSUCCESSFULLY ATTEMPTING KEEP SIMS AWAY FROM FOXTROT. KOTLIN 388, KASHIN 529 AND PETYA 883 UN-SUCCESSFULLY ATTEMPTING BLOCK PRATT. KASHINS FLYING "TURNING TO PORT," "TURNING TO STBD" AND "MANEUVERING WITH DIFFICULTY" SIMULTANEOUSLY. BELIEVE KASHIN 182 SUFFERED ENG CASUALTY AFTER PLANT WHEN TRYING TO MATCH SIMS GOING FROM FLANK TO STOP. KASHINS REGULARLY MANEUVERING WITHIN 100 FEET OF SIMS WITH PETYA HAVING CLOSED PRATT TO 20 FEET. AS AO AND FOXTROT CUS 180/SP8 SINCE 0550Z. ARGENTINA 30 ON STA UNDER PRATT CONTROL. MY 0600Z POSIT 33-35N4 19-49E3. SOVIETS MUST REALLY WANT TO SPRING THIS FOXTROT TO DEVOTE THREE KASHINS, ONE KOTLIN AND ONE PETYA. SONAR CONDITIONS COMMENCING TO IMPROVE GIVING SIMS INCREASINGLY LONG RANGE. CURRENTLY HOLDING CONTACT ON SURFACED FOXTROT AT 4500–5500 YDS.[17]

At 0813, the Foxtrot submerged and an overhead P-3 Orion swooped in and dropped smoke flares marking the Foxtrot's entry point. Despite the continued shouldering, sonarmen on both American ships reported themselves "hot" on the Foxtrot. To counter Soviet attempts to divert his ships away from the Foxtrot, Hilton set up a pick play. While *Pratt* slowed, *Sims* swung around, accelerated to twenty-five knots, and charged the *Pratt* nearly head on, forcing the escorting Soviet ships abeam of the *Sims* and *Pratt* into head-on-collision situations. The Kashins dogging *Sims* broke off as they could see their comrades coming at them. To avoid hitting the Kashin 529, the skipper of the Kotlin escorting the *Pratt* ordered back full, and the Russian destroyer went dead in the water, with thick smoke billowing out of her stacks. The Soviets' drastic evasive maneuvers freed the two American ships to pursue the prey now hiding near the sub tender. Meanwhile, to ward off the circling P-3 Orion, the Soviets on the sub tender fired flares into the sky.[18]

Throughout the morning, the intensive maneuvering continued. Repeatedly, using pick and double-pick plays, *Sims* and *Pratt* broke free to prosecute the Foxtrot contact. When Soviet shouldering tactics succeeded in diverting the American surface ships, the P-3 Orion maintained contact with the submarine. Both sides attempted to communicate their intentions by using flaghoist signals. At one point, as Kashin 184 pulled alongside the *Sims*, Hilton grabbed the microphone for the 6MC and wished the Soviets a happy Easter and complimented the Soviet captain on the appearance of his ship. The Soviet captain waved and attempted to respond using a bullhorn.[19] After noontime, the two American warships had the Foxtrot under full sonar surveillance as sea conditions were perfect for underwater acoustics. Somewhat frustrated, the Soviet escorts acted less aggressively during the afternoon hours.[20] At 0558 the next morning, the Foxtrot dove, apparently to serve as a target for an ASW exercise. On the surface, Soviet warships began maneuvering in search patterns in an effort to locate their undersea comrade. Throughout the morning below the surface, the Foxtrot took evasive actions to thwart her comrades' tracking efforts. The Foxtrot's maneuvers seemed to succeed, as by midday the four Soviet surface ships involved in the exercise appeared to have gone cold. In the meantime, the two American ships stayed hot. Fitted with superior sonar arrays, the *Sims* and the *Pratt* had no difficulty following the movements of the Foxtrot while staying clear to allow the Soviet surface ships to conduct their training. The Foxtrot resurfaced at 1013. A few hours later, the Kashins departed the area, leaving the sub tender, Kotlin, and Foxtrot alone with the Americans.[21]

With numbers again evened out, Hilton's ships, along with supporting ASW aircraft, maintained contact with the Soviet sub for the next three days despite a series of dives and evasive maneuvers. On the *Sims*, Hilton reviewed videotapes of some of the dramatic encounters of Easter Sunday, which had been shot from the signal bridge, noting the outstanding quality of the footage in one of his sitreps.

On the Sixth Fleet flagship, USS *Springfield,* at Gaeta, Italy, Vice Admiral Miller closely followed Hilton's sitreps. The existence of the videotape especially caught Miller's attention. The Sixth Fleet commander ordered the *Pratt* and the *Sims* up to Gaeta and invited Hilton and the two ship skippers for lunch that following Friday.[22]

At noon Friday, Hilton, along with *Pratt* and *Sims* skippers Jack Beck and Gerry Flynn, entered the Flag Mess aboard *Springfield.* After discussing the events of the past few days over lunch with the Sixth Fleet commander, the men viewed and talked about the videotape. Impressed with what he heard and what he saw, Miller arranged for Hilton to travel to London to make a presentation to Adm. William F. Bringle, Commander in Chief, U.S. Naval Forces Europe (CINCUSNAVEUR).[23] In London Admiral Bringle watched the tapes for seventy-five minutes during a ninety-minute session and peppered Hilton with questions about the various maneuvers. To Bringle the action depicted in the tapes was substantial enough to warrant presentation to Admiral Zumwalt and the new Secretary of the Navy, John W. Warner.[24]

Hilton now found himself making a trans-Atlantic journey. His arrival in Washington would precede by a week a delegation of Soviets who were due to meet with Warner to continue negotiations on preventing incidents at sea between the two navies. Hilton's presentations reaffirmed positions that the Americans held versus the Soviets over the contentious issue of establishing fixed-distance zones around ships of the two navies. Eventually, the impasse would be worked out in accordance with the American viewpoint that such an arrangement would be unworkable.

On 25 May 1972 Secretary of the Navy Warner and Admiral of the Fleet of the U.S.S.R. Sergei G. Gorshkov signed an agreement designed to modify the aggressive behaviors of both navies. The "Agreement between the Government of the United States of America and the Government of the Union of Soviet Socialist Republics on the Prevention of Incidents On and Over the High Seas" (INCSEA) became a reality after a series of increasingly dangerous incidents between Soviet and American ships and aircraft, as portrayed by Hilton's tapes, led to concern within both governments that a "chicken of the sea" game might well escalate into actual combat.

As Hilton's experience illustrated, confrontations between the two navies on and over the high seas during the late 1960s and early 1970s had reached a point requiring discussions and bilateral negotiations. Such intense naval interactions were a relatively recent phenomenon associated with the growth of Soviet sea power. But even in the immediate post–World War II era, when Soviet sea power was still weak, there had been confrontations between the two militaries. With an American strategy of containment, most military contacts were confined to the skies along the Soviet periphery. From 1945 through 1960, a series of air duels took place, costing more than 100 American and Soviet aviators their lives. These duels, and how the two respective governments reacted to them, provide the contextual background for a much more complex Cold War at sea.

« **2** »

CONFRONTATION
ALONG THE
PERIPHERY

The contacts in the Mediterranean Sea between American and Soviet maritime forces described in chapter 1 represent just a sampling of many such encounters that had occurred at that time. The mission of Captain Hilton's destroyers entailed locating and tracking surface warships and submarines of the Soviet Mediterranean fleet. Conversely, the Soviet naval ships had a mission of locating and tracking the carrier battle groups of the U.S. Sixth Fleet. By the late 1960s, and continuing through the end of the Cold War, the locating and tracking game had become an essential mission for both navies and naval alliances.

In contrast, during the first decade after the end of World War II, the U.S. Navy maintained maritime supremacy, steaming unchallenged over the high seas. American naval leaders hardly viewed their Soviet counterparts as a threat. In presentations to the president and Congress, Vice Adm. Forrest P. Sherman noted that the 700 to 800 ships the Soviet Navy possessed were "of low combat value except for submarines and motor torpedo boats."[1] In reality, the U.S. Navy's greatest challenge in the immediate postwar period came not from the Soviet Navy, but from proponents of air power who were questioning the need for a traditional navy.

Still, during the late 1940s, the U.S. Navy developed a maritime strategy to support Joint Staff planning for a confrontation with the Soviet Union. This maritime strategy emphasized a balanced blue-water navy that was capable of conducting traditional conventional missions in areas of the globe far from the United States. While the U.S. Navy maintained a presence in the western Pacific, there was a significant shift of resources toward the oceans and seas surrounding Europe. For example, during this period the U.S. Navy established a permanent presence in the Mediterranean Sea.

As he attempted to cut defense spending in the late 1940s, President Truman wavered in his commitment to support the naval forces necessary to sustain a forward deployment strategy. For a while, proponents of strategic air power held sway and the Navy suffered severe budget cuts, including the cancellation of the aircraft carrier *United States*. With the coming of the Korean War, the Navy reasserted its traditional missions, providing critical logistical, close air, naval gunfire, and amphibious sea-lift support to United Nations (UN) forces. Still, throughout the rest of the 1950s, the maritime strategy that had been developed in the late 1940s and that centered on a balanced fleet faded as the Navy attempted to share a piece of the strategic nuclear-attack mission emphasized in Pres. Dwight D. Eisenhower's "New Look." Supercarriers were built capable of launching nuclear-bomb–laden aircraft against the Soviet periphery. More significantly, the Navy undertook a massive research and development effort to develop submarines that could launch nuclear-tipped ballistic missiles. Meanwhile, U.S. Navy ships maintained a dominating presence in the Pacific and Atlantic Oceans and in the Mediterranean Sea.[2]

Devastated by the Germans, and restricted to supporting land operations during World War II, the Soviet Navy could muster no challenge even to a greatly reduced postwar U.S. Navy. The Soviets also faced an ongoing internal struggle over the employment of naval forces and the types of forces to deploy. With origins long predating World War II, the struggle pitted "old school" officers favoring a traditional Mahanian battle fleet against a "young school" that argued for a navy with a *guerre de course* strategy centered on submarines, light surface ships, and aircraft.[3]

Learning from World War II and noting how the United States deployed its fleets to support its foreign policy, Stalin selected a modified "old school" approach. He wanted a big navy, capable of deterring Western sea powers from employing their maritime supremacy. Stalin's proposed force structure combined elements of the "young school" strategy with a "fortress fleet" of small-craft and shore-based elements designed to provide coastal defense.

There would also be a "fleet in being" to form the foundation of a blue-water navy centered on aircraft carriers. American naval actions off Korea at the start of the Korean War only reinforced Stalin's conviction that the U.S.S.R. needed a large ocean-going navy. The Soviet leader pushed forward a large construction program that began producing cruisers and fast destroyers at about the time of his death in 1953.[4]

After Stalin's death, the plans for the large navy also died. The Soviet Union's top security nightmare was surprise attack by Strategic Air Command (SAC) bombers, and the new leadership shifted resources to improve air defenses and build up the U.S.S.R.'s own strategic forces. The Soviets curtailed large surface-ship construction and concentrated instead on submarines, light surface craft, and land-based naval aviation. While the shift marked an apparent victory for the "young school," the dearth of resources allocated by the Kremlin made implementing even the envisioned lighter force structure a challenge. Years later, Adm. Sergei G. Gorshkov wrote that with the development of atomic weapons, influential authorities believed that the Navy had completely lost its value as a branch of the armed services. Future wars could be fought without Navy participation. With such a mindset, the Soviets allowed the navies of the United States and the Western alliance to steam uncontested on the world's oceans through the end of the 1950s.[5]

Since the Soviet Navy remained a coastal defense force, contact between the two militaries occurred only when U.S. forces came close to the Russian motherland. Often, this close contact occurred in the skies along the Soviet periphery and occasionally over the Soviet Union itself. Thus, the first period of the maritime confrontation during the Cold War was marked by a series of air-to-air confrontations and diplomatic efforts to contain the violence.

Two incidents occurred within six months after the September 1945 Japanese surrender ending World War II. On 15 October 1945, and again on 20 February 1946, U.S. Navy patrol aircraft monitoring the Japanese evacuation from China came under fire over the Yellow Sea from pursuing Soviet fighters. In the 15 October case, the Navy plane had flown within the twelve-mile limit established for Soviet-occupied Port Arthur by an agreement between the Nationalist Chinese and the Soviet Union. The 20 February incident occurred after the American plane reportedly lost its bearings and buzzed a Soviet airfield near Port Arthur. In both cases the American aircraft managed to escape with no casualties.[6] The ensuing diplomatic notes typified exchanges that would occur over the next quarter-century after confrontations between American and Soviet military units on and over the high seas. In the 15 October case, the Soviets rebuffed an American protest that the Soviet-Chinese twelve-mile limit lacked international recognition.[7]

The two Yellow Sea incidents, insignificant in themselves, added to a chronology of events souring the relationship between the two major military powers to emerge from World War II. For reasons that continue to fuel debate among historians, the Soviet Union and the United States became major adversaries during the postwar era. Whereas the Navy Yellow Sea patrol missions had targeted departing Japanese forces for observation, future American flights would focus on the Soviet Union to gather information.

"At this time we were really babes-in-the-woods as far as intelligence was concerned," reflected retired Air Force Gen. Curtis E. LeMay in a 1971 interview discussing the American situation versus that of the Soviets after World War II. The Soviet Union presented a perplexing challenge for war planners. If postwar tensions escalated into confrontation, the planners had to determine what strategic targets to attack, then they had to overcome Soviet air defenses to reach these strategic targets, and, finally, they had to determine what Soviet offensive capabilities could threaten the United States and how to counter them.[8]

To help provide the war planners with the necessary targeting information, SAC began to build a long-range reconnaissance capability. From 1947 to 1950 the number of strategic reconnaissance wings increased from two to nine.[9] Photo reconnaissance flights along the Siberian Pacific coastline from late 1946 to early 1948 alleviated concerns that the Soviets were building offensive bomber bases in eastern Siberia. However, the large cameras, mounted within high-flying reconnaissance planes patrolling along the Soviet periphery, could only peek so far into the vast expanse of the U.S.S.R. After strong Soviet diplomatic protests in mid-1948, the United States further limited how much photographic intelligence it could collect by restricting reconnaissance aircraft to fly no closer than forty miles from the Soviet coast. (With the detonation of the Soviet atomic bomb in August

1949 and Communist triumph in China, the standoff restriction was cut to twenty miles.)[10] This factor, combined with limited intelligence derived from other sources, left American planners so lacking in knowledge about the Soviet military-industrial complex that the basic war plan into the early 1950s simply called for the atomic leveling of the largest Soviet industrial cities. Significant breakthroughs in acquiring targeting information would not occur until overhead photography could be obtained by the U-2 and by later spy satellite programs.[11]

The importance of obtaining accurate information on Soviet defensive capabilities became evident after the downing of two Air Force C-47 cargo planes that had drifted over Yugoslavia in August 1946. The secret of Yugoslav success was resolved when a B-17 bomber, modified to carry receivers to conduct electronic intercepts (ELINT), detected signals from a German Wurzburg fire-control radar. Apparently, the Yugoslavs had successfully refurbished a captured piece of German electronic gear. Were the Soviet air defenses similarly improving?[12]

To test Soviet defenses, both Navy and Air Force aircraft began operating off Soviet coastlines to provoke and detect Soviet search and fire-control radar emissions. Known as "ferrets," these airplanes were coordinated at the direction of the military chiefs in a program called Special Electronic Airborne Search Projects (SESP). The two services divided the flights geographically, the Air Force having responsibility for the Baltic, Gulf of Bothnia, Murmansk, the Caucasus, and Far East, and the Navy being responsible for patrolling the Mediterranean and Black Sea areas. However, this division did not preclude one service from operating in the other service's areas with the consent of that service.[13] Thus, on the morning of 8 April 1950, a Navy Privateer patrol plane departed from Wiesbaden, West Germany, to fly a Baltic route. An afternoon attempt by an Air Force communications station to contact the plane by radio failed.[14]

The fate of the plane was quickly resolved. On 11 April, with the American search effort in progress, Soviet Foreign Minister Andrei Y. Vishinsky presented the American ambassador, Alan G. Kirk, with a formal protest note. The note claimed that a "B-29"–type plane had penetrated twenty-one kilometers into Soviet territory. He added that not only did the intruder fail to obey Soviet fighter directives to land, the plane fired on the Soviets. "Owing to this, an advanced Soviet fighter was forced to fire in reply, after which the American plane turned toward the sea and disappeared." A week later, Ambassador Kirk called on Deputy Foreign Minister Andrei Gromyko to present a sharply worded response. He demanded a Soviet investigation, punishment of those responsible, and no further repetitions of such acts. The Soviets ignored the American demands.[15]

On 17 April the SESP program was suspended for thirty days for re-evaluation. The military quickly reconfirmed the necessity for the program. On 5 May Chairman of the Joint Chiefs Gen. Omar Bradley wrote to Defense Secretary Louis Johnson, "It is recognized that there is a risk of repetition of such incidents upon resumption of these flights, but it is felt that there would be more serious disadvantages accruing to the United States if the cessation of these operations were to be extended over an excessively long period." Bradley recommended one change: future flights along the Soviet periphery would no longer be unarmed. Reviewing the memorandum on 19 May, President Truman commented on this recommendation in the margin, "Good sense it seems to me."[16] On 6 June the president gave his permission to resume the program.

While the Air Force and Navy modified ferret aircraft to carry defensive weapons, regular bomber and patrol aircraft began flying along the periphery of the Soviet Union to establish predictable operating patterns for ferret aircraft to slip into. However, the resumption of ferret operations in Europe would be held up during the summer of 1950. In the wake of the North Korean invasion of South Korea, Assistant Secretary of State for European Affairs George W. Perkins urgently requested that the Air Force not resume Baltic missions in view of the "hyper-tension" in Europe. The Air Force heeded the request, but only until it became apparent that the "hot" war would remain confined to Korea.[17]

The Korean War provided the background for some of the most violent air-to-air confrontations between U.S. and Soviet air forces because of the proximity of the Soviet Union to the Korean peninsula. On 4 September 1950 the destroyer USS *Fletcher* directed a four-plane combat air patrol from the aircraft carrier USS *Valley Forge* to intercept an unknown aircraft approaching from Port Arthur toward the Yellow Sea–based UN task force. After intercepting a Soviet twin-engine patrol bomber, the flight leader claimed that the Soviet aircraft fired on him. In self-defense, the American fighters shot down the Soviet aircraft.[18] In Moscow, two days later Foreign Minister Vishinsky called in Ambassador Kirk to present a protest note. Kirk refused to accept it, informing Vishinsky that the issue needed to be directed to the United Nations because the aircraft were under UN command.[19]

This diplomatic dodge came back to haunt the United States. On 6 November 1951 Soviet fighters shot down a Navy P2V Neptune flying on a UN reconnaissance mission over the Sea of Japan. Because of the precedent set a year earlier in Moscow, State Department officials felt it ill-advised to approach the Soviets at a government-to-government level. Instead, the State Department, to the dismay of the Navy, took no action except to provide a letter explaining the U.S. version of the incident to the UN Secretary General. This was distributed to members of the Security Council where the Soviet Union maintained a veto.[20]

Thirteen days after the Neptune downing, an Air Force C-47 was forced down in Hungary. The Russians held the flight crew and then turned them over to the Hungarians, who released them after payment of a ransom. After exhausting diplomatic channels, the State Department decided to use international claims procedures to seek redress. Samuel Klaus, assistant to the State Department's legal advisor, who had been documenting cases of human rights abuses in Eastern Europe, was assigned the job of preparing the petitions for a hearing at the International Court of Justice (ICJ).[21]

In Klaus, the State Department selected an individual with an outstanding reputation for investigative thoroughness. Prior to his coming to the State Department, Klaus had worked at the Treasury Department, where he performed an invaluable counterintelligence role prior to World War II by tracking the financial sources of subversive activities and identifying and eliminating Axis-controlled enterprises. During World War II Klaus served in the Army as a legal consultant, holding the rank of brigadier general. His investigative and military background would serve him well over the next decade.[22] In the case of the C-47, the Soviets and Hungarians ignored the ICJ jurisdiction. However, Klaus argued that his effort presented the United States as the government of law and order and created an international historical record that would be beneficial over the long term.[23]

While Klaus worked on the C-47 case, the confrontational environment established with the outbreak of the Korean War led to a dropping of distance restrictions for electronic and photographic reconnaissance aircraft. Subsequently, in the spring of 1952, the Navy and Air Force teamed up to conduct a series of electronic-photographic reconnaissance missions along the Siberian coast. Flying ahead, a Navy P2V-3 ferret actually made shallow penetrations of the Soviet landmass to provoke Soviet defenders to turn on search and fire-control radars. With the radar locations pinpointed, a tailing Air Force camera-laden RB-50 snapped pictures of the sites. On two of these overflight missions Soviet fighters scrambled and intercepted the intruders but did not attack.[24]

On 7 October 1952 an Air Force RB-29 aircraft was conducting a photo-mapping mission off the coast of northern Japan and southern Kuriles. A ground radar operator tracking the flight near Yuri Island spotted another blip on the screen that approached the American aircraft. At the same time, a ground communications station received a distress call in which the scream of "Let's get the hell out of here" could be heard in the background. A Japanese fisherman later told an Air Force investigator that a Russian fighter had dived from above and fired at the American plane, causing its tail section to break off. Search efforts failed to recover any of the eight crewmembers.[25]

Because this RB-29 was involved in a non-UN-related photo-mapping mission, the State Department did not feel diplomatically constrained as it did in the November 1951 P2V Neptune case. The two sides exchanged diplomatic protests. The Soviet note protesting an intrusion into Soviet airspace arrived on 12 October. The United States counterprotested five days later. In a note sent on 24 November, the U.S.S.R. responded negatively to U.S. inquiries concerning survivors. The Americans reissued their protest in a note passed on 16 December 1952.[26]

As in past incidents, after the exchange of diplomatic volleys, the United States returned to its corner unsatisfied and frustrated. In this case, however, Samuel Klaus also insisted that the United States challenge the Soviets before the ICJ. He shrugged off Air Force concerns of potentially undesirable revelations on the nature of the flights, arguing that the aircraft's mission would be irrelevant in a court of law. In stating his case, Klaus emphasized that American unwillingness to pursue claims in the April 1950 Privateer incident had not served the national interests and had only encouraged the Soviets to repeat the atrocities.[27]

Yet the Air Force had good reason to be concerned about Klaus's initiative. Throughout the summer of 1952, reports filtered in that the Soviets had begun massing Tu-4 bombers throughout eastern Siberia. To verify the reports, in mid-August President Truman approved a reconnaissance flight to fly deep over the Chukotskiy Peninsula bordering the Arctic Ocean. On 15 October, a week after the ill-fated RB-29 flight, an RB-47 lifted off from Alaska and proceeded to fly over some 1,000 miles of Soviet territory. Soviet radar tracked the big six-engine jet as it violated Soviet territory, but Soviet fighters could not catch up with the high-flying jet. In addition, Air Force tactical reconnaissance aircraft and SAC RB-45C aircraft stationed in Japan were flying over Soviet Siberian maritime provinces during this period to conduct Korean War–related reconnaissance. Given this context of clear American violations of international law, the Air Force's reluctance to press the Soviets on the RB-29 was understandable.[28]

Klaus prevailed. In the 7 October 1952 incident, Klaus saw not only an unwarranted assault but also a question of Soviet sovereignty over Yuri Island. By revisiting the agreement reached at Yalta and tracing subsequent events, Klaus argued that the Habomai island group, of which Yuri Island was a part, should not have been occupied by Soviet forces at the end of World War II since those islands were distinct from the neighboring Kurile Islands. By injecting a territorial argument into a court battle over the loss of the RB-29, Klaus saw an opportunity to curry favor with Japan. Given permission, Klaus began an extensive personal investigation to prepare the U.S. case to go before the ICJ.[29]

In the fall of 1953, Klaus found himself in Japan conducting interviews and collecting key documents to bolster his case. While in the Far East investigating the downing of the RB-29, he also took a thorough look at events surrounding two additional air incidents that had occurred that summer.[30] The first transpired during the waning hours of the Korean War, on 27 July, when four American fighters shot down a Soviet Il-12 passenger plane en route from Port Arthur to the Soviet Union. In a protest note presented on 31 July, the Soviets claimed the "piratical attack" occurred over Chinese territory and had resulted in twenty-one fatalities. Responding the next day, the United States deplored the loss of life, acknowledging responsibility for the attack, but claimed that the Soviet plane had been in a zone of hostilities in North Korean airspace at the time of the incident.[31] In another note, the Soviets stated that a B-50 violated the Soviet frontier in the vicinity of Vladivostok in the early morning hours of 29 July and that the plane fired on Soviet fighters, which were compelled to return fire. Consequently, the "American aircraft departed in the direction of the sea."[32] The Navy rescued one survivor and two more bodies were later found adrift in the Sea of Japan.[33] The remainder of the crew of seventeen remained unaccounted for. The Soviets ignored demands for apologies, reparations, and information about the missing airmen. Months later, after reviewing detailed testimony, Klaus reiterated U.S. charges that the Soviets were withholding information on the status of survivors. He argued that this case also needed to be brought before the ICJ: "Failure to push this case, particularly in the light that Soviets are lying about survivors, may embarrass us with the American public and the next of kin."[34]

As Klaus methodically conducted his preparations of cases to be presented before the ICJ, the United States initiated additional overflights of the Soviet Union. In the Far East, modified fighters of the 15th Tactical Reconnaissance Squadron conducted nine overflights of Soviet territory between April 1954 and February 1955. On the other side of the Eurasian landmass, British and American reconnaissance aircraft were launched to determine Soviet bomber depositions. On 28–29 April 1954 three RAF RB-45Cs lifted off to fly over different portions of western Russia. All returned, although one RB-45C confronted heavy antiaircraft fire while flying over Kiev. Just over a week later, on 8 May, an American RB-47E conducted a deep overflight of the Kola Peninsula. This time MiG fighters caught up with the intruder and fired several shells into the fleeing photo-reconnaissance plane. The RB-47E photography revealed that the Soviet long-range bombers had yet to deploy on the Kola Peninsula.[35]

While the Soviets repeatedly failed to bring down Allied aircraft over their territory, they still brought down aircraft outside of their borders. Later in 1954, a U.S. Navy patrol plane became the victim of another attack. In the report describing the 4 September 1954 incident off the east coast of Siberia, Comdr. John B. Wayne told how a MiG-15 had made repeated strafing passes. Forced to ditch, one of the ten crewmembers did not clear the aircraft and subsequently drowned as the patrol plane sank in the calm Pacific seas.[36] In addition to protesting the attack and preparing a case for World Court (ICJ) adjudication, the Eisenhower administration took the issue before the UN Security Council. On the morning of 10 September, after a failed Soviet attempt to prevent the issue from being placed on the agenda, U.S. Ambassador Henry Cabot Lodge Jr. began his presentation:

> Mr. President:
>
> I have been instructed by the United States Government to bring to the attention of the Security Council a problem which has great concern and which, if it were allowed to go unchallenged, might endanger the maintenance of international peace and security.

Lodge then detailed the attack and recalled other "wanton attacks" against American aircraft. The American diplomat suggested that the case could be brought before the ICJ for adjudication of claims. In conclusion, Lodge hoped that the U.S. decision to bring the case before the Security Council would focus world opinion on the situation and could "contribute materially to prevent the repetition of these incidents."

Foreign Minister Vishinsky restated previously given Soviet versions of events and brought up incidents such as the downing of a Soviet bomber in the Yellow Sea in September 1950 and the shootdown of the Il-12 plane in July 1953. Vishinsky taunted Lodge on the purpose of the flights and concluded by placing clear responsibility on the U.S. government "for the incident of 4 September and for further attempts to exploit these incidents with the objective of creating international tension."[37]

A few days after the UN Security Council debate, an explanatory article appeared in the *New York Times*. Titled "The Price of Survival — 45 U.S. Airmen Have Died in Incidents with Soviet Planes Since April 1950," the Hanson W. Baldwin piece discussed the importance of missions flown around the periphery of the Iron Curtain. Noting that the Soviets also flew reconnaissance missions,[38] Baldwin wrote, "This mutual search for information about what the other fellow is doing is symptomatic of the insecurity of the atomic age and the awful penalty that can be paid today by any nation that is not alert to the terrible dangers of surprise atomic attack." The article accurately discussed the various missions of the U.S. Air Force and Navy reconnaissance aircraft and concluded, "It is this silent war, this ceaseless search for information that must be inevitably a part of the

Cold War. We have no confidence in the intentions of the Soviet government, yet we know that the Soviet government has the capabilities of devastating destruction against the United States unless we are alert."[39]

On 7 November 1954 another RB-29 fell to MiG gunfire. This incident occurred not far from the Yuri Island incident of two years previous. One airman drowned after he became entangled in his parachute. Again, the two sides exchanged protest notes containing different versions of the story. Senate Majority Leader William F. Knowland charged that the incident was deliberately timed to cause "loss of face" for the United States during the visit of the Japanese premier, Shigeru Yoshida. The conservative California Republican demanded that more drastic action be taken than sending notes to Moscow. Previously he had suggested that the United States should respond to such provocation by severing diplomatic relations. Although disagreeing on such extreme action, other senators joined Knowland in expressing a desire for additional action. At the State Department Samuel Klaus received another case to bring before the ICJ. Eventually, the United States would apply to have the case heard on 7 July 1959.[40]

As Klaus began his investigation into "RB-29 II," he was wrapping up his legal work on the RB-29 incident of October 1952. On 25 September 1954, two weeks after the Lodge-Vishinsky showdown at the United Nations, the United States submitted a diplomatic claim against the Soviet Union seeking compensation for the lost RB-29 and crew, information about the crew's fate, and Soviet withdrawal from the Habomai island group. Anticipating Soviet rejection of the claim, Klaus continued preparations for a challenge in the ICJ.

On 2 June 1955 U.S. Ambassador H. Freeman Matthews presented a petition before the ICJ to contest the Soviet Union's shootdown of a RB-29 near Yuri Island on 7 October 1952. The United States demanded compensation of $1,620,295.01 plus interest, as well as a court finding that Japan should have title to the Habomai Islands. The case was the second brought before the court concerning an air incident. An attempt to challenge Czechoslovakia over the 10 March 1953 shootdown of a USAF F-84 fighter was earlier rejected when the Czech government refused to acknowledge ICJ jurisdiction.[41] As with the Czechs, the Soviets ignored the court's summons. Eventually the U.S. petition would be dropped from the docket. Although the Soviet action had been anticipated, Klaus still believed that the effort could pay dividends in the future, especially in light of the Soviet Union's efforts to remake its image in the post-Stalin period. Klaus's vision was prophetic.

On 22 June 1955, three weeks after the petition had been submitted to the World Court, one or two Soviet fighters ambushed a Navy P2V Neptune flying on a routine shipping surveillance patrol over the Bering Sea. The plane's pilot managed to fly the crippled aircraft forty miles to St. Lawrence Island and safely crash-land on the marshy tundra. All the crew survived.[42]

The timing of the attack could not have come at a worse time for a Soviet government preparing for a "Big Four" summit meeting scheduled for the following month in Geneva. As the Neptune crashed, Soviet Foreign Minister Vyacheslav M. Molotov was in San Francisco attending the tenth anniversary session of the United Nations. President Eisenhower, upon learning of the incident, directed his representative to the session, Secretary of State John Foster Dulles, to meet with the Soviet envoy. Dulles caught Molotov uninformed about the incident and received a promise of an investigation. Meanwhile, the downing received bipartisan condemnation in the Senate.

Obviously embarrassed, the Kremlin leadership wired Molotov his instructions. Three days after the incident, the two chief diplomats met, and Molotov presented Dulles with a conciliatory note that admitted the incident could have been "due to a mistake." For the first time the Soviets expressed regret. Molotov also expressed the Soviet willingness to compensate the United States for half of the requested reparations on the Neptune incident. Secretary Dulles, gratified by this unprecedented example of Soviet frankness, immediately notified his boss. The incident would not jeopardize the upcoming summit.[43]

The number of violent encounters beyond Soviet borders diminished over the next few years. Responding to continued American penetrations of Soviet airspace, the Soviets issued diplomatic protests. One note was delivered on 14 May 1956, in the wake of an extensive SAC photo-mapping effort of the northern tier of the Soviet Union. RB-47Es, flying from Thule, Greenland, flew 156 missions over Soviet territory from 21 March to 10 May 1956. Only on three or four occasions did the Soviets attempt to intercept the flights. With the overflight program ended, the Eisenhower administration responded on 29 May with a note expressing regret if navigational errors had caused unintentional violations of Soviet territory.

Again the Soviets vigorously protested when the first U-2 penetrated Russian skies on 4 July 1956. The U.S. response to the 10 July Soviet note denied a military overflight.[44] With this protest, and his desire to improve relations with the Soviet Union, Eisenhower became uncomfortable with additional reconnaissance missions. Still, he gave permission for three Air Force RB-57D-0 planes to penetrate deep into Siberia after being told the fast high-flying aircraft would not be detected by Soviet radar. However, on 11 December, the Soviets did detect the flights and sent fighters to chase the American planes. Again Eisenhower received a strong Soviet protest note. Embarrassed, Eisenhower ended reconnaissance missions by the military over the Soviet Union.[45]

Perhaps in the "spirit of Geneva," Soviet leaders had ordered the Soviet Air Force to refrain from hostile action against American aircraft beyond the Soviet periphery despite the continuing U.S. overflights of Soviet territory. If so, the spirit of Geneva faded in 1958. Ironically, as American military aircraft ceased to reconnoiter the U.S.S.R., Soviet aircraft became more aggressive. During the latter half of 1958, six major incidents occurred involving U.S. and Soviet aircraft along the Soviet periphery. In the two cases where Soviets shot down U.S. Air Force planes, the incidents occurred over land. On 27 June 1958 Soviet fighters shot down a USAF C-118 transport plane over Armenia, injuring two of the nine-man crew. Two weeks later, on 10 July 1958, an Air Force RB-50 patrolling off Petropavlosk exchanged gunfire with Soviet fighters. No damage was reported. Two months later, on 10 September 1958, Soviet fighters shot down an Air Force–modified C-130 that was conducting ELINT duties over Soviet Armenia. The American release of the dramatic cockpit conversations of the intercepting fighter pilots effectively refuted the Soviet denial of the attack. The Soviets eventually returned six bodies from an aircrew of seventeen. On 31 October 1958 a Soviet fighter attempted an intercept of an Air Force RB-47 on patrol over the Black Sea. Five days later, on 4 November 1958, a Soviet fighter harassed an Air Force C-130 transport flying over the Sea of Japan.

Then on 7 November 1958, in the vicinity of Gotland Island in the Baltic Sea, a Soviet fighter fired at an Air Force RB-47, while over the Sea of Japan Soviet fighters buzzed another RB-47.[46] Throughout 1959, as both sides positioned themselves over Berlin, the skies around the Soviet Union remained incident-free. Perhaps resraints were placed on the Soviet Air Force due to the Kremlin decision to apply pressure on Berlin. On the American side, the U.S. Air Force had discontinued provocative RB-47 flights from Greenland.[47] Tensions between the superpowers eased in the aftermath of Soviet leader Nikita Khrushchev's September 1959 visit, as people spoke of a "spirit of Camp David."

In the spring of 1960 there were predictions of a productive "Big Four" Paris summit, followed by a triumphant tour of the Soviet Union by the American president, causing many to believe that the end of the Cold War was at hand.[48]

The stories of the U-2 incident and the consequential downturn in East-West relations as a result of the breakup of the Paris summit, the showdown at the United Nations, and the trial of Francis Gary Powers are well known. The 1 May 1960 Soviet downing of the CIA spy flight over Sverdlovsk is only briefly mentioned to place the final known U.S.-U.S.S.R. air-to-air confrontation involving fatalities in proper context.

On 1 July 1960 an RB-47 left from RAF Station Brize Norton, England, to develop improved ECM capabilities by collecting electronics intelligence from Soviet radar installations. The RB-47 was assigned to the 55th SRW, headquartered at Forbes Air Force Base in Kansas. In the summer of 1960 Brize Norton and bases in Turkey, Japan, and Alaska served as advanced overseas bases for the wing.[49] Over the Barents Sea, a MiG passed from above and behind, then reappeared astern and commenced firing. The big six-engine jet was knocked out of the sky. Two of the six crewmembers survived and were recovered by a Soviet fishing trawler. The Soviets also retrieved the body of the pilot.[50]

On 11 July the Soviets formally protested the latest violation of Soviet airspace and announced their intention to try the two Americans as spies. Soviet rhetoric intensified the next day as Khrushchev held a press conference to reemphasize the charges. In Washington, State Department officials distributed copies of the U.S. response to the Soviet note. Critical of the Soviet attempt to link the RB-47 with the U-2, the note demanded the release of the two captives and the remains of the pilot, as well as reserved the right to demand compensation at a future date.[51] On the following day, the Soviets requested that the issue of "American aggressive actions" be brought before the UN Security Council. The Eisenhower administration announced it would welcome a full investigation into the "wanton shooting down" of the aircraft. Security Council President Jose Correa from Ecuador agreed to allow the body to debate the issue upon conclusion of the ongoing discussion over the Belgian Congo crisis.[52]

On 22 July the debate opened in New York at the United Nations. First Deputy Foreign Minister Vasily V. Kuznetsov began by restating the Soviet version of the event. He followed with a condemnation of U.S. foreign policy in general. Getting back to the focal point of his presentation, the Soviet diplomat challenged the Americans to offer proof that their airplane had not flown in Soviet airspace. Kuznetsov charged that the RB-47 "committed an aggressive act with espionage in mind" and argued "there can be no distinction between the flight of the RB-47 and the U-2."[53] He then submitted a resolution condemning the provocative actions of the United States.

After a weekend adjournment, on Monday, 25 July, Ambassador Lodge began his long, deliberate, and dramatic presentation. Using an annotated chart, Lodge traced the actual flight path of the ill-fated plane. He emphasized that the aircraft never penetrated Soviet airspace: "This astonishing and criminal fact is established beyond doubt by the evidence of our scientific devices, which followed the RB-47 through all of the events which I have described." Lodge confidently declared that the plane, after being slightly driven off course by the Soviet fighter, had turned away from the Soviet landmass on a northeasterly heading and had cruised for twenty minutes before being attacked. Lodge claimed the actual time as 1522, nineteen minutes after the Soviet claim. The American ambassador then proposed to have the case investigated by an unbiased third party such as the ICJ or by a commission with members appointed by the two parties.

Responding, Kuznetsov cast aside Lodge's appeal, restating that the responsibility for all of the "sadness and tears" rested squarely on the United States and belittling Lodge's call for an investigation as only "confusing an already clear issue."[54] The Security Council voted the next day. The outcome was seven to two against the Soviet resolution. Only Poland supported the Soviet Union.[55]

The RB-47 story did not conclude with the UN debate. Two Americans captive in Lubyanka remained a contentious issue in Soviet-American relations during the final six months of the Eisenhower administration. In September Ambassador Llewellyn E. Thompson privately assured Khrushchev that the United States would not pursue the RB-47 case at the World Court if the two aviators were released. Still, Samuel Klaus began preparations to take the case to court.[56]

Throughout the summer of 1960, as Klaus began to collect material to build his case, he became disturbed about the accuracy of Lodge's UN presentation. The U.S. reconstructed the route of the reconnaissance plane, which indicated that it had actually approached the Soviet border more closely than indicated on Lodge's chart. Klaus also realized he would have difficulty explaining the American search pattern in view of the supposed accuracy of U.S. "scientific devices."[57]

As a goodwill gesture to newly sworn-in Pres. John F. Kennedy, Khrushchev ordered the release of the two Air Force prisoners. Despite Thompson's promise to Khrushchev, Klaus continued to pursue facts, arguing that the United States should still challenge the Soviet claim that territorial airspace had been penetrated. In addition, with the return of the two aviators and subsequent debriefings, further discrepancies in Lodge's UN statement became even more brutally apparent. Klaus called Lodge's speechwriter, Peter Thacher, to point out that the RB-47 had not been forced off course as claimed and to inquire about the 1522 shootdown time. Klaus indicated that the evidence was more supportive of the Soviet time of 1503.[58]

From what Klaus could determine, the RB-47 never did penetrate Soviet airspace, although it came close to an imaginary line over the White Sea that the Soviets declared extended from Svyatoy Nos to Cape Kanin. Klaus believed that allowing this demarcation line to remain unchallenged could set an unfortunate precedent for freedom of navigation on and over the high seas. In October 1961, after several months of intensive work, his protest note challenging the Soviet sovereignty claim was ready for delivery. However, because of overriding political considerations, the note was never delivered. Klaus advocated reconsideration, but the new administration wanted to avoid additional antagonisms with the Kremlin leadership.[59] The July 1960 RB-47 downing would prove to be the last incident of this type for which Samuel Klaus would apply his considerable legal talents. He died after a heart attack in August 1963.

The effectiveness of Klaus's and Lodge's efforts is difficult to evaluate.

Critics of international law regimes could argue that their efforts were for naught, given the Soviet Union's refusal to be held accountable before the ICJ and its ability to veto censure at the UN Security Council. Such critics could argue that the outcomes of the air-to-air cases illustrate the ineffectiveness of an international system, given the lack of a powerful legislative body, the lack of a third-party dispute-settlement mechanism, and the lack of a mechanism to effect sanctions on lawbreakers.

Yet the converse could be argued. Molotov did meet with Dulles in June 1955 to offer reparations for a Navy patrol plane that had been shot down. Although refusing to acknowledge ICJ jurisdiction, perhaps the Soviet leaders began to realize they were losing a battle in the world court of public opinion. By attacking foreign aircraft flying in international airspace, clearly acting against norms established by international law, the Soviets might have found their credibility challenged in other areas of diplomacy. In addition, Soviet aggressiveness ran counter to Soviet stated desires at this time to establish détente with the West.

While it may be difficult to evaluate how the American diplomatic effort affected the Soviet leadership, it is clear that Soviet protest notes had an impact on the Americans. Reacting to Soviet protest notes in 1948, Truman placed restrictions on photo-reconnaissance flights. These restrictions were lifted during the Korean War. Still, Eisenhower proceeded cautiously in permitting overflights of the Soviet Union. While Soviet protest notes could be dismissed or responded to with regrets about navigational errors, the possibility of losing an American aircraft to Soviet defensive fire would have undercut the propaganda edge he sought to maintain. Finally, in response to a Soviet protest in December 1956, Eisenhower did end military reconnaissance of the Soviet Union. Soviet diplomacy, backed by improved air defenses, succeeded in stopping one part of the American reconnaissance effort.

In the end, however, it may have been technology rather than diplomacy that ended the confrontations. The summer of 1960 represents a milestone in U.S.-Soviet military relations for reasons beyond the downing and subsequent showdown at the United Nations over the RB-47. Launched into orbit almost a month after the UN debate, Discoverer XIV made several successful photo passes over the Soviet Union before reentering the earth's atmosphere. The film-laden payload, dangling from the end of a parachute, never touched the ground; instead it was scooped up in mid-air by a specially rigged C-119 Flying Boxcar. A new era of satellite reconnaissance dawned for the United States, reducing the need for risky aerial missions. However, as later proven by the Cuban missile crisis, U-2s and follow-on reconnaissance craft would still play an important role for U.S. defense planners throughout the rest of the Cold War and beyond.

Forced to accept the new reality of an America capable of conducting photo-reconnaissance at will, the Soviets may have turned away from their focus on the threat posed by conventional spy planes. Consequently, the July 1960 RB-47 incident became one of the last violent superpower air-to-air encounters in the Cold War.

« **3** »

SURFACE
CONTACTS

During the summer of 1960, the Soviets became concerned over another event posing a far greater threat than any overhead photo-satellite capability. On 20 July 1960, two days prior to the UN debate over the RB-47, the USS *George Washington* fired a ballistic missile from under Atlantic waters off Cape Canaveral — a remarkable achievement. As of late 1956, top American scientists projected the first deployment of a ballistic-missile submarine would occur in 1965. Four new technologies converged to make Polaris deployment feasible in 1960: proven nuclear propulsion, reliable solid-rocket propellant, inertial shipboard navigation development, and miniaturization of nuclear warheads. The imminent deployment threat posed by Polaris missiles on board American nuclear-powered submarines was one the Soviets were unprepared to handle. The new mobile undersea strategic missile bases were simply beyond the reach of the Soviet submarines, warships, and land-based aviation that had been amassed to counter the nuclear threat from the new big-deck carriers being commissioned by the U.S. Navy.[1]

Facing this new threat, Admiral Gorshkov began a deliberate campaign to urge Nikita Khrushchev to reverse his naval outlook. As of January 1960 the Soviet leader still retained his view that the surface ships had a diminished role in the modern Soviet Navy. Gorshkov first succeeded in preventing the scrapping of the *Sverdlov*-class cruisers built as part of Stalin's postwar shipbuilding program. In 1960 and 1961 additional reassessments of naval strategy apparently took place within the Kremlin leadership. By the spring of 1962, the conversion had almost been completed as Khrushchev toured a Leningrad shipyard and praised the work on new surface ships under construction.[2]

Although the arrival of a challenging Soviet fleet was still years away, growth in the Soviet maritime presence already had been under way. In 1960 the physical volume of Soviet seaborne trade totaled 44.3 million tons, up from 8.3 million tons in 1950. By 1970 this figure would reach 121.3 million tons. Furthermore, Soviet vessels carried an increasing percentage of this growing trade. While Soviet ships carried only 5.9 percent of the U.S.S.R.'s seaborne trade in 1950, by 1960 this number had grown to 18.2 percent, and by 1970 to 69.9 percent.[3]

The United States kept close tabs on Soviet shipping, a process that became a source of constant Soviet irritation. For example, during the posturing prior to the UN RB-47 debate and during the debate itself, the Soviets complained of some 250 "buzzings" of their merchant and fishing vessels plying the high seas in the first five months of 1960. American aircraft flying low over Soviet shipping gave cause for Kremlin leaders to file additional protest notes throughout the coming decade.[4]

Not all of the vessels "buzzed" had strictly commercial purposes, and the American side made this an issue before and during the RB-47 debate. Two days after the Soviet revelation of the RB-47 shootdown, the U.S. Navy revealed the late-April presence of a Soviet spy trawler off the U.S. East Coast. Noting the craft's similarity in appearance to fishing trawlers lying off the Newfoundland Grand Banks, a naval intelligence officer displayed huge slides of the vessel *Vega*, pointing out eleven portable antennas protruding from a van mounted on the bridge. The Navy's Chief of Information (CHINFO), Rear Adm. Charles Kirkpatrick, complained that at one point while off Long Island the 600-ton trawler attempted to interfere with the recovery of a dummy missile by a Navy tug participating in a Polaris missile-firing maneuver. Kirkpatrick emphasized that the trawler remained unmolested because of its location in international waters: "We are a legal people and abide by international law." Asked if he made that statement to contrast American behavior with the Soviet downing of the RB-47, Rear Admiral Kirkpatrick smiled and said, "I'm talking about this incident — nothing else."[5]

Although the Navy's press conference attempted to portray the Soviet spy trawler as a new provocation, by 1960 the presence of these rugged little ships on the world's oceans had become a fact of life for Western navies. The Intelligence Directorate of the Alaskan Air Command first became suspicious of a group of "trawler-type" vessels in the summer of 1955. The question posed was: "Have the Soviets set up a line of picket ships in the Bering Sea for offshore surveillance and early warning?" Throughout the spring and summer of 1955, Navy P2V Neptunes, including the one shot down on 22 June, lifted off to determine an answer. From May through August, the Navy patrol planes made twenty-seven sightings of vessels so equipped, leading intelligence officers "to speculate the possibility of a primary purpose other than fishing." Operating in waters not normally frequented by the Soviet fishing fleet, only one of the spotted vessels appeared to have nets in the water. Some of the vessels had nets and fishing equipment stowed on deck, while others had no nets or net floats in sight. The radar and elaborate communications equipment installed aboard all these craft seemed most significant to the Alaskan Air Command intelligence analysts, who speculated that these vessels may have provided tracking information to the aircraft that shot down the Neptune on 22 June.[6]

Eventually, Western navies designated these trawler-type vessels as Auxiliary, General, Intelligence (AGIS). During the late 1950s the Soviets built more of these ships, using trawler designs for blueprints. Trawler designs were adaptable because the insulated refrigeration compartments provided ideal space for electronic equipment. Trawlers also possessed the necessary stability for operating in heavy seas.[7] During the 1960s AGIS became a common sight off American submarine bases, at shipping chokepoints, off Cape Canaveral, near test facilities such as those at Kwajalein Atoll, and among U.S. Navy carrier task forces. Because of the assertiveness of some of these spy ships in gathering intelligence, many American skippers probably believed that "Be a nuisance" must have been part of the AGI mission statement.

In a 1972 study of six years' worth of incidents involving Soviet ships and aircraft on the high seas, thirty-two of seventy-nine cases involved one or more of these spy ships.[8] However, this number probably represented only a fraction of the actual instances in which one navy's ship maneuvered so as to impede the movements of the other navy's ship, because many incidents simply were not reported to higher command authorities. Those that were reported often became a subject of diplomatic notes passed between the two governments. For example, on 30 June 1964, the USS *Daniel A. Joy* nearly collided with Soviet AGI *Randa* some 450 miles east of New York. The American destroyer escort claimed that she had to blow her horn four times to signal danger and make sharp speed adjustments to avoid hitting the Soviet vessel, which had closed to within 150 yards. Six months later, on 7 January 1965 off Iceland, the Soviet AGI *Vertikal* approached within seventy-five feet of the USNS *Dutton,* which was flying flags and warning signals to indicate that there was a tow astern. Ignoring these warnings, the Soviet ship passed beneath the stern of the research ship, cutting a magnetometer cable that had been deployed to measure magnetic fields. As the crew of the *Dutton* reeled in the cut cable, the *Vertikal* illuminated their actions by directing two arc searchlights and again closed on the American ship despite danger signals blasted on *Dutton*'s whistle. When the *Dutton* later reeled out a second cable to resume operations, the *Vertikal* again returned to harass the movements of the American ship. On 24 February 1965, near the coast of California, the AGI *Arban* positioned herself ahead of the oncoming aircraft carrier USS *Hornet* refueling from the USS *Ashtabula,* forcing the two American ships to execute an emergency breakaway to clear the Soviet vessel. A week later, on 2 March 1965, in Narragansett Bay off Rhode Island, the AGI *Sverdlovsky* harassed the USS *Courtney,* the USS *Hartley,* and the naval tug *Keywadin* for a half hour as the three American ships attempted to perform training maneuvers. The "reckless harassing maneuvers" of the Soviet spy ship forced the destroyer escort *Courtney* to turn to starboard to avoid a collision.[9]

A former commander of a destroyer stationed in the Tonkin Gulf in 1965, Robert P. Hilton Sr. observed that Soviet AGIS had a habit of cutting across refueling formations and cutting across carrier bows. He added, "I think they were a little reluctant to cut across the bow of a carrier going at full speed because I think they discovered that if the carrier had the right of way, it was not going to alter course." Hilton further explained that task force commanders assigned destroyers to keep the AGIS out of the way, using shouldering tactics if needed. He noted, "Of course, we were instructed to comply with the Rules of the Road even when it came to shouldering."[10]

No collisions are recorded between aircraft carriers and AGIS. In a game of chicken between a truck and a motorcycle, the fellow on the motorcycle invariably gives way. Thus, many carrier skippers maintained course and speed when challenged by an oncoming Soviet trawler. Some carrier skippers even took deliberate steps to let the uninvited guests know that their mischief-making was not welcome. Former CNO Adm. Thomas B. Hayward recalled being confronted by an AGI when his aircraft carrier, USS *America,* initially arrived in the Gulf of Tonkin during the Vietnam War. Reacting to the AGI's aggressive maneuvers, Hayward ordered all aircraft tied down securely and then executed a hard starboard turn into the path of the AGI, "sending an immediate signal to its captain that we didn't appreciate his action and that he should clear the area immediately. It worked."[11] Another former CNO, Adm. James L. Holloway III, acted with equal assertiveness in 1965 when he took the USS *Enterprise* on its first combat deployment to Vietnam. When the Soviet eavesdropper showed up in the Gulf of Tonkin, Holloway ordered the 90,000-ton carrier to flank speed and headed right for it. "And he got the hell out of our way." Holloway would continue to use that tactic to keep AGIS at bay. Still, Soviet AGI harassment of *Enterprise* would eventually be discussed at a diplomatic level. In the Mediterranean, COMSIXTHFLT Vice Adm. William I. Martin commented in 1967 on Soviet AGIS in the Mediterranean stating, "There have been times when Russian electronic intelligence ships have moved in the way seemingly to embarrass us; either we change course or [we would] ram them."[12]

J. P. "Blackie" Weinel did not share the assertive philosophy displayed by the two former CNOs and fleet commander. As a rear admiral in command of a carrier task force later in the Vietnam conflict, Weinel one day observed one of his big carriers being challenged to a game of chicken by one of the Soviet AGIS. As the scenario unfolded, Weinel considered the consequences of a collision and the odds of being put out of action. "Was it worth it to prove to some twenty-three-year-old ensign that we were not going to be chicken?" he asked himself. Concluding this was silly, Weinel asked the carrier captain about his intentions. When the captain stated he would not give way, Weinel recalled responding, "You ever thought what would happen if you got hit? Get the hell out of his way! We are fighting a war and we don't have time for this!"[13]

Often getting out of the way was also a risky proposition. A ship operating aircraft, whether it be an aircraft carrier launching supersonic fighters or a destroyer receiving supplies from a transport helicopter, was restricted in maneuvering courses and speeds partly because of wind conditions. Still, if a Soviet AGI crossed ahead, there was usually enough flexibility to maneuver and continue flight operations with only slight delay. Often the transgressions were overlooked. However, on 18 January 1966, Deputy Undersecretary of State U. Alexis Johnson, during his meeting with Soviet Ambassador Anatoly Dobrynin, noted the persistent efforts of AGI *Gidrofon* to disrupt the flight operations of *Enterprise* operating off North Vietnam. At the meeting Johnson formally protested three recent occasions when the Soviet spy ship had crossed ahead of the American nuclear carrier conducting flight operations and one instance in which *Gidrofon* crossed into the path of USS *Kitty Hawk,* which was receiving fuel from an oiler.[14]

The ability to replenish at sea was and is a hallmark of a true blue-water navy. By the 1960s the Navy was employing specially designed supply ships to meet the logistical challenge of providing food, supplies, fuel, and ammunition to the fleets operating several thousand miles from home. During underway replenishment (unrep), the supply ship would maintain a set course and speed (usually about 12 knots). The ship to be replenished then approached from astern. To maneuver several thousand tons of floating steel through the ocean to a position about eighty yards off another large moving object was and remains one of the toughest tests for a young shiphandler. When making this approach, sea state and winds must be considered, along with the ship's handling characteristics.

Once alongside a variety of methods can be employed to exchange men and material. During the 1960s the Navy introduced the Fast Automatic Shuttle Transfer (FAST) system, which incorporated a tensioned wire arrangement. The supply ship reeled out a steel cable, and deckhands on board the receiving ship secured it to an exterior bulkhead at a "replenishment station." The supply ship activated a system of hydraulic rams tensioning the wire highline. On this wire highline traveled either a "trolley" to transport stores or ammunition or a series of pulleys carrying a fuel hose to the receiving ship.[15]

Frequently, the supply ship serviced ships to port and starboard simultaneously. Three ships strung together were particularly vulnerable to the antics of undesired visitors. When confronted with an obstruction ahead, such as an intruding AGI, the ship skippers had three choices. They could hold course and hope that the intruder would move on, conduct an emergency breakaway, or turn. The first option ran the risk for disaster if for some reason, such as mechanical breakdown, the intruder could not move on. An obstruction hitting a tensioned wire could drag the replenishment formation together. With exposed ammunition or full fuel hoses crashing together, loss of life, severe injuries, and damage would almost be certain. The second option, an "emergency breakaway," was simply an expedited decoupling of the ships. When one of the ships blasted the danger signal, crews rushed to break down the replenishment rigs. Unfortunately, the pressure to perform quickly often increased the chances of accidents due to the overlooking of safety steps. If the unrep had to be completed, the third option was to turn the formation — a touchy maneuver even in fair weather and calm seas, let alone high winds and heavy seas. To turn steaming ships bound together with tensioned steel cables, the guiding replenishment ship altered course in small two- to five-degree increments. In addition to shifting course, the other ship or ships adjusted speed to keep abreast of and parallel to the guide. One commander recalled having to turn nearly 270 degrees in this nerve-wracking manner to avoid hitting one persistent Soviet AGI. In one incident on 10 January 1965 in the Mediterranean, the *Kotelnikov* disrupted a pending unrep by blocking the path of the oiler USS *Neosho,* which was being approached from astern by the USS *Saratoga. Neosho* changed course 30 degrees to starboard to avoid collision, and the trailing *Saratoga* reversed engines to avoid hitting the Soviet ship.[16]

As indicated by Rear Admiral Hilton, attempts were made to avert a showdown by sending the cavalry forward to head off the intruder. The cavalry usually took the form of an escorting destroyer that would speed ahead to shoulder the AGI out of the path of the oncoming formation. Sometimes the cavalry would be a low-hovering helicopter that irritated the intruder with noise and prop wash. Often these preemptive measures were successful. Several complaints registered against the Soviets between 1965 and 1972 dealt with scenarios of the type just described. Another complaint concerned AGI actions against surfaced submarines.

AGIS kept station off U.S. submarine bases to monitor submarine arrivals and departures. In doing so, they often made dangerously close approaches, sometimes blocking the path of an oncoming submarine to photograph and discern intelligence about outward features of the boat to assist Soviet ASW and submarine design programs. For example, on 9 September 1969, Capt. C. A. H. Trost, the commanding officer of the ballistic-missile submarine USS *Sam Rayburn,* came upon the AGI *Teodolit* off Charleston, South Carolina. The Russian ship ignored danger signal blasts and steamed ahead of the submarine, blocking its path. Trost took the conn and maneuvered around *Teodolit,* which immediately turned to chase outbound attack submarine USS *Sunfish.* The United States formally protested the *Teodolit* activity on 27 October 1969.[17]

Again, sometimes assistance was needed to shoulder AGIS out of the way. Retired Capt. Robert Rawlins recalled how his submarine tender off Rota, Spain, diverted attention from one pesky AGI just long enough to allow a harassed submarine an opportunity to dive safely.[18]

Often to avoid AGI detection, submarines arrived or departed at night and surfaced or dove closer to the shoreline. Such evasive actions added risk. For example, sometime during the late 1960s or early 1970s the missile submarine USS *Theodore Roosevelt* reportedly ran aground underwater off Holy Loch, Scotland, while attempting to avoid detection, causing extensive damage to her sonar dome. Submerged submarines operating close to shore also must contend with other undersea obstructions. Over the years, Navy lawyers have been constantly busy settling claims with fishermen who have had nets and other fishing gear destroyed.[19]

Surface ships also took measures to avoid observation. Admiral Weinel recalled one deceptive measure employed while he commanded the aircraft carrier USS *Ticonderoga* when he wanted to conduct some nuclear weapons–related exercises. Somewhat concerned that the nearby Soviet spy trawler that steamed within his task force formation might obtain intelligence on U.S. tactics, Weinel desired to get the AGI out of the vicinity. Ordering one of his destroyer captains to divert the AGI, Weinel admired the scheme that was employed. Sailors on the destroyer took a frame of a bunk with the springs exposed and tied a line to each corner. The sailors lowered the bedsprings in the water and then pulled it up. One sailor stood by, wearing a set of big earphones, and wrote notes on a clipboard. After awhile this routine caught the AGI's attention, and the Soviets stayed with them for the next day while Weinel went off and completed his exercises. Reflecting, Weinel wondered what Moscow thought of these intelligence data.[20]

The Soviets did not maintain a monopoly on spy ships. In 1960 the U.S. National Security Agency (NSA) received permission to acquire ELINT ships for the purpose of intercepting the communications of Third World countries. Transmissions originating from these countries could yield valuable information — especially diplomatic traffic from Eastern-bloc embassies. By 1963 two small converted coastal transports operated by the Military Sea Transportation Service (MSTS) were conducting "hydrographic survey cruises" off the coasts of Africa, South America, and in the Caribbean.

The Navy became interested in the NSA spy-ship concept. While the NSA ships focused on gathering diplomatic and political intelligence, the Navy desired a platform primarily dedicated to intercepting foreign naval communications. The Navy struck a compromise with NSA eventually, allowing it to place three Liberty hulls and two Victory hulls back in service to perform electronic snooping duties. One of these ships, the USS Liberty, achieved notoriety during the 1967 Six-Day War when she came under savage attack by Israeli aircraft and torpedo boats.[21]

The NSA and Navy spy-ship fleets mostly cruised in areas void of Soviet naval activity and consequently avoided confrontations. However, this would not always be the case for a new class of American spook ships coming into service at the time of the Liberty incident. Dissatisfied with the time-share arrangements with NSA, the Navy strapped antenna-laden vans on destroyers and destroyer escorts. For example, USS Maddox was performing an ELINT mission in the Gulf of Tonkin when it came under attack on 2 August 1964.[22] However, deploying a warship to perform ELINT duties wasted most of the ship's combat capabilities: it was not a cost-effective use of Navy manpower. Also, a foreign country could interpret the appearance of an American warship steaming slowly off its coastline as a hostile move.

Inspired by the Soviets, the DoD's Deputy Director of Defense Research and Engineering, Dr. Eugene G. Fubini, proposed constructing an American AGI fleet. Eventually, three veteran light-cargo transports underwent conversion. With the operational evaluation of these three ships, plans could go ahead for the construction of additional listening platforms.

The USS Banner became the first of the three-ship class. At 935 tons, this veteran of many Pacific cargo runs matched her Soviet counterpart's average displacement. As for appearance, the American spy ship differed from many of her Soviet contemporaries. The deck house, containing the pilot house, crew's quarters, and engineering spaces, was located aft of amidships. As the ship underwent conversion at the Puget Sound Naval Shipyard in Bremerton, Washington, during the summer of 1965, workers replaced the cargo with operational spaces crammed with electronic equipment. Under the command of Lt. Robert P. Bishop, her first deployment in November 1965 from Yokosuka, Japan, turned into quite an adventure. In addition to conducting electronic eavesdropping duties, the 176-foot ship would also challenge a Soviet claim of sovereignty to waters across the mouth of Cape Povorotny Bay. The United States did not recognize this claim, and the *Banner* would demonstrate U.S. freedom to navigate in these waters and electronically monitor the Soviet response. Steaming in total EMCON (all radio emissions secured) and taking advantage of the Japanese coastline to conceal its presence, the little American spy ship attempted to get as close as possible to the Soviet-claimed waters without being detected. However, *Banner* steamed into an oncoming Siberian storm. As the ship pushed forward into the hostile seas, ice built up on the deck, making the former cargo ship dangerously top-heavy.

As if this were not enough, on 13 November Soviet destroyers and patrol craft appeared to show their displeasure with the intruding American by conducting a series of harassing maneuvers. A Krupnyy-class guided-missile destroyer signaled *Banner* that she was violating Soviet territorial waters. On 19 November the United States formally protested this Soviet territorial claim. On 17 December the Soviets again asserted their territorial claim and noted that the *Banner* had once again violated Soviet territorial waters on 24 November. The United States immediately rejected this note.[23]

During the next year *Banner* continued to deploy up and down the Soviet coastline to listen to Soviet communications. Repeatedly, the Soviets made the crew feel unwelcome. On 24 June 1966, on the approaches to Peter the Great Bay in the Sea of Japan, the Soviet AGI *Anemometr* and the *Banner* collided. Each side blamed the other for causing the collision. The State Department reacted immediately. The next morning in Washington, Ambassador-at-Large Llewellyn Thompson met with Ambassador Dobrynin to inform him of the incident and the forthcoming protest. Thompson told Dobrynin that the Soviet trawler had cut ahead of *Banner* in violation of the international regulations for preventing collisions at sea and that only last-second actions by the American ship had averted serious damage. The telegram containing the protest was sent that afternoon. The Soviet protest note, containing a different version of the incident, arrived at the U.S. Embassy, Moscow, on 28 June.[24]

With the *Banner* providing a high-quality yield of Soviet communications intercepts, conversion work continued on two additional mothballed ships, commissioned together on 13 May 1967 as the USS *Pueblo* and the USS *Palm Beach*. On 6 November the *Pueblo* departed from San Diego to Japan. Meanwhile, the *Palm Beach* was already en route to Norfolk, from where she would make deployments to the North Sea and Mediterranean before being withdrawn from service.[25] The plight of the *Pueblo* is well known. On 23 January 1968 North Koreans seized the ship and held the crew captive for the next eleven months. The disastrous consequences of the capture of a ship filled with the latest ciphering and deciphering equipment was not fully recognized until the arrest of a former Navy warrant officer fifteen years later. John A. Walker Jr. would be convicted for selling the Soviets key lists, cryptographic materials, and other publications allowing Soviet access to classified Navy communications.[26]

In the wake of the *Liberty* and *Pueblo* fiascoes, the Navy considered providing armed escorts for its fleet of spy ships. This was not a cost-effective option. With the increasing maintenance costs associated with operating World War II–vintage ships and a war in Southeast Asia competing for funds, in July 1969 CNO Adm. Thomas H. Moorer recommended that the ships be decommissioned. Within six months the Navy retired all from service. Other methods would have to be used to conduct communications interceptions.[27]

As noted earlier, the Soviet merchant marine and fishing fleets also were expanding during this period. Owned and operated by the state, these ships contributed to Soviet economic objectives and could be used to support military operations. For example, in 1955 Alaskan Air Command intelligence analysts commented on a recent sighting of the whaling ship *Aleut* and four small whale-killing ships sixty miles west of Attu:

> The *Aleut* was obviously whaling; the carcasses on her deck could almost be smelled through the stereoscope. However, each of the ships in the group

carried the electronic array of the probable "So" type radar. Although such gear has obvious usefulness in whale hunting, a secondary role in offshore picketry is technically feasible.[28]

Some believed that the Soviet fishing fleet had other, malicious intentions. A background paper prepared for the 1960 Paris summit expressed concern over the increase in transatlantic cable cuttings. After an average of only fifteen breaks per year between 1954 and 1958, fifteen breaks had been reported in the first four months of 1959 and twenty in the first four months of 1960. However, the paper emphasized that no positive evidence proved that Soviet trawlers were the culprits. Yet in coming to a conclusion of Soviet culpability, the paper cited the case of the *Novorossisk*. Between 21 and 25 February 1959 a total of five American Telephone and Telegraph (AT&T) and Western Union cables were severed off the coast of New-foundland. Being the only vessel in the vicinity, the *Novorossisk* was approached and halted by the radar picket destroyer USS *Roy O. Hale*. Citing the section of the Convention for the Protection of Submarine Cables that allowed naval ships to examine official documents of ships suspected of damaging cables, a five-man American party boarded the Soviet trawler. Later, at a press conference, the head of the search party stated that during his seventy-minute inspection no incriminating evidence could be found; however, it seemed "definitely possible and probably quite likely the trawler had something to do with the breaking of the cables."[29] In a note to the Soviet Union, the United States provided a detailed explanation of its action and pointed out that the Soviets recognized the 1884 Paris Convention. Despite the explanation, Radio Moscow reacted by calling the boarding "a premeditated act of provocation."[30]

In the ensuing years, Soviet fishing fleets in the Western Atlantic would demonstrate greater care in avoiding the cables. The same could not be said for the Soviet ships in the Pacific. In the aftermath of AT&T cable failures in November 1965 and February 1966, aerial reconnaissance revealed Soviet fishing trawlers operating over the cable route. AT&T asked for State Department assistance in obtaining Soviet cooperation to end the problem.[31]

Besides the alleged cable-cutting episodes, the growing Soviet fishing fleet activity off America's coastlines created another source of tension, albeit nonmilitary, between the United States and the Soviet Union. As noted in connection with the *Novorossisk* incident, Soviet trawlers had been operating in the cod-rich Grand Banks east of Newfoundland since the mid-1950s. By 1963 Soviet fishing vessels were working off the mid-Atlantic states from Massachusetts, south to North Carolina, and also in the Gulf of Alaska. By 1967 Soviet fishing trawlers had established a permanent presence off California and the Pacific Northwest.[32]

In contrast with the American fishing fleet, much of which was operated by individual owners, the Soviets fished with flotillas as large as 100 to 200 trawlers working together, supported by large factory and refrigerated cargo ships. With the U.S. territorial waters set at three miles during the 1960s and early 1970s, these ships could often be easily seen from the U.S. shoreline. Occasionally, the Coast Guard seized aggressive Soviet fishermen on the inshore side of the three-mile zone. One seizure occurred on 2 March 1967 when the USCG *Storis* came upon a Soviet trawler fishing within the three-mile limit off the Shumagin Islands near Alaska. The case was handled quickly since the trawler's captain agreed to pay the imposed fine, and the vessel and crew were released.[33]

American fisherman resented the Soviet "invasion" of U.S. coastal fishing waters. They depended on fish caught off the U.S. coast for their economic survival. Not surprisingly, a series of incidents would come to the attention of the Coast Guard, the media, and politicians. On the night of 26 July 1966 the fishing vessel *Pierce* was the victim of a hit-and-run incident in the Pacific off the coast of Washington. Sigvart Brevik, master of the *Pierce,* along with a witness on board another American fishing vessel, alleged that a Russian trawler bore responsibility. The incident received wide attention in the regional press, yet the State Department refused to press the Soviets for compensation because the witnesses had not positively identified the culprit. In the ensuing years the State Department received additional complaints about the Russians from fishermen on both coasts, including charges of malicious destruction of fishing gear.[34]

During the late 1960s the United States and the Soviet Union implemented a series of agreements to prevent future fishing disputes. Examples include the 5 December 1965 Agreement on Catching King Crabs and an agreement signed in 1967 and subsequently renewed to regulate fishing off the Middle Atlantic and Pacific Northwest regions. Still, fishermen and politicians remained unhappy with the situation. Joseph

Curran, president of the National Maritime Union, frequently wrote to challenge government policy toward handling Soviet trawlers. The U.S. government resisted any extensions of territorial seas for fear of sending a signal encouraging other nations to shift their maritime borders outward. As a nation dependent on navigational freedoms to assure trade, the United States clung to a three-mile limit during an era when most nations were adopting a twelve-mile zone. Eventually, the Law of the Sea negotiations in the 1970s settled on the twelve-mile limit and made allowances for economic exclusion zones. With the 1977 decision to establish a 200-mile economic exclusion zone around its shorelines, the United States could directly control the fishing activities of domestic and foreign fishing fleets within the zone and impose strict limits on the catch.[35]

The Soviet merchant fleet also became a factor in the growing confrontation on the high seas. With Fidel Castro taking Cuba into the communist camp, Soviet shipping along the eastern U.S. seaboard dramatically increased. Throughout 1961 and 1962 Soviet merchant shipping en route to Cuba underwent thorough photographic scrutiny. By August 1962 the National Photographic Interpretation Center (NPIC) in Washington, D.C., had identified ships containing military cargo reaching the island nation. Despite persistent complaints about "buzzings" lodged by both the Cubans and the Soviets, the American reconnaissance effort continued. Photos taken on 15 September of the ss *Poltava* showed the large hatched vessel riding high in the ocean as she made her way to Cuba. In retrospect, it is believed that *Poltava*'s cargo consisted of medium-range ballistic missiles. Later that month, the ss *Kasimov* was spotted en route to the Caribbean with ten sixty-foot crates amidships. Analysts later declared that these boxes contained fuselages for Il-28 medium bombers.[36]

On Monday, 22 October 1962, President Kennedy addressed the nation and the world about the discovery of the Soviet installation of medium- and intermediate-range missile facilities in Cuba. In announcing the American response, Kennedy stated that the first step would be to impose "a strict quarantine of all military equipment under shipment to Cuba." The next day, Kennedy signed the order making the quarantine effective beginning at 1000, Wednesday, 24 October. Would the Soviets challenge the quarantine?[37]

Late on Wednesday, reconnaissance flights revealed that several Soviet dry-cargo ships had halted in the mid-Atlantic, and eventually they reversed course and returned to Russia. Meanwhile, other ships continued toward the Caribbean. The first direct contact with a Soviet merchant ship occurred the following day at 0745 when the destroyer USS *Larve* hailed the Russian tanker *Bucharest*. Because the tanker was not carrying weapons, the White House allowed her to proceed. Later that day U.S. warships hailed the Cuba-bound East German passenger ship *Volkerfreundschaft* and the Greek merchant ship *Maritsa*, which had taken on cargo in Leningrad.[38]

On Friday morning, 26 October, the SS *Marucla* became the first and only ship to be boarded. American-built, Panamanian-owned, Lebanese-registered with a Greek master, the *Marucla* was under Soviet charter carrying material from the port of Riga to Cuba. Appropriately, a team mostly from the USS *Joseph P. Kennedy Jr.*, a ship named for the president's fallen brother, conducted the boarding. The boarding went without incident.[39]

The case closest to a direct high seas confrontation occurred the following day when the Soviet tanker *Groznyy* failed to heed the warning of a tailing American destroyer. Other American warships closed in and loaded their guns. When the U.S. Commander in Chief Atlantic (CINCLANT) ordered the picket ships to discharge their ammo by firing into the sea, *Groznyy* promptly reversed course and proceeded beyond the quarantine line to wait. A few days later, the Soviet tanker had permission to proceed to Cuba. By that time, the crisis had been resolved, the Soviets having agreed to remove their offensive weapons from Cuban soil.[40]

A touchy issue remained. How was the United States to be assured that the offensive missiles and aircraft had been removed? An irate Fidel Castro, furious at the Kremlin for backing down, refused to allow UN inspectors to violate Cuban sovereignty. Thus, to assure the United States of its pledge, the U.S.S.R. allowed the Americans to inspect the cargoes visually. Between 8 and 11 November nine departing Soviet freighters removed the forty-two missiles known to have been on the island. American warships intercepted the ships as they departed from Cuban territorial waters. Nearly all of the Soviet merchant ships begrudgingly cooperated with American requests to remove the tarps to expose the cargo. DESRON SIX commander Capt. Charles R. Calhoun recalled being embarked on the destroyer USS *Vesole* fifty feet abeam of one Soviet missile-laden merchant making headway at 15 knots.

Looking across, he observed the ship's skipper. "We could clearly see his countenance, which was very unhappy." The Soviet ignored hails made in English. Calhoun then directed a Soviet linguist to call over. "The moment he spoke in Russian, the Soviet captain's face lit up; he smiled, and waved and said, 'Good Morning' in English!" He quickly directed his crew to uncover the missiles. "We counted five on that ship as I recall, and we thanked him and made a report."

Some at-sea meetings were quite amiable. The skipper of the *Ivan Polzunov*, having just heard about the passing of Eleanor Roosevelt, expressed his sympathy to the captain of the uss *Newport News*. Upon completion of the verification, the American cruiser signaled, "GOODBYE AND GOOD LUCK." The Soviet merchant responded with "THANKS TO YOU — GOODBYE."

One Soviet freighter, the ss *Volgoles*, refused to heed the requests of the uss *Perry* to expose its load of missiles. At the United Nations American representative John McCloy protested to Vasily Kuznetsov. The Soviet diplomat suggested that, after a brief period, the American destroyers should reestablish contact with the *Volgoles*. Later, when the *Perry* asked the Soviet ship to expose the missiles, the *Volgoles* complied.

Some of the Soviet merchant skippers felt that the American verification techniques were overly aggressive. Kuznetsov complained to Ambassador Adlai Stevenson about demands made on three of the departing merchant ships, claiming that the American demands for them to open their cargo hatches under threat of force constituted a gross misunderstanding of the U.S.-U.S.S.R. agreement. In one case the missile destroyer uss *Biddle* made a close pass at the *Leninskiy Komsomol* to take photos. Unnerved, the Soviet master sounded the danger signal. American aircraft also overflew the Soviet ships to take photos for verification.[41]

The wake of the Cuban missile crisis must have been an adventurous time for Soviet merchant sailors. They could depend on the monotony of voyages being broken up by low-flying reconnaissance aircraft or passing Western warships. Even in port, the Soviet merchant seamen could encounter some unique circumstances. For instance, during port calls to Cuba and Vietnam Soviet ships were occasionally exposed to hostile actions.

Two such incidents occurred in Cuba in September 1963. On the night of 17 September, the Soviet cargo vessel *L'Gov*, berthed at Cuba's Port Isabela

La Sagua, was fired upon by heavy-caliber machine guns from a cutter that had entered and quickly departed the harbor. Just over a week later, during the night of 26–27 September, another attack occurred. This time a cutter fired at the *Baku*, which had just completed taking on a cargo of sugar at the Cuban port of Caibarien. Although Cuban counterrevolutionary groups took credit for the attacks, the Russians held the American government accountable.

American ships were not immune from attacks either. On 15 July the ss *Sister Katingo* departed from Novorossisk without the permission of the port authorities and was chased, fired on, and boarded by the crew of a Soviet patrol vessel. The American ship's master had decided to depart after a dispute over stevedoring charges. The U.S. government recognized that the Soviets had the legal right to act as they did. However, a protest was lodged as a result of overly abusive conduct by the Soviet authorities involved.[42]

During the war in Southeast Asia, a steady stream of Soviet ships called at North Vietnamese ports to unload the weapons Hanoi needed to sustain its effort to reunite the country under the communist banner. Often ships carrying these war materials steamed right past American warships posted on Yankee Station in the Gulf of Tonkin. Not surprisingly, each side issued several complaints regarding the conduct of ships of the other when in close proximity. For example, the Soviets claimed that on 1 August 1966 the merchant ship *Ingur* was steaming in the Tonkin Gulf when four American destroyers ordered her to stop.[43] Until mid-1966, Soviet ships in port were relatively safe. During the Rolling Thunder air campaign against North Vietnam, which began in March 1965, American aircraft were instructed to stay outside of a ten-mile radius around Haiphong. On 29 June 1966 this policy changed. To cut the fuel to the trucks carrying supplies down the Ho Chi Minh Trail, Pres. Lyndon Johnson authorized raids against petroleum receiving and storage facilities in the Hanoi-Haiphong area.[44]

No Soviet ships were in Haiphong to witness the air attack on 29 June. However, Soviet sailors were around to observe the second American raid, on 7 July. In a protest note the Soviets charged that the raid created a direct threat to Soviet seamen and claimed that fragments and machine-gun fire landed near three ships moored near Haiphong and that large metal objects fell around another ship at anchor in Halong Bay.[45] During a third raid on 2 August the Soviets alleged that U.S. Air Force planes strafed the cargo ship

Medyn. In this case, the U.S. Embassy in Moscow refused to accept the subsequent Soviet protest note, citing the abusive language it contained.[46]

Soviet ships received no actual damage during these 1966 episodes. However, on 2 June 1967, at the port of Cam Pha, fifty miles north of Haiphong, the Soviet cargo ship *Turkestan* was hit by a bomb, killing one crewmember and critically injuring another. That day, Foreign Minister Andrei A. Gromyko handed U.S. Embassy Chargé d'Affaires John C. Cuthie a protest note demanding punishment of those responsible and asking for assurances against future attacks. The next day, the Soviet chargé d'affaires in Washington received a note denying U.S. responsibility. Meanwhile, the incident received widespread media attention in the Soviet Union. Protests occurred at an American exhibit in Leningrad.[47]

The incident quickly declined in importance as leaders of both nations concentrated on events in the Middle East that erupted into the Six-Day War. However, on 17 June the United States sent a note to the Soviet Embassy. Delivered three days before the Glassboro summit meeting, the note explained that on 2 June an Air Force aircraft operating in the Cam Pha vicinity might have been responsible for the damage and injuries sustained by the Soviet ship. Nine days after receiving the note, the Soviets claimed that U.S. planes hit the Russian freighter *Frunze,* which was berthed at Haiphong. Upon investigation, the State Department officials conceded that American planes might have been responsible, because of the close proximity of a target.[48]

The Americans admitted possible responsibility for one more incident. On 4 January 1968 the captain of the *Pereyaslavi-Zalessky* claimed that a bomb had landed six feet from the side of his ship and exploded, causing extensive damage. The Soviet merchant ship had been berthed at Haiphong during an American air attack. The next day, Secretary of State Dean Rusk called in Ambassador Dobrynin to express regret.[49] The *Pereyaslavi-Zalessky* incident would be the last of its kind for several years. On 31 March 1968 President Johnson announced his decision to halt the bombing campaign in the north and his decision not to seek reelection.

Once on the high seas, some Soviet merchant-ship masters failed to heed the Rules of the Road when in proximity to American warships. A 1966 State Department survey listed thirty-six Soviet harassment incidents against

American ships in a one-year span, crediting one-quarter of the incidents to Soviet merchant ships failing to abide by the Rules of the Road. For example, on 13 May 1966 in the Pacific, the ss *Makhachkala* had responsibility to yield in a crossing situation with the uss *Terrell County*. The Soviet ship failed to maneuver until the American ship took last-minute action to avoid a collision.

The State Department survey was an attachment to a 20 August 1966 letter written by Deputy Undersecretary of State U. Alexis Johnson to Deputy Secretary of Defense Cyrus Vance. Johnson expressed concern over the growing number of encounters between U.S. and Soviet ships and aircraft. He noted that with more Soviet vessels operating off Vietnam the risk of a serious incident increased, and his concern extended to areas other than Southeast Asia. Understanding that U.S. commanders conformed to the Rules of the Road, Johnson worried that some on both sides might "shade" the instructions to engage in "a test of wills." The undersecretary had no recommendations for Vance except to make sure that American commanders adhered rigidly to their instructions. He closed by asking Vance for suggestions.[50]

Johnson's letter precipitated a review of instructions to commanding officers and started a search for ideas on how to manage the situation better. On 30 November Vance wrote a letter to Deputy Undersecretary Johnson's successor, Foy D. Kohler, proposing that the United States reach an understanding with the Soviets on the subject of encounters between U.S. and Soviet ships. Vance attached to the letter a proposal of "Basic elements for an understanding with the Soviet Union regarding operations of ships proximate to ships of the other nation." The basic elements contained the following proposals:

a. Ships of one nation will not operate in dangerous proximity to the ships of the other nation in such a manner as to create a possible hazardous situation.

b. The right of ships to close for identification purposes is recognized; however, the ship initiating the surveillance should maneuver in a manner that will neither embarrass nor endanger the ship being identified.

    c. Once identification is complete, the ship initiating the procedure should break off. Prolonged close accompaniment on the high seas, in absence of a reason therefore, is not justifiable.

    d. Ships of both nations will be required to adhere strictly to the letter and spirit of the International Regulations for Preventing Collisions at Sea, and respect the rights of others in their exercise of freedom of the seas.[51]

On 12 December 1966 Deputy Undersecretary Kohler responded to Vance, acknowledging receipt of the proposal and stating that it would be studied.[52]

Naval power is a major component of a nation's maritime power. However, counting aircraft carriers, destroyers, and submarines tells only part of the story. A strong merchant marine can significantly contribute to national economic viability, visibility, prestige, and security. Because of the growth of Soviet maritime activities and a changing world geopolitical situation, during the early to mid-1960s the two superpowers came into increasing contact on the high seas. However, because these contacts involved one or both of the parties being unarmed, there never was a serious threat of escalation into direct combat at the scene of the incident. Concerned about the nature of the incidents and aware that Soviet maritime power was continuing to expand, during 1966 the United States began to consider other options besides exchanging diplomatic volleys in the form of protest notes.

THE RISE OF THE
SOVIET NAVY

Direct contacts between the combatant ships of the two superpowers remained a rarity during the early 1960s. As noted, this period represented the nadir in Soviet surface naval capability. Soviet surface ships could not sustain operations over an extended period without replenishment ships. Occasionally, the Soviets did conduct "show the flag" missions. For example, the first post–World War II Soviet surface-ship deployment to the Mediterranean occurred in May–June 1954 when Black Sea Fleet Commander Vice Adm. Sergei G. Gorshkov took a cruiser and two destroyers and visited Albania. Additional Soviet surface-ship forays in the following years included brief visits to Egypt and Syria. Then, in 1958, the Soviets obtained basing rights at Vlone, Albania. Given the vulnerability of their surface ships, the Soviets chose to station eight Whiskey-class submarines and a submarine tender at the Albanian port. Having this base allowed the Soviets to conduct their first major Mediterranean naval exercise in September 1960. However, with the sudden break in Soviet-Albanian relations in 1961, the Soviets lost their base and were forced to scale back their regional presence.[1]

A more significant deployment of naval forces away from the homeland occurred in October 1962 during the Cuban missile crisis when Soviet submarines feebly challenged American naval supremacy. Later in the decade the Soviets began to mount a more serious challenge. If incidents with noncombatant ships caused policymakers in Washington to consider approaching the Russians about behavior at sea, the growing presence of the Soviet Navy on the world's oceans only added to the concern.

A portent of things to come occurred in March 1962 when the USS *Dewey* entered Baltic waters to show the flag and demonstrate U.S. resolve to navigate freely in international waters close to the Soviet Union. One morning, as the newly commissioned 5,800-ton warship proceeded farther into Baltic waters, a Soviet Riga-class frigate lay ahead. Because of previous run-ins with the Russians in these waters, the *Dewey*'s commanding officer, Capt. Elmo R. Zumwalt Jr., had secured special instructions from the fleet commander to stand fast if harassed, even if it meant possible collision. No match for the powerful *Dewey* in combat, the Soviet 1,300-ton frigate could still engage Zumwalt in a war of nerves.

Having taken station on a parallel course ahead of *Dewey*'s bow, the Riga began making a series of S-turns. As the *Dewey* maintained course and speed, the distance between the two warships decreased. When she was 1,000 yards off *Dewey*'s port bow, the Riga steadied on a course that would slowly lead to a collision. As the captain of the "privileged" vessel in accordance with the International Rules of the Road, Zumwalt kept his ship on course. As a precaution, the future CNO sounded General Quarters to upgrade *Dewey*'s watertight integrity. The skipper of the smaller warship maintained his course and speed as the American sailors ran to their battle stations and closed all open interior hatches. Finally, with collision seemingly certain, the Soviet skipper ordered "All stop" and reversed his engines. Momentum carried the frigate to within fifty feet of the *Dewey*'s hull. Because of her quick reversal, the Riga lost power. Zumwalt brought the *Dewey* around and ordered flank speed. Zipping past the stalled frigate, the American skipper then ordered his ship to come to a slower speed. The Riga resumed pursuit but maintained a distance astern throughout the rest of the day and into the evening. The next morning the little frigate again made an approach on the American ship but backed off after an exchange of flaghoists where the two ships conveyed their intentions by using signal flags.[2]

Seven months after this incident, during the Cold War's most serious crisis, the Soviet surface navy's inability to conduct sustained open-ocean operations forced the Soviet leadership to use submarines in an escort role — a mission alien to this type of warship. However, despite the Soviets' limited capability, President Kennedy's decision to establish the quarantine was not a risk-free move. Soviet submarines posed a threat for several reasons, including a direct tactical threat to American warships deployed to establish the quarantine; Khrushchev had warned visiting American businessman William Knox that Soviet submarines would sink any American ship attempting to enforce a quarantine.[3]

Soviet submarines also posed a threat because they could be used to circumvent the blockade. President Kennedy raised this concern at the morning meeting with his advisors on 16 October. Could this be the means by which the Soviets would transport the nuclear warheads to the island of Cuba? To make the quarantine effective, Soviet submarines would have to be included in the list of ships subject to inspection. This decision set the two navies on a course of direct confrontation. In stopping an unarmed merchantman to board and search, the U.S. Navy would use procedures long recognized by the seafaring nations of the world. But how does a navy enforce the procedure against a submerged warship?

That was the question Defense Secretary Robert McNamara had for Deputy Chief for Fleet Operations Vice Adm. Charles D. Griffin on the evening of 23 October. Griffin contacted the Atlantic Fleet staff, and together they created a unique set of signals for contacting Soviet submarines. With McNamara's approval, the signals were transmitted to the fleet five hours before the blockade would take effect. A Notice to Mariners announcing the signals was broadcast to the world on 25 October; Moscow may have received an advance copy a day earlier.[4]

To signal the submarines, the Navy used a combination of explosive devices and sonar signal transmissions. The type of explosive device dropped depended on the delivery vehicle. ASW aircraft dropped Mark 64 practice depth charges. Known as PDCs, these small explosive charges were used routinely in U.S. Navy exercises observed by Soviet submarines, so the Navy leaders assumed that Soviet skippers would recognize the sound. Surface warships simply dropped hand grenades over the side to send the signal. By causing four to five underwater explosions, the Navy signaled its demand that the Soviet submarine surface, head on an easterly course, and identify itself. Simultaneously, Navy warships used underwater communications equipment to pass the code signal "IDKCA," meaning "rise to surface." The Americans created this signal for this occasion, published it in a Notice to

Mariners, and hoped that the Soviets would transmit its meaning to its deployed submarines.[5]

After the crisis was over, CNO Adm. George W. Anderson boasted to an audience that the Cuban missile crisis had provided the best opportunity to exercise ASW tactics since the end of World War II. His Navy classified as confirmed contacts five diesel boats of the Foxtrot class and tracked them throughout the crisis. One of these submarines, located on the morning of 24 October apparently en route to escort merchant vessels heading toward Cuba, was the focus of attention for three American destroyers under instructions only to tail the boat. Later that day, when the Foxtrot had to surface to recharge batteries, one of the destroyers passed alongside the exposed submarine to ask, "Do you need any help?" The Russians responded by frantically shaking their heads and waving the offending warship off.[6]

This story repeated itself throughout the missile crisis. Constantly working to avoid or escape detection, surfacing diesel boats found warships of the U.S. Navy standing by. Two of the Foxtrots had to surface to make extensive repairs. The Americans observed men working on the deck of one of these damaged submarines, leading the observers to speculate about a faulty hatch seal. The other submarine to surface for repair eventually had to be towed, suggesting a propulsion problem. It is doubtful that American signaling devices caused either of these casualties, as some have suggested.[7]

The effectiveness of the special submarine signals was questionable. Even if Moscow transmitted the signals, many of the sub skippers may not have received them because of the actions they were taking to dodge the American ASW effort. However, three of the Soviet submarines that surfaced did so on an easterly heading. That could have been just a coincidence, but to recharge batteries these submarines merely had to snorkel.[8] Other submarines were not so cooperative. For example, the destroyer USS *Charles P. Cecil* located a submerged Foxtrot in the western Atlantic on 30 October and kept "almost continuous" contact despite repeated attempts by the diesel boat to escape. Throughout a thirty-six-hour period, this American warship coordinated and controlled assisting aircraft and ships and eventually flushed the Soviet boat to the surface for identification.[9]

After the conclusion of the crisis, Khrushchev reportedly summoned Admiral Gorshkov. The soon-to-be-deposed Ukrainian told his navy chief that neither he nor any successor should ever have to back down again in

THE RISE OF THE SOVIET NAVY » 51

such a situation. Gorshkov assured his leader that plans were being implemented to prevent a repetition of such humiliation in the future.[10] Gorshkov had reason to offer such reassurance. As the Cuban missile crisis unfolded, Soviet shipyards were beginning to produce the types of warships that could be deployed away from home waters. Late in 1962 the Soviets completed the first of four Kynda-class cruisers. Armed with large deck canisters containing SS-N-3 antiship cruise missiles, this first modern Russian warship class displaced 5,500 tons fully loaded. Early in the following year, the Kynda was joined by another revolutionary ship class: the Kashin. Featuring a gas turbine propulsion plant over a decade before any American warships did, the Kashin offered high speed and an ability to get under way at the flick of a switch. These sleek warships packed an intimidating array of sensors and weapon systems, some modified to carry the SS-N-2 Styx surface-to-surface missile. With the addition of these modern warships to a fleet that already held an inventory of fourteen *Sverdlov*-class light gun cruisers completed during the Stalin shipbuilding program, plus assorted conventional destroyers and frigates, Admiral Gorshkov finally could begin to challenge Western supremacy on the high seas.[11] "Could the Soviet Union agree to the age-old dominance on seas and oceans of the world by western maritime powers, especially in conditions which allow the extension of these areas as nuclear launch platforms? Of course not!" wrote the Soviet Navy commander in chief.[12]

Under Gorshkov the submarine remained the capital ship in the naval inventory for countering American submarine and surface forces. However, to complement Soviet submarine deployments and contribute to the hunt for American ballistic-missile submarines, Gorshkov ordered his growing surface fleet away from home waters. The need to deploy to the Mediterranean became a major priority, given the American deployment of Polaris missile submarines into this basin beginning in 1963. Despite relative inexperience, lack of training, and logistical difficulties, by mid-1964 Soviet warships had established a continual presence in the Mediterranean Sea which would only grow larger. Soviet naval units also ventured farther out into the Atlantic and Pacific. As additional modern combatants joined the fleet, Soviet naval deployments would eventually cover all areas of the globe — including the Caribbean. The Cold War at sea entered a new era.[13]

In the summer of 1966 the uss *Walker* departed Vietnamese waters to participate in a joint U.S.-Japanese antisubmarine exercise in the Sea of Japan.[14] On 24 July 1966 the *Besslednyy* (DD 022), a Soviet Navy Kotlin-class destroyer, joined up with the allied task force and assumed a tailing role. *Walker* kept an eye on the *Besslednyy*, with orders to screen away the snooping Russian visitor should she try to charge toward the center of the allied ship formation. A lieutenant (junior grade) on board the *Walker* later recalled that during this transit the Soviet warship was not really persistent in her attempts to break into the formation. Apparently American screening efforts were effective enough to draw a formal Soviet protest issued on 10 August 1966.[15]

Ten months later, the *Walker* again entered these waters. As part of TG-70.4, *Walker* joined the destroyer USS *Taylor* and destroyer escort USS *Davidson* to provide a screen for the aircraft carrier USS *Hornet*. At 1030 on 9 May 1967 the *Besslednyy* reappeared to assume shadowing duties. Throughout the day, the *Besslednyy* turned into the screening *Taylor* on several occasions and backed off only when the American destroyer refused to yield. At one point only 50 feet separated the two ships. As night fell, the Soviet ship retreated, keeping five miles away from the formation.

About 0845 the next morning, the CO of the *Walker*, Comdr. Stephan W. McClaren, received orders to relieve the *Taylor* of her shouldering duties. At approximately 0900 McClaren assumed the conn of the *Walker* and within fifteen minutes had his ship positioned between the Soviet and the *Hornet*. For the next two hours *Walker* strove to keep the Russian destroyer at bay. One observer counted fourteen approaches during which the *Besslednyy* came within 100 yards. Four of these approaches were within fifty yards, and two came within fifty feet. At 1106 the two ships had maneuvered themselves into a collision situation. With the Soviet ship approximately thirty-five feet off *Walker*'s starboard beam and still closing, the Officer of the Deck (OOD), Lt. (jg) John C. Gawne, USN, dashed for the 1MC (the ship's public address system) and passed the word: "Standby for collision starboard side, that is standby for collision starboard side." He then sounded the collision alarm.[16]

As the two ships closed, the officers on the bridge of the Soviet destroyer seemed unconcerned and, in fact, jovial until a minute or so before the collision. However, with collision imminent, several became very concerned. In the words of one American observer, "It was as if they didn't realize we would collide until just before it happened." The two warships rubbed up against each other for about a minute with the bridge of the *Besslednyy* positioned just aft of the *Walker's* bridge. After the two vessels separated, both skippers brought their respective vessels to a stop to inspect the damage. No personnel appeared to be injured on either ship. As for damage, the *Walker* suffered a torn radio antenna, a mangled paint-stowage locker, and a dented vent opening. On the Soviet ship the whaleboat dangled in the water off one of the port davits.

Shortly after the collision, the *Walker* sent the first of many radio messages to the task group commander, Rear Adm. Harry L. Harty Jr. The collision details were then sent via "flash" message precedence to the Joint Chiefs in Washington. As Harty's staff received amplifying reports, they prepared and sent additional sitreps to Washington. The *Walker* situation was not the only problem concerning the commander. An hour before the collision, one of his ASW helicopters detected a possible contact in the vicinity of the two dueling destroyers. Perhaps the Soviet surface warship had been acting to divert attention from an undersea comrade.[17]

The news of the collision reached Washington early on the tenth. By midday Assistant Secretary of State for European Affairs John M. Leddy met with Soviet Chargé d'Affaires Yuri N. Chernyakov and lectured him about the "dangerous performance" of the Soviet warship. As Leddy protested to the Soviet envoy, a new day broke in the Sea of Japan.[18]

In the early dawn, the *Besslednyy* departed, relieved by an older Krupnyy-class (DDGS 025) destroyer. Shortly after her arrival, the Krupnyy transmitted a flashing light message to the *Hornet*:

TO COMMANDER OF TASK FORCE, DURING 9TH AND 10TH OF MAY THE U.S. NAVAL SHIPS TAYLOR AND WALKER SYSTEMATICALLY AND ROUGHLY VIOLATED INTERNATIONAL RULES OF THE ROAD AT SEA AND MADE DANGEROUS MANEUVERING WHICH CAUSED DANGER OF COLLISION WITH SOVIET NAVAL SHIP. AS A RESULT OF SUCH A HOOLIGANS ACTION THE DESTROYER WALKER RAN DOWN THE PORT SIDE OF SOVIET DESTROYER 022 AND CAUSED DAMAGE TO HER. SUCH ACTIONS OF NAVAL SHIPS CANNOT BE AFFORDED. REQUEST STOP THE VIOLATIONS OF INTERNATIONAL RULES OF SHIPPING AT OPEN SEA IMMEDIATELY. COMMANDER SOVIET TASK FORCE.

At 1059 on 11 May the *Walker* received orders to resume shouldering duties. For the next three hours, the Krupnyy stayed approximately a mile off

Walker's starboard quarter, paralleling the American ship's course and matching her speed. Relieved for an hour and a half to refuel, *Walker* again resumed her watchdog duties. At the request of Commander McClaren, Lieutenant (jg) Gawne had been the OOD since 1030. Gawne recalled that in the late afternoon, after the formation had reversed course, the Soviet destroyer made several attempts to break past the *Walker* to approach the carrier. Each time the American destroyer blocked the Soviet's path. After one series of maneuvers, the Soviet ship had positioned itself ahead of the *Walker*'s starboard bow. Suddenly, DDGS 025 came left, placing both ships *in extremis*. Gawne signaled, "YOU ARE STANDING INTO DANGER" and "DO NOT CROSS AHEAD OF ME." The OOD then sounded the danger signal — six short blasts on the whistle — and passed the word over the 1MC, "Standby for collision starboard side forward, standby for collision starboard side forward."

After the two ships collided, the Krupnyy continued to the right and then stopped about 1,000 yards from the twice-hit American destroyer, which now sat dead in the water with her crew again scampering to battle stations. In contrast to DD 022, the Americans noted that the Krupnyy had secured all of her hatches and ports (indicating a higher degree of watertight integrity) and that she had her lifeboat rigged and griped down.[19]

As the signal lights blinked between the two ships, damage control teams assessed the conditions of the ships. Again no injuries were apparent on board either ship. Damage to the *Walker* consisted of dented frames on the starboard side near the bow and a six-inch puncture above the waterline. The Soviet ship sustained damage to her port quarter which included bent stanchions, an eight-inch-diameter hole above the waterline, and a ten-foot-long dent in her gray hull. In this case, the American skipper believed his ship was deliberately rammed. He stated that his suspicion was confirmed when the Soviet destroyer immediately flashed: "TO SKIPPER OF DESTROYER WALKER. YOU STARTED BY VIOLATE INTERNATIONAL RULES OF ROAD AT SEA." McClaren believed such a message, sent within two minutes of the collision, could have been sent only if it had been preprepared. Twenty minutes later the *Walker* responded: "YOU VIOLATED RULE 21 OF INTERNATIONAL RULES OF THE ROAD FOR PREVENTING COLLISIONS BY NOT MAINTAINING COURSE AND SPEED."[20]

Within two hours after the *Walker* completed her initial reports, Rear

Admiral Harty released another flash message for transmission to the Joint Chiefs. Again Chargé d'Affaires Chernyakov was summoned from the Soviet Embassy to the State Department to relay a message to his government urging that it should "take prompt steps to halt such harassment." Elsewhere in Washington, House Republican Leader Gerald R. Ford asserted that Soviet leaders were "seeking to challenge the United States." He further stated that "we certainly can't tolerate other such incidents." The future president suggested that American skippers should be given specific guidance to protect their ships, including utilizing their weapons. The White House press secretary stated that President Johnson "deeply regrets the incidents" and "considers them a matter of concern."[21]

Meanwhile, Radio Moscow blamed the United States for the collisions. Two days later the Soviets summoned Ambassador Thompson to deliver a formal protest, claiming that the acts of the United States warships were of "a premeditated, arrogant nature." A few days later, Admiral Gorshkov, in an article in *Izvestiya,* accused McClaren of acting with "malicious intent," and ridiculed the war-monger Gerald Ford for his "irresponsible statement." The Soviet Navy commander concluded: "It is not hard to imagine what might happen if warships were to begin shooting at each other when they collide."[22]

As the *Walker* jousted with Soviet destroyers in the Sea of Japan, the long-standing dispute between Israel and its Arab neighbors again threatened to erupt into violence. Additional American warships moved into the eastern Mediterranean. The Soviets also augmented their surface-combatant presence in the region. By 5 June 1967 thirteen Soviet warships, nearly double the normal presence, were within striking distance of the two U.S. carrier groups. With most of his ships at Kithira, an anchorage located in international waters between mainland Greece and Crete, the Soviet commander kept abreast of U.S. fleet movements through reports received from his "tattletales."

One of the "tattletales," an AGI, intercepted the USS *Saratoga* and her escorts entering the region about 23 May. A few days later, a Riga-class frigate did likewise when the USS *America* and escorts entered the eastern Mediterranean. On 4 June a speedier Kashin-class destroyer relieved this small Riga of her shadowing duties. The Americans were not the only ones being spied on. Soviet minesweepers kept tabs on the British carrier HMS

Victorious. On 2 June a Kotlin-class destroyer joined these sweeps in the vicinity of Malta.[23]

On 6 June Israeli air strikes against Arab airfields set the tempo for what would eventually prove to be a remarkable military success. Egypt claimed American participation in these devastating raids; however, due to its tattletales, Moscow knew otherwise. Still, tensions between the two maritime forces increased. A pool of seventeen reporters embarked on the *America* kept Americans informed of the growing activities of the Soviet Navy.[24] As the fighting continued on land on 7 June, *America*'s commander received a report of a Soviet submarine in his vicinity and ordered ASW forces to locate and track this potential threat. As U.S. destroyers, helicopters, and patrol planes began their intensive search, the Soviet tattletale became more assertive. After a near collision with the destroyer USS *William C. Lawe,* the Soviet Kashin received a message from COMSIXTHFLT Vice Adm. William I. Martin, directing her to clear the formation, which she did.[25]

By the evening of 7 June, *America*'s destroyer screen believed it had a Soviet submarine under sonar surveillance. The next day, another Soviet destroyer returned, accompanied by a smaller corvette. These two ships also tried to be disruptive. For example, the corvette (PC-160) had been trailing the *America* when the carrier came about to conduct flight operations. The corvette turned into the path of the turning carrier and onto an intercepting course. Had the carrier continued to turn to its intended course, the two ships would have been placed *in extremis. America* cut its turn short and cleared the Soviet ship. As the carrier passed within 700 yards of the Soviet vessel, Capt. Donald D. Engen sent the little ship a stern warning to remain clear. Captain Engen, supported by his chain of command, held fast when the Rules of the Road dictated that he had the right of way. Later, he recalled, "I held firm and would have run down a Soviet ship if I was right."[26]

As the *America*'s CO confronted the annoying Soviets, the distress call received from the USS *Liberty* presented a new problem. Who was the culprit? Fortunately, because the American commander knew the relative positions of Soviet surface units, he quickly eliminated them as a possible aggressor. With two speedy destroyers dispatched to the scene of the attack, word finally came that Israeli Defense Forces had attacked the *Liberty.*

As the dead and wounded were transferred from the *Liberty* to the

America on the following day, Israeli ground forces made spectacular gains against the armies of Syria, Jordan, and Egypt. A Soviet threat to intervene in the conflict was sternly met by the Johnson administration on 10 June through the movement of the *America* and *Saratoga* closer to the shores of Syria. With the Soviet Navy transmitting American carrier movements to Moscow, the Soviet Union backed down from committing belligerent action and supported the uneasy cease-fire that eventually took effect.

As the cease-fire held, more Soviet warships and support vessels slipped into the Mediterranean to bolster its naval presence. By mid-June, the Soviet order of battle in the region included some seventy vessels. The June 1967 war constituted a definite watershed: for the first time a Soviet surface fleet had been deployed to demonstrate support for client states and counter the influence of U.S. sea power in a region away from the Soviet Union. Because the Egyptians were desperate to reequip their armed forces after their stunning defeat, they gave in to Soviet demands for basing rights. With port facilities in Alexandria and Port Said, the large naval force placed in the Mediterranean would be sustained, improved, and in position to challenge the United States in a future crisis.[27]

The growing seriousness of at-sea confrontations with the Soviet combatant vessels, in conjunction with incidents with merchant ships, fishing trawlers, and AGIS, caused concern within the American government, especially in the Navy. Yet the State Department refused to approach the Soviets, despite the *Walker* incidents in the Sea of Japan and reported harassment in the South China and Mediterranean seas. In a letter to Rear Adm. James W. Grady sent on 3 July 1967, Assistant Secretary of State Leddy agreed that the proposed understandings with the Soviets on safety at sea submitted by Cyrus Vance the previous November were sound. However, he believed that the Soviets would not be interested in discussing the issues constructively, given the international situation at that time. He did suggest that the United States could approach the Soviets at some future date.[28]

Meanwhile, the two sides continued to exchange protest notes. For example, on 22 August 1967, the Soviets protested dangerous and provocative maneuvers by the USS *Davis*. The Soviets alleged that the American destroyer had cut at full speed across the bow of a surfaced Soviet submarine operating in the Mediterranean. The Americans, disputing the allegations, rejected the note.[29] After another near collision on 30 October 1967 between U.S. and Soviet destroyers, Comdr. J. W. Robertson, an OpNav Action Officer, drafted a memorandum for the Deputy Chief of Naval Operations (DCNO) for Plans and Policy to recommend the State Department reconsider approaching the Soviet Union to propose an understanding. On 9 November 1967 Secretary of the Navy Paul R. Ignatius forwarded the recommendation to Deputy Secretary of Defense Paul H. Nitze. The paper then sat in his in-basket.[30]

On 17 December 1967 the fleet tug USS *Abnaki,* operating with the USS *Ranger* at Yankee Station, was assigned the mission of screening the AGI *Gidrofon* away from the carrier. *Gidrofon* had been especially pesky over the previous three days, hazarding operations for the carriers *Ranger* and USS *Oriskany.* As *Gidrofon* closed on the *Ranger,* the fleet tug interposed itself between the two ships. With the *Gidrofon* within 200 yards of the carrier, *Abnaki* physically shouldered the Russian away, brushing up twice against the Soviet trawler's hull. Neither ship was seriously damaged.

Within the DCNO's Plans and Policy office, an action officer drafted another memorandum for Secretary Ignatius to forward. Signed by Ignatius on 11 January 1968, the memorandum for Nitze summarized the *Abnaki-Gidrofon* collision. The leading paragraph referred to the previous memorandum and Vance's letter of 30 November 1966, and restated the need for developing with the Soviet Union "parameters for surveillance procedures in order to avoid unnecessary and undesirable encounters between U.S. and Soviet ships, which could be extremely serious. This need is becoming urgent."[31]

On 23 January 1968, seven months after tragedy befell *Liberty,* North Korea captured the USS *Pueblo.* President Johnson, on the advice of Secretary of State Rusk, declined to send U.S. forces into military action elsewhere in Asia. Instead, he initially opted for a show of naval force off the Korean coastline.[32] Responding, the Soviets set out to disrupt the USS *Enterprise* task force that was steaming in the Sea of Japan. On the same day the North Koreans captured the *Pueblo,* the Soviet AGI *Gidrolog* blocked the carrier's path and forced the *Enterprise* to stop and reverse engines. Throughout the following weeks, while eighty-three men remained captive in North Korea, Soviet ships dogged the American task force.[33]

A week later, a more urgent crisis diverted the attention of those who advocated a more aggressive response against the North Koreans. On 31

January the Tet offensive challenged U.S. and South Vietnamese positions throughout South Vietnam. To compound the perception of American vulnerability created during the previous month by different events in the Far East, on the morning of 1 February the destroyer USS *Rowan* and the Soviet merchant ship *Kapitan Vislobokov* collided in the Sea of Japan. It was a crossing situation in which the Soviet ship failed to give way. Neither ship's crew sustained injuries. The American warship suffered a three-foot gouge in her port bow, while the *Vislobokov* reported a two-meter dent in her stern.[34]

The next day in Washington, Paul Nitze finally signed the letter that again asked the State Department to make a prompt approach to the Russians to come to an understanding. On 9 February Undersecretary of State Nicholas deB. Katzenbach responded, stating that correspondence with the Russians over the *Pueblo* incident had included American suggestions on talks to prevent incidents at sea. Katzenbach wrote that if the Russians did not respond in a month or two, he would have "the Soviet desk go back at them again."[35]

Meanwhile, incidents continued in the Sea of Japan. On 22 February 1968 Commander in Chief, U.S. Pacific Fleet (CINPACFLT) Adm. John J. Hyland sent a message to his boss, Commander in Chief Pacific (CINCPAC) Adm. Ulysses S. G. Sharp, stating that the harassing incidents near Japan were increasing in frequency and that the nature of the incidents indicated that "many or all were deliberately intended." Hyland cited fourteen recent examples to illustrate his case and called for prompt diplomatic action. On 8 March the DCNO for Plans and Policy responded by sending a draft protest note on the recent Sea of Japan incidents to Deputy Secretary Nitze to pass on to the State Department for delivery to the Soviets.

Earlier, on 1 March, Sharp reported Hyland's communiqué to the Joint Chiefs of Staff, emphasizing that if Soviet harassing actions were allowed to go on with impunity, they would "constitute an infringement of the basic right to freedom of navigation on the high seas." The Joint Chiefs formed a panel to consider the problem that asked for full Joint Chiefs backing of the previous DCNO for Plans and Policy position calling for negotiations.[36] With the Joint Chiefs supporting the Navy position and no progress made with the Russians in discussions related to the *Pueblo* incident, the State Department finally acted. On 16 April 1968 a proposal was delivered to the

Soviet Ministry of Foreign Affairs requesting that discussions be held on "safety of the sea" issues.[37]

On 25 May 1968 the USS Essex and her escorts were on a submarine-hunting mission off the coast of Norway. However, the hunter could also be the hunted. During preceding days, Soviet jet or prop-driven bombers flew over the Essex on eight separate occasions. On this day, Essex lookouts spotted the silver fuselage of a twin-engine Tu-16 Badger.[38]

The arrival of the Badger did not deter the ship from conducting her assigned mission. After the lifeguard helicopter was launched — as a precaution, to make a quick rescue should one of the planes to be launched plunge into the ocean — an S-2 Tracker ASW aircraft moved into position over the forward port catapult. The plane's pilot, Comdr. Russ Dickens, was told to "hold up a few minutes." It bothered Dickens that no one could explain the reason for the delay. Suddenly, he looked up to see the top ten feet of the tail section of a Badger pass in front of the bow. "The fuselage of the Badger was actually below the flight deck level!" Dickens observed it turn about two miles from the ship and noted, "It appeared to me that after the initial low level turn, the pilot took a peek at his position with regards to the aircraft carrier, and that is when he dipped his left wing and cartwheeled into the water."[39]

Essex's rescue helicopter found no survivors. Small boats placed in the water did recover debris and human remains. Flash message traffic entered the airwaves to alert Washington of the situation in order to preempt any misunderstandings that could draw a hostile Soviet reaction. As the Soviet Embassy received news of the unfortunate incident, the American destroyer USS Warrington passed a similar message to a Soviet destroyer patrolling some 100 miles away from the crash site. That Soviet destroyer immediately proceeded to the vicinity of the Essex.[40]

After the Soviet warship joined up with the Essex in the late afternoon, arrangements were made for the transfer of remains. Comdr. Edward Day, the operations officer, had the solemn task of escorting the remains to the Soviet ship. As Commander Day's boat was placed in the water, the Soviet destroyer took station astern of the American carrier. As a tribute to the fallen naval aviators, the Americans flew the "missing man" formation in S-2 Trackers. The Soviets also rendered honors in the form of a gun salute.[41]

On 13 August 1968 Adolph Dubs of the State Department Bureau of European Affairs called in Soviet Counselor for Political Affairs Y. M. Vorontsov. While discussing the crash of the Badger, Dubs also offered to lease navigational equipment in the wake of the Soviets forcing down an American chartered airliner full of military personnel that had strayed over the Kuriles. The Americans offered electronic navigational beacons to the Soviets to prevent future occurrences. Dubs presented Vorontsov with copies of film and photographs of the Badger incident and used the opportunity to remind the Soviets of the U.S. offer to hold safety at sea talks. Three days later Undersecretary Katzenbach wrote to Deputy Secretary Nitze about the meeting and expressed pessimism on a positive Soviet response.[42]

It is possible to speculate that the Soviets did respond positively, if not directly. In a Pentagon study of incidents, the Badger crash was recorded as the eighteenth U.S.-U.S.S.R. incident at sea in 1968. Only four more incidents would be recorded for the rest of the year, and only ten during the following year. If numerical decline actually represented a change in guidance from Moscow to Soviet ship skippers, several factors may have brought this about. First, the American proposal to hold "safety at sea" talks, combined with the Badger crash, may have sobered Soviet naval leaders and underlined to them that this was a serious issue that could get out of hand. Second, other foreign policy objectives also may have contributed. The Kremlin leadership hoped to take advantage of circumstances such as President Johnson's declaration at the end of March that he would not seek reelection, and his decision to cease bombing in North Vietnam, to gain leverage in various negotiations with the United States. In late June a nuclear nonproliferation accord was signed, and the two sides reached an agreement to hold bilateral nuclear arms talks. Soviet Navy mischief-making could only hurt Soviet diplomatic initiatives. Finally, the Czecho-slovakian "problem" eventually led to the invasion of that country by 300,000 Warsaw Pact troops in mid-August. Suffering a world public-opinion disaster, the Soviets may not have wanted to exacerbate the situation on the high seas.

There is also a possibility that the statistics merely represented a disengagement of Soviet and U.S. maritime forces in the wake of President Johnson's decision to cease bombing North Vietnam and an American drawback in the Sea of Japan after the initial response to the seizure of the uss *Pueblo*. The consistency or, rather, inconsistency of the types of incidents reported and the types of statistics maintained by the Navy staff also needs to be factored into any thesis that the Soviets responded unofficially to the American overture. A future participant in talks with the Soviets, Capt. Robert Congdon, recalled that a Soviet destroyer harassed his ship, the uss *Buchanan*, in the Sea of Japan in the spring of 1969. However, Congdon maneuvered his ship away from a hazardous situation.[43] This incident is not listed in the 1969 statistics. In all probability, Captain Congdon felt the incident was not worth reporting. Whether the Soviet Naval Headquarters issued a dictum urging greater restraint at this time awaits the declassification and release of Soviet records. However, the large statistical drop, even considering possible tainting by poor bookkeeping, points toward some move toward greater prudence on the high seas on the part of the Soviets.

Buchanan's presence in the Sea of Japan was due to another crisis. On 15 April 1969 a North Korean fighter shot down a Navy EC-121M aircraft off the east coast of North Korea, killing all thirty-one on board the electronic surveillance plane. Back in Washington, the shootdown tested the new Nixon administration crisis action team. Henry Kissinger, at the time Advisor to the President on National Security Affairs, later wrote that in this case the White House performance was lacking. The decision to deploy carrier task groups to the Sea of Japan merely mimicked the ineffective reaction of the Johnson administration during the 1968 *Pueblo* crisis.[44]

To protect future airborne ELINT missions from attack, the Navy deployed the ground-controlled intercept picket ships uss *Wiltsie* and uss *Benjamin Stoddert* to the Sea of Japan. Throughout the summer of 1969 low-flying high-speed Soviet aircraft frequently buzzed the two ships. CINCPAC expressed concern that the flights were harassing and provocative, causing additional tensions on the picket ships due to crew knowledge that the aggressive North Koreans also flew similar aircraft. Consequently, Secretary of Defense Melvin Laird forwarded a draft proposal to Secretary of State William Rogers to modify surveillance behaviors in the Sea of Japan. Rogers turned the letter and attached proposal over to his European Branch for consideration.[45]

On 27 October 1969 Adolph Dubs again met with Yuly M. Vorontsov, this time to discuss the USS *Rayburn*–AGI *Teodolit* incident off Charleston, South Carolina, and to complain about the Soviet seizure of research buoys that had been placed in the central-north Pacific Ocean. During the meeting Dubs reminded Volontsov that the 16 April 1968 offer for safety at sea talks remained open.[46]

On 9 December 1969 the State Department finally brought to the Soviets' attention the June *Wiltsie* and *Stoddert* incidents, along with reports of subsequent buzzings of American warships in the Sea of Japan. The protest note did not propose talks to address specifically the Sea of Japan situation as Secretary Laird had asked; however, Dubs reminded Soviet Embassy Minister-Counselor Yuri N. Chernyakov of the April 1968 offer.[47]

A year after the EC-121 shootdown and the subsequent interactions with Soviet naval and air forces, the Soviet Navy made its presence known to the West in a very big way. John Warner, Secretary of the Navy from 1972 to 1974, later called it a coming-out party for the Soviet Navy. A naval maneuver of immense complexity and proportions, Okean 70 ranked as one of the largest exercises ever to be conducted in peacetime. The April 1970 simulated battle included over 200 submarines, surface combatants, and support vessels as well as aviation units. Global in scope, the maneuver demonstrated Soviet capabilities in antisubmarine and antiaircraft carrier warfare, sea-lane interdiction, and amphibious operations.

Commanding the guided-missile destroyer USS *Waddell*, Capt. Peter K. Cullins closely observed Soviet Pacific Fleet Okean 70 operations in the Sea of Japan. To collect intelligence, Cullins said he repeatedly breached guidelines set by his superiors and often brought his ship within 100 yards of the Soviets, yet the Soviets never seemed to mind his close maneuvers. To gain Soviet acquiescence to his close approaches, Cullins placed the ship's dog on his bridgewing chair and the ship's rock band on the fantail to entertain the Russians with "Back in the U.S.S.R." and other tunes. Occasionally, the band took requests.[48]

From intelligence reports fed back from *Waddell* and other sources, American leaders were placed on notice that U.S. control of the seas could no longer be assumed. Without aircraft carriers, the Soviet Navy could not hope to seize overall control of the seas, but with its blue-water fleet of submarines and missile ships it was developing a capability to deny certain ocean areas to U.S. forces. For the United States, it was a bad time to be placed on notice. The backbone of the U.S. fleet had been built during World War II and faced block obsolescence. Congress declined to expend funds to build needed replacement hulls because of the expensive conflict in Southeast Asia.[49]

Faced with the relative decline of American sea power, Defense Secretary Laird convinced the president to make a radical choice to provide leadership to the Navy. The man Laird recommended had impressed him during a recent visit to South Vietnam by demonstrating that "Vietnamization" could work. Selected over dozens of more senior officers to become the youngest CNO ever, Adm. Elmo R. Zumwalt Jr. took the helm on 1 July 1970.[50]

As the new 49-year-old CNO took command, tension remained between the two navies on the high seas. Soviet planes frequently flew out of bases in Egypt to conduct mock attacks on Sixth Fleet units. In March there had been a collision between an American Phantom fighter from the carrier USS *Franklin D. Roosevelt* and a Badger bomber with Egyptian markings. Since the United States suspected that the plane's pilot spoke Russian as a native tongue, the State Department brought the incident to the attention of the Soviets. In early July the United States claimed that Badger and larger Bear aircraft had made recklessly low passes over the USS *Wasp* in the Norwegian Sea. On 3 July one Badger diagonally buzzed across the carrier's bow as an aircraft was about to be catapulted.[51]

In August more alleged Soviet nautical mischief occurred off Cape Canaveral when a Soviet AGI entered into a restricted area offshore to attempt to retrieve materials from a missile-firing exercise being conducted by the ballistic-missile submarine USS *James Madison*. The aggressive movements of the *Khariton Laptev* around the American escorting vessels nearly caused a collision. Later that month, the *Laptev* gave grief to a surfaced submarine operating off Block Island, Rhode Island. On 27 August State Department officials Herbert S. Okun and William T. Shinn summoned Soviet Embassy Counselor Igor D. Bubnov to the State Department. When the Soviet envoy arrived, Okun delivered two written protests and an oral protest concerning the *Wasp* and two *Laptev* incidents. Okun reminded Bubnov of the long-standing U.S. offer to formally discuss "safety on the seas."[52]

Naval interaction would continue to be a factor in U.S.-Soviet relations, as illustrated by the Jordanian crisis of September 1970. On 6 September members of the Popular Front for the Liberation of Palestine hijacked a PanAm 747 and had the jumbo jet flown to Cairo, where it was blown up. Simultaneously, a TWA Boeing 707 and a Swissair DC-8 were being flown at gunpoint to a dirt runway near Amman, Jordan, where they were joined a few days later by a British VC-10 that had also been seized by terrorists. In reaction, on 9 September, in conjunction with other military preparations, President Nixon directed that the USS *Independence* and her escorts move to a position off Lebanon. On 12 September, after removing the passengers, the Palestinians blew up the three airplanes and released some hostages. The remaining captives, coming from many countries, served as trade-bait to gain the freedom of Palestinian terrorists held in prisons throughout Western Europe and Israel. With the American task force off the coast of Lebanon waiting for further instructions from Washington, rumors flowed in Jordan of imminent American intervention. Meanwhile, Soviet Navy warships posted themselves near the American fleet as Moscow preached "restraint."[53]

On 17 September King Hussein ordered his army into action to regain control of his country. As Hussein's army moved against Palestinian concentrations in Amman and the rest of the country, the question became: Would there be outside intervention? To support the king, the United States ordered two additional carrier battle groups toward the region. As the USS *Saratoga* and escorts headed east from Malta, the USS *John F. Kennedy* steamed across the Atlantic at best speed. In addition, an amphibious task force that had been operating off the coast of Crete moved toward Lebanon, while additional marines made ready to deploy from the American East Coast. In Chicago, President Nixon announced that if Syria or Iraq tried to intervene on behalf of the Palestinians, the United States or Israel would be provoked to step in, adding that he preferred the United States to take the action.[54]

Reports received in the White House on the morning of 20 September indicated that Syria was moving forces into Hussein's kingdom. Preparations were made for American intervention as U.S. and Israeli intelligence monitored the battle unfolding between the two Arab neighbors. Off the coast of Lebanon, Soviet warships became more aggressive toward the growing U.S. fleet. The Soviet Navy warships went to battle stations in the presence of the American carriers, running missiles to their launcher rail and tracking American aircraft with their fire-control radar. As a precaution, the COMSIXTHFLT assigned escorts with rapid-fire guns to trail the Soviet missile ships so as, in the words of Admiral Zumwalt, "to prevent them from preventing us from launching our planes by knocking out most of their cruise missiles before many of them took off."[55] Events in Jordan developed to preclude the need for outside intervention. By 22 September an estimated 120 Syrian tanks had been rendered inoperable by Jordanian arms or mechanical malfunction. In the face of such losses and the possibility of American-Israeli intervention, the Syrians were forced to withdraw. Although American sea power did not directly play a part, its presence contributed to resolving the crisis to America's advantage. The Soviet naval attempt to influence American moves still proved feeble in the wake of preponderant American sea power.[56]

Still, the prospects for future naval confrontations on the high seas seemed certain as the Soviet Navy demonstrated worldwide capabilities during the 1970 Okean exercises and deployed overseas in support of Soviet foreign policy objectives. In late 1970, with the Jordanian crisis, the continuing conflict in Southeast Asia, and other contentious foreign policy issues, Soviet-American relations were far from harmonious. Then a strange string of unforeseen events occurred in mid-October to further worsen matters between Moscow and Washington.

« **5** »

THE ROAD TO
MOSCOW

"Nadya rushed into the pilot's compartment, screamed 'hijacking' and began to close the door. A shot rang out. Nadya fell and a man of about 50 burst into the cabin. He had a sawed-off shotgun in his hands and shouted 'Turkey, Turkey!'" exclaimed Aeroflot copilot Suliko Shavidize to a newspaper correspondent in the aftermath of the first successful hijacking of a Soviet passenger aircraft. On 15 October 1970 a Lithuanian truck driver and his son forced an Antonov twin turbo-prop flight to divert to the Turkish city of Trebizond. The incident created instant tension between the Soviet and Turkish governments as the Turks ignored Soviet extradition requests for the two men, who had murdered a Russian stewardess. On 18 October a Turkish court further infuriated the Kremlin by declaring the hijacking a political offense, meaning that the hijackers could not have criminal charges pressed against them or be subject to extradition.[1]

As this political storm raged between the Soviet Union and one of America's closest allies, the commander of the U.S. Military Aid Mission to Turkey, Army Gen. Edward C. D. Scherrer, prepared to depart from Ankara for the border region to take a tour of forward Turkish military installations. On 21 October Scherrer, joined by Brig. Gen. Claude M. McQuarrie and Turkish Col. Cevdat Denilg, were in a U-8 Beechcraft, piloted by Maj. James P. Russell, battling heavy weather. Seeing a break in the clouds, Major Russell brought the twin-engine plane down to the airstrip in Leninakan — in Soviet Armenia.[2]

Obviously, no connection existed between the two incidents. Yet Vasiliy Grubyakov, the Soviet ambassador to Turkey, observed, "There are now two Russian murderers in Turkey and one Turkish colonel in Russia. Both must be returned."[3] The subsequent Soviet handling of the captured Americans and Turk further soured relations between the two superpowers. The Soviet media exploited the incursion, equating it with the U-2 incident that had occurred a decade earlier. The Soviets further enraged the Americans by denying timely consular access to the prisoners as specified in an agreement, and by suggesting that the captured Americans be exchanged for Igor Ivanov — a convicted Soviet spy. Both sides lodged protests. Boris H. Klosson, the American chargé d'affaires in Moscow, boycotted October Revolution festivities. Perhaps after American hints that the situation could have an adverse impact on the newly started Strategic Arms Limitation Talks (SALT), the Soviets came around. On 9 November the Soviet government indicated that the three Americans and the Turk would be released the next day.[4]

After the release, Klosson met with veteran Soviet diplomat Georgiy M. Korniyenko to discuss the Scherrer incident. At the end of that discussion, Korniyenko changed the topic and stated that "competent organs" within the U.S.S.R. were now prepared to accept the U.S. proposal to hold bilateral meetings on how to avoid incidents at sea between ships and aircraft of the two countries. He proposed that the meetings take place in Moscow in early 1971. Korniyenko further stated that no decision had been reached regarding who would lead the Soviet delegation, but it probably would be a naval officer. Korniyenko told the American diplomat that Moscow would await concrete proposals from the United States. Korniyenko's offer surprised Boris Klosson. In a 10 November 1970 telegram to the Secretary of State, the chargé d'affaires did not offer any special insights. He speculated that the Soviets might have desired to "send a positive sign involving the military to help offset the negative effect of the Scherrer case or the *Ark Royal* case may have bestirred on them." The previous day, the British aircraft carrier HMS *Ark Royal* had collided with a Soviet destroyer, resulting in loss of life on the Soviet vessel.[5]

The Americans were surprised, if not shocked, by the sudden Soviet decision to accept the long-standing American offer. On balance, Admiral Zumwalt thought that the Soviets' offer was good news, but he held some suspicions regarding their true motivations "as they had a tremendous reputation for perfidy."[6] Consequently, the American side was not immediately prepared to respond with concrete proposals. How the United States formulated its positions would be the subject of a long and tedious but vital interdepartmental review process.

The initial battle developed over who would head the American delegation. John Stevenson, from the State Legal Branch, and George S. Springsteen, Acting Director of the European Branch, sent Secretary of State William P. Rogers a memorandum arguing that State expertise was needed as the success or failure of negotiations would depend on complex political and legal issues. The two men recommended that the talks focus on ship-ship and ship-aircraft situations. Territorial violation issues were to be avoided. They also suggested Deputy Assistant Secretary of State for European Affairs Richard T. Davies as best qualified to head the U.S. delegation. On 3 February 1971 Rogers sent Secretary of Defense Melvin R. Laird a letter naming Davies to lead the American contingent and politely asked Laird to name a naval officer to serve as Davies's assistant.[7] Laird balked. The Russians had already indicated that they intended to have an admiral head their delegation, and the issues to be discussed dealt with technical aspects of ship and aircraft operation. A DoD representative ought to head up this delegation. But who? The choice came down either to Lawrence S. Eagleburger, the Deputy Assistant Secretary for International Security Affairs, or John W. Warner, the Undersecretary of the Navy.

Laird consulted with the Chief of Naval Operations. Admiral Zumwalt felt that Warner would be a good choice, particularly because he had some experience as a U.S. representative to the Law of the Sea conferences. Laird concurred. He was grooming the young Virginian for the Secretary of the Navy (SecNav) job. Warner had asked to be appointed SecNav after Nixon's victory in November 1968. He had supported Nixon in 1960 and cochaired "Citizens for Nixon" in 1968 and, with victory, he argued that he had the credentials for the position, noting that he had enlisted Navy experience in World War II and had served as a Marine officer in Korea. During the transition Laird sat down with him and said, "Now look — we are going to put in a former governor, because you need to have some learning experiences on how to deal with the press and how to deal with Congress." Thus, John H. Chafee served as President Nixon's first Secretary of the Navy.

On 19 February Laird sent his response to Rogers, recommending Warner and requesting that State's representative contact him to discuss talk preparations, delegation composition, and dates for negotiations.[8]

On that same day, Henry Kissinger issued National Security Study Memorandum (NSSM) 119 directing State to lead an interdepartmental working group to outline the issues, examine alternative U.S. proposals and their implications, estimate probable Soviet positions and their implications, and develop a negotiating plan. The group would have representatives from the Office of the Secretary of Defense/International Security Affairs (OSD/ISA), the Joint Chiefs of Staff (JCS), the National Security Council (NSC), and the Central Intelligence Agency (CIA). There was to be no representative from the Office of the Chief of Naval Operations (OpNav). Kissinger expected a response by 8 March.[9]

Assistant Secretary of State for European Affairs Martin J. Hillenbrand reviewed NSSM 119 and the Laird proposal. Despite some grumbling from his underlings, Hillenbrand recommended to his boss that he concur with Warner's selection. He had heard from the legal branch that Warner had been extremely helpful to the department on Law of the Sea matters and that the department could gain more cooperation from Defense on other issues as a result of giving in on this one. Hillenbrand also reminded Rogers that with its representative assigned to chair the interdepartmental working group, State would still be running the show. With Rogers deferring to Laird's selection of Warner, invitations were sent to the designated agencies for representatives to attend the first interdepartmental working group meeting, to be held at 1500 on 1 March in Room 4217 at the State Department.[10]

Meanwhile, on 26 February in Moscow, Davies, who had been excluded from the delegation, made a courtesy call on Korniyenko. Korniyenko noted that nearly four months had passed since the Soviet proposal and that nothing had been heard. Davies assured him that a response would soon be forthcoming.[11]

Although Kissinger had left the OpNav off the interdepartmental working group, the CNO's staff fully intended to contribute to the policymaking process. At the Pentagon, a new officer had recently settled in at his new desk. Coming from commanding a submarine tender based at Rota, Spain, Capt. Robert D. Rawlins had taken charge of OpNav's Ocean

Policy Branch and assumed responsibility for tracking Soviet harassment at sea. After one week on the job, on a cold February morning, Rawlins's boss called him in. Rear Adm. Walter L. Small, the Director of the Political-Military Policy Division (OP-61), questioned the submarine officer on progress in getting fleet commanders' inputs for the Navy's position paper for the upcoming talks. Unaware of what his new boss was talking about, Rawlins recalled responding, "Sorry, Admiral, I was not briefed on that item." Not noted for his tolerance, Small directed Rawlins to "get his lawyer off his duff."

Captain Rawlins had his assistant draft a message to the fleet explaining the proposed talks and asking for recommendations. As he waited for responses, Rawlins began analyzing the branch files of reported incidents. Other than the serious cases, such as the *Walker* collision in the Sea of Japan, there was little documentation. With what records he had, Rawlins created a matrix of incidents by type, thus identifying the incidents that occurred most frequently. He augmented this matrix with information from copies of State Department documentation on cases that had been formally protested to the Soviets. Fleet responses to Rawlins's message were unenthusiastic. Fleet commanders insisted that the U.S. Navy could not afford to get tied down by establishing fixed approach distances between the ships and aircraft of the two sides.[12] The sentiments of Second Fleet Commander Vice Adm. Gerald "Jerry" E. Miller reflected those of his colleagues:

> Put it on the man that he shall not do anything that will jeopardize his ship or the safety of his crew — basic and fundamental. But don't say how close he can get or how far away he must stay. When the responsibility is on him to determine the distance, you'll find he'll stay farther away than he would if you gave him a fixed limit.[13]

Rawlins sought input from the various directorates within OpNav and was surprised to receive little substantial comment from the surface-ship or the aviation directorates. But while the surface sailors and aviators were indifferent, the submarine directorate adamantly opposed discussing submarines with the Soviets.[14]

The members of the naval intelligence community strongly supported the fleet commanders' position because they felt that the Soviets would be given an unfair edge in intelligence gathering. U.S. ships needed to "get close" to Soviet ships to monitor technological advances effectively. The United States could perform this intelligence gathering only at sea, whereas the Soviet Union could easily perform the function during any of hundreds of overseas port visits during which American ships would open their gangways to visitors.[15] With inputs from the fleet and from Navy staff within the Pentagon, Rawlins began putting the pros and cons together to form a Navy position paper to the interdepartmental working group.

At OSD/ISA Capt. Robert N. Congdon received the invitation and was assigned as the OSD/ISA action officer. The former destroyer skipper would hook up with Rawlins and play a key role in relaying OpNav's concerns to the interdepartmental working group.

As Congdon teamed up with Rawlins, another two-man team formed. Selected to head the interdepartmental working group and be the deputy head of delegation, State's Herbert S. Okun would prove to be an ideal choice for the dual role. He was familiar with the issues and had deep experience in dealing with Soviet diplomats in his position as Alternate Director of the Office of Soviet Affairs. His diplomatic experience included a posting to Moscow during the Cuban missile crisis. More important, while some in the diplomatic corps avoided relations with the military in that era, Okun relished working with military professionals. He recently had attended the Naval War College. Upon getting the nod, Okun immediately made an appointment to meet with the Navy undersecretary. The Soviet expert had never met Warner, and he had heard some uncomplimentary comments about the man. "Some said, 'Who was John Warner? Oh, he's married to Kathy Mellon — a billionaire — a playboy.'" Okun would soon have the opportunity to evaluate Warner for himself.[16]

Sitting in Warner's spacious office, the Soviet expert presented his ideas on how to tackle the task ahead. The Navy undersecretary listened intently. Okun explained that they were breaking new ground with the Soviets, since talks had never been held on controlling the juxtaposition of the two powers' naval forces to prevent undesired incidents. As Okun continued, Warner became more impressed with his visitor. Likewise, Warner impressed Okun with his attitude and his insightful questions. Although on paper Warner headed the delegation, the two men established a quiet and unofficial partnership.[17]

The first meeting of Okun's interdepartmental working group convened on 1 March 1971. Already Kissinger had received a request for and granted an extension of the NSSM deadline to 15 March. State asked for and received another extension to the twenty-sixth. By that date, Okun's working group had prepared several revisions to the draft.[18]

Okun recalled how his group approached the problem by forming a red team, a blue team, and a documents team. The red team took the Soviet perspective and explored possible Soviet objectives. The blue team explored U.S. positions. The two groups worked separately and then came together to negotiate. The "docs" team acted as umpire for the negotiation.[19]

Congdon would disagree with the above description in that it could imply an equal distribution of work — clearly not the case. Congdon explained that he and Rawlins, away from the working group, had drawn up the initial proposals for handling ship and aircraft interactions, using the previously developed Ocean Policy Branch positions. OpNav, OSD, and the Plans and Policy Directorate within the JCS (J-5) then reviewed the draft proposals. Congdon also put himself in Soviet shoes and spent much effort drafting Soviet proposals and possible U.S. responses. These papers also had to snake around Pentagon corridors for comment.

Once Rawlins and Congdon cleared their papers through OpNav, OSD, and J-5, Congdon came before the working group to present and discuss the drafted positions. Congdon recalled that the State and CIA representatives provided little additional input, because the issues were maritime in nature. State Department representatives expressed concern over the Navy's unwillingness to show much flexibility on the issue of the fixed approach distance. As a result, the group adopted a fallback position under which a fixed approach distance of no more than 500 feet would be acceptable if pursued by the Soviets.[20]

Disagreement also pervaded within Okun's working group over the real motivations behind the sudden Soviet willingness to discuss safety at sea issues. Although the group consensus held that the Soviets seriously wanted to address safety at sea, there was some concern that the Soviets might use the talks to expand into broader areas such as the Law of the Sea.[21] To prepare for this contingency, provisions were made to include in the delegation two lawyers with expertise in Law of the Sea issues. To guard against the unexpected, Comdr. William C. Lynch, a trusted legal advisor to

Undersecretary Warner, would be paired with Charles Pitman from State to stuff the documents footlocker with materials pertaining to such issues as chokepoints, straits, and the history of the Dardanelles.

Okun's working group also addressed the allies about the expected negotiations. News of the pending talks had already leaked to the British government. British Rear Admiral Dunlop had called on Rear Admiral Small in mid-February to discuss the Soviet proposal for safety at sea talks. The British naval attaché suggested that the United States could represent the United Kingdom in Moscow during the proposed talks. Small replied that Dunlop's suggestion needed to be considered at a higher level. Armed with the knowledge of Britain's special interest in the subject, and desiring to maintain the "special relationship," the group recommended that the British receive a special briefing on the proposed talks when preparations were completed, in addition to the planned NATO consultations.[22]

On 1 April Hillenbrand chaired a meeting of the standing National Security Council Interdepartmental Group/Europe (NSC/IG/EUR). Senior representatives from six government agencies met with Okun's working group to review the drafted "U.S.-Soviet Incidents at Sea" study. The study explored the context of incidents at sea talks within the framework of U.S.-Soviet relations, examined how U.S.-Soviet talks could affect relations with allies, spelled out what was nonnegotiable, looked at possible Soviet positions, and then detailed nine U.S. proposals. The nine proposals were:

1. That both sides observe the letter and spirit of the International Regulations for Preventing Collisions at Sea (Rules of the Road), emphasizing adherence to meeting, crossing, or overtaking situations.

2. That in ship encounters between a surveillant and a ship or group of ships, the surveillant will exercise good seamanship.

3. That individual ships remain well clear so not to endanger or hinder the maneuvers of an aircraft carrier while conducting flight operations or ships conducting underway replenishment operations.

4. That aircraft remain well clear of a ship conducting flight operations so as to cause no danger to the operations in progress.

5. That illumination of the bridge of ships and of helicopters when dipping sonars be prohibited.

6. That improper or false use of international signals be prohibited.

7. That provocative practices, such as training of guns/missile batteries and the opening of bomb bays by aircraft, be avoided.

8. That the two sides increase use of the nonobligatory international signals, which indicate status or intentions.

9. That a Navy-to-Navy arrangement for reporting and discussing incidents at sea be established on a trial basis through attaché channels.[23]

Accepting the study with few changes, the Hillenbrand group discussed and recommended that Congress and the media be given some background materials prior to the NATO consultations and that the Soviets be given an interim response. In addition, the group agreed that the delegation's size should be kept to about ten people. Congdon and Rawlins attended the meeting and received the responsibility for preparing and providing the needed point papers, speeches, and other background documents to these yet-to-be-determined ten people. On the basis of the work already completed, Hillenbrand felt confident that the United States would be ready to meet with the Soviets by the end of June.[24]

On 13 April Hillenbrand sent Okun's working group proposals to Kissinger for review by the Senior Review Group. Helmut Sonnenfelt, who had attended the 1 April meeting as Kissinger's representative, saw no need to call together Deputy Secretary of Defense David Packard, Deputy Secretary of State U. Alexis Johnson, and Director of Central Intelligence Richard M. Helms to debate the NSSM response. Okun's working group had been fairly harmonious in its recommendations. Kissinger agreed there was no need to call a formal meeting. Instead, the National Security Advisor directed the Senior Review Group members to have their staffs review the NSSM 119 response and comment. Kissinger sent the NSSM 119 response to Packard, Johnson, and Helms on 28 April, commenting that the U.S. negotiating position needed to be more flexible.[25]

Meanwhile, the Soviets were becoming impatient. On the morning of 6 May 1971, the destroyer USS *Hanson*, patrolling in the Sea of Japan, came upon a Soviet floating dry dock under tow. As the *Hanson* approached the dry dock from astern, the Soviet tug *Diomid* moved to intercept the intruding American. When the *Hanson* passed astern and steamed up along the dry dock's port side, the *Diomid* aggressively maneuvered around the American ship while pleasantries were exchanged over loudspeakers. As the conversation concluded, *Diomid* continued to close on the American ship and slowly accelerate.

At midday, the *Hanson* increased speed to ten knots. The Soviet ship kept up and continued to close. After a series of maneuvers, *Diomid* positioned herself off *Hanson*'s starboard beam. Comdr. Richard Fleeson, *Hanson*'s commanding officer, recalled:

> When forward of the beam, the *Diomid* Commanding Officer and others on the port wing were smiling and obviously intending to ram. I ordered left rudder, all stop and all back full in succession at 1214. The *Diomid* made a definite turn to port apparently aiming abaft of *Hanson*'s starboard anchor. She struck the anchor at 1214 and 40 seconds as *Hanson* swung to port and her port side rolled into *Hanson*'s starboard side. *Diomid* bounced off then sheared off to starboard, tearing the wooden bumper from the port bow. The *Diomid* Commanding Officer's face and those with him on the bridge first reflected consternation, then anger, as they saw the wooden bumper splinter and tear off.

Fleeson suspected that higher echelons ordered the *Diomid* to ram the *Hanson*. Fortunately, no one on either ship suffered injuries.[26] *Hanson*'s ramming in the Korean Straits broke a pattern of Soviet good behavior that had lasted since the November 1970 Soviet offer to conduct talks. In the Mediterranean, COMSIXTHFLT Vice Adm. Isaac C. Kidd told an interviewer that there had been no cases of what he considered to be harassment during the first half of 1971.[27]

Suddenly, on 10 May, Korniyenko called in the U.S. defense attaché to protest simulated attacks by U.S. Air Force jets on Soviet warships in the Aegean Sea on the fourth and mock attacks by U.S. Navy aircraft on a Soviet warship south of Crete on the seventh. The next day the Soviets called the U.S. representative to protest the *Hanson-Diomid* collision. He also heard an oral statement complaining about the carrier USS *Franklin D. Roosevelt* and two destroyers that cut in front of a Soviet merchant vessel in the Aegean Sea on 9 May. In addition, there were charges of dangerous maneuvering by a U.S. frigate in the vicinity of a Soviet ship in the Gulf of Tonkin on the tenth.[28]

On 12 May the Soviet press played up the *Hanson-Diomid* collision, carrying portions of the protest note delivered by Korniyenko. Obviously, the target audience of the news stories was not the Soviet public. Ambassador Jacob Beam reported the news items to Washington.[29] Six months had passed since the Soviets had responded to Washington's long-standing overture for talks, and Washington had yet to react. The wait would soon be over. President Nixon reviewed and approved the NSSM 119 findings. Issued on 26 May, National Security Decision Memorandum (NSDM) 110 directed the Under Secretaries Committee to oversee interagency preparations for the upcoming negotiations and determine the appropriate sequence for consulting with the allies, informing the Soviets, and scheduling the talks.[30]

Two days later, the State Department directed Ambassador Beam to notify the Soviets informally of the forthcoming positive response to their November overture. As this message was being transmitted to Moscow, joint State-DoD messages were sent to U.S. embassies in twenty-two NATO-allied countries directing them to brief appropriate authorities and seek feedback. The ambassador to Great Britain had special instructions to inform Her Majesty's Government that the U.K. legation in Washington would receive a special briefing on the proposed talks.[31] In Moscow Boris Klosson arranged an appointment with Korniyenko on 9 June to inform him that a formal response could soon be expected.[32]

On 17 June officials from the British Embassy were briefed. Rear Admiral Dunlop questioned whether the United States intended to have third parties benefit from a possible agreement. He was told that the issue of allied participation would be brought up after the initial talks.[33] Moscow continued to await the formal response. As if to keep up the pressure, the Soviet media continued to feature stories of American harassment. For example, on 14 June, *Izvestiya* carried an article discussing how a cruiser, carrying Defense Minister Marshal Andrei A. Grechko in the Mediterranean, had been harassed by American planes and warships earlier in the month. The article claimed that at one point Grechko dictated a message sent by flashing light to the tailing American destroyer USS *Claude V. Ricketts* that stated, "SIR, THIS IS NOT BROADWAY. FIND A SAFER PLACE FOR YOUR PROMENADES."[34]

At the end of June, the U.S. Embassy in Moscow finally received instructions to seek an appointment at the Ministry of Foreign Affairs for the purposes of formal notification of U.S. willingness to hold talks promptly and presentation of the U.S. delegation list containing mostly naval personnel.[35] This list broke from the standard practice of replicating the interdepartmental working group. Okun later pointed out that this all-Navy delegation composition "was essential." He later reflected, "If the State Department had headed this thing there would have been no way you could have kept all those other people off. We would have had a fifteen-man delegation with representatives from fifteen agencies, and that never would have led to an agreement!"[36]

The list sent to Moscow included Undersecretary John W. Warner, Herbert S. Okun, Vice Adm. Harry L. Harty, Capt. Robert D. Rawlins, Capt. Robert N. Congdon, Capt. Edward R. Day, Comdr. Ronald J. Kurth, Comdr. William C. Lynch, Charles J. Pitman, and Edward A. Mainland. At the time of the talks, Harty served as Assistant Vice Chief of Naval Operations, Director of Naval Administration, and had orders to be the Vice Chairman of the U.S. Delegation, UN Military Staff Committee. Although Harty was not involved in the interdepartmental group review process, as the commander of the Sea of Japan task group that had included the USS *Walker* he was familiar with the topic at hand. The veteran aviator kept the CNO briefed. With Harty's frequent updates, Zumwalt maintained a hands-off approach toward the delegation and the talks.

Rawlins had a background in submarines. Even though he was not on the interdepartmental group, he was placed on the team because he was the one individual within OpNav who had conducted the background research and understood the historical background. He would head up a team to discuss surface issues. Congdon, a surface sailor with command experience, worked for Lawrence Eagleburger in OSD/ISA and with Rawlins in preparing the NSSM 119 response. Day served in the Bureau of Political-Military Affairs at the State Department on loan from the Navy to State as part of a long-standing exchange program. Day would head up a team in discussions on aviation-ship issues. Day had previous experience with this issue back in

May 1968 in the Norwegian Sea. Kurth, as Assistant Head, Europe and NATO Branch in the OpNav Policy and Plans directorate, had been pushed on Warner by Rear Admiral Small. Small noted that Kurth had expertise in naval operations — both surface and air — an understanding of Soviet politics, and a masterful comprehension of the Russian language. The aviator had taught Russian at the Naval Academy and later earned his Ph.D. in Soviet studies at Harvard. With his aviation experience, Kurth was paired with Day for aviation-ship discussions. Lynch and Pitman were the delegation's lawyers. Lynch had been assigned to Undersecretary Warner's office and teamed up with Warner on Law of the Sea discussions. Pitman was the ocean affairs expert from the State Department's Office of the Legal Advisor. He supported Lynch on Law of the Sea questions and provided the delegation with legal counsel on other issues. Mainland, of the Office of Soviet Union Affairs, provided another State contribution to the delegation. Another Russian speaker, Mainland proved invaluable in the preparation of cables to Washington covering delegation progress.[37]

On 5 July the formal acceptance was delivered to the Soviet Foreign Ministry. Korniyenko's deputy accepted the message and stated that it would be difficult to arrange the talks before the summer vacation period. Eventually, the two sides agreed to hold the talks in early October.[38] Warner did have an opportunity for some preliminary discussions on an agenda for the forthcoming negotiations. Attending a session of the Geneva Law of the Sea Talks held in late July–early August, the undersecretary cornered Senior Legal Advisor to the Ministry of Foreign Affairs Khlestov to press the American view of subjects to be covered. Khlestov agreed to persuade officials in Moscow responsible for the talks to restrict the agenda to naval operational subjects.[39]

With the start date projected for the fall, the delegation now had time for additional preparations. Rawlins and Congdon worked long hours preparing the traditional three-ring black binders stuffed with position papers for each delegation member. Speeches were prepared for every eventuality. Warner's opening remarks were fine-tuned so that "if the Soviets responded by saying A, B, or C, then Warner had remarks that said either X, Y, or Z." Warner spent long hours consulting with Okun and reading everything he could get his hands on regarding Russian and Soviet history.[40]

As the delegation was finishing its preparations for the talks, a new player suddenly came on the scene. Newly promoted Rear Adm. James H. Doyle, assigned to head the new International Negotiations Division within the Policy and Planning Directorate of the JCS, saw a role in the forthcoming talks. A former ship skipper and law-school graduate, Doyle had previous experience, including a tour with the Navy's international law branch, that provided him a solid understanding of Law of the Sea issues. Upon reviewing the interdepartmental working group response to NSSM 119 and the U.S. negotiating positions laid out in NSDM 110, Doyle foresaw problems with having a U.S. fallback position on fixed approach distances. Doyle firmly believed that any agreement between the United States and the Soviet Union creating "no trespassing" zones around ships would set a very bad precedent for ongoing talks on law of the sea at a time when countries were trying to extend territorial waters, restrict free passage of ships, and establish maritime economic zones. Believing that a fixed-distance fallback position in the delegation's instructions did not serve the interests of the Chairman of the Joint Chiefs of Staff (CJCS), Doyle had Warner approached to request direct JCS representation on the delegation. On September 9 Warner asked the Secretary of Defense for permission to approach the CJCS to obtain a nominee.[41]

With the request rejected, Warner met with Doyle's boss, Vice Adm. J. P. "Blackie" Weinel, in mid-September to assure the JCS Policy and Plans Directorate head that his representative would be kept informed and have a role in negotiation preparations. Although denied a seat at the negotiating table, Doyle had positioned himself to play a key role in determining the content of any final agreement.[42]

The Soviets rejected the idea of a joint press release on the forthcoming talks but had no objection to an American announcement after some suggested modifications had been made. On 8 September 1971 State Department spokesman Charles Bray III announced the upcoming negotiations at the noon press briefing. He emphasized that the United States anticipated the talks would lead to an informal understanding and it was the first time since World War II that the two sides would sit down to reduce tension due to the juxtaposing of their forces. In addition, he noted that more than 100 incidents had been registered in the past decade and that fishing disputes would not be discussed.[43]

While the words for the press announcement were being crafted, a message from CINCPAC Adm. John S. McCain Jr. requesting permission for the USS Fox to transit the Sea of Okhotsk came to Warner's attention. The undersecretary, while recognizing the importance of demonstrating freedom of navigation in waters claimed by the Soviets as territorial, vehemently argued that this was not the moment to conduct such a maneuver. In a 7 September memorandum to Secretary Laird, Warner opposed the demonstration as untimely. He feared it could provide a pretext for the Soviets to provoke an incident, which, in turn, could hinder efforts to limit the scope of the discussions as directed by NSDM 110. Laird dismissed Warner's plea. On the day after the press briefing announcing the safety at sea talks, the Fox proceeded into the Sea of Okhotsk. A month later, just three days before the start of the talks, the Soviets presented Ambassador Beam with a formal note protesting the Fox transit.[44]

With less than a month to go, logistical support for the delegation became a focal point. The Soviet side agreed to pay for hotel, food, transport, and cultural activities. As for cultural activities, the Soviets recommended the program could be discussed after arrival when Undersecretary Warner called on Adm. Vladimir A. Kasatonov. Beam and Klosson would have preferred to have a tentative schedule in advance for planning purposes as the embassy faced handling the visits of several other American delegations. When informed of the Moscow Embassy's concerns, Washington responded by telling Beam not to worry.[45] The embassy action officer assigned to look after the visiting Navy-State delegation would have to be "flexible." For the assigned action officer, Comdr. William H. J. Manthorpe, the upcoming visit proved a godsend. The young intelligence officer had just settled into his new job as assistant naval attaché, and preparations for the negotiations allowed him the opportunity to meet a variety of Soviet officials and establish contacts that would prove helpful to him later during his Moscow tour of duty.[46]

Henry Kissinger wrote the following in White House Years on Soviet negotiating tactics:

Soviet diplomacy is extraordinarily persevering; it substitutes persistence for imagination. It has no domestic pressures impelling it constantly to put forward new ideas to break deadlocks. It is not accused of rigidity if it advances variations of the same proposal year after year. There are no rewards in the Politburo for the exploration of ever new schemes, which turns much of the American diplomacy into negotiating with ourselves. Like drops of water on a stone, Soviet repetitiveness has a tendency sooner or later to erode the resistance of the restless democracies.[47]

To prepare the U.S. delegation to handle such tactics, Okun arranged for a series of briefings. On 7 October 1971, a few days before departure, Paul H. Nitze and Llewellyn E. Thompson visited with the delegation to give their spin on what could be expected in Moscow. Of the two, Thompson, who would die in 1972, made the deeper impression. When Warner asked the ambassador about the symbolic impact of the United States sending a naval delegation to Moscow and reaching an accord, Thompson unequivocally responded, "Take whatever you can get, when you can get it."[48] Of all of the experts who briefed the delegation, only "Tommy" Thompson saw a clear-cut possibility for success. There was some justification for his optimism. There was a flourish of diplomatic activity during the summer of 1971. On 13 July, after Kissinger made a secret trip to Peking, Nixon made the stunning announcement that he would go to China. Suddenly the Soviets became interested in fulfilling a long-standing Nixon desire to visit the Soviet capital. On 10 August the Soviet Union extended an invitation to the American president to attend a summit meeting in Moscow in May or June 1972. Kissinger privately conveyed to Ambassador Dobrynin on 17 August that Nixon would accept and that a formal announcement would be forthcoming.[49] However, the delegation that would travel to Moscow in October had no clue of the pending Nixon summit in Moscow, since Kissinger had handled Dobrynin through "back channels." Thus, the highest ranking U.S. military delegation to visit Moscow since the end of the World War II was being set up for a pleasant surprise.

On the evening of 10 October 1971 the American delegation boarded an overnight flight to Copenhagen. Last-minute additions to the party included Warner's military aide, Capt. C. A. H. Trost, and two secretaries to provide administrative support. Arriving in Copenhagen early on the eleventh, the American delegation switched aircraft, boarding a Wiesbaden-based U.S. Air Force C-118 transport plane. The old propeller-driven airplane had its Air Force markings removed to look inconspicuous in Moscow. A Soviet escort crew joined the American flight crew to ensure safe navigation over Soviet territory. The C-118 lifted off from the Danish airport at 0800.[50] Meanwhile, Rear Admiral Doyle continued to advocate a cautious position for the U.S. delegation. On 9 October CJCS Adm. Thomas Moorer sent a memorandum to Secretary Laird reflecting the Doyle view-point — that the United States needed to be inflexible on the issue of fixed distance and that air-to-air and undersea situations needed to be kept off the table. Secretary of Defense Laird apparently approved, for Doyle received Vice Admiral Weinel's blessing to transmit a message to Moscow that would greet the delegation upon its arrival.[51]

« **6** »

NEGOTIATIONS

He had been First Deputy Commander in Chief of the Navy since June 1964. As such, Admiral of the Fleet Vladimir Afanas'evich Kasatonov was considered to be very close to his boss, Admiral of the Fleet of the Soviet Union Gorshkov. They met at the M. V. Frunze Higher Naval School, graduating in 1931. They chose different career paths and Gorshkov became the Soviet Navy's commander in 1956. Kasatonov started in submarines. During the war, Kasatonov served with the Main Naval Staff. In 1949 he was assigned as Chief of Staff for the Pacific Fleet. He then held several fleet commands before attaining the number-two post. Yet Kasatonov was not content with driving a desk. As first deputy, Kasatonov took ample opportunities to escape from Moscow. In 1965 he participated in submarine operations under the Arctic ice pack which would lead to his decoration as a Hero of the Soviet Union.[1] The award was just one of many that seemed to cover the whole left side of his service dress blue jacket as he stood at the base of the portable stairs that were being rolled up to the arriving C-118 at Sheremetyevo Airport. The sight of their Soviet entourage lined up left to right with medals, buttons, belt buckles gleaming, and shoes spit-polished impressed the Americans as they slowly stepped off the aircraft. With the Soviet reception committee were U.S. Embassy representatives and photographers to record the historic handshake between the two naval leaders. Behind the crowds, Zil limousines lined up to take the delegations to the Hotel Rossiya. After the two delegation heads exchanged pleasantries at the base of the stairs, the Americans and the Soviets stepped into the Zils for the trip to Moscow.[2]

With police escort, the Zils raced at an exhilarating speed while the Soviet hosts welcomed their guests to Moscow and repeatedly pointed out that, as this was a navy-to-navy affair, the Soviet Navy was running the program. The Americans need not worry about typical hindrances.[3] The limousines pulled up to the Rossiya, a modern hotel that stood near Red Square, and dropped off members of the visiting delegation. The senior officials were assigned plush rooms on the top floor. Some of the delegates took a short walk, but most, exhausted from the trip, bedded down shortly after the evening meal.

The next morning after breakfast, Undersecretary Warner made a courtesy call on the head of the Soviet delegation. During the short visit, Kasatonov proposed the social agenda and stressed the need to maintain confidentiality during the talks. Kasatonov then handed Warner a copy of the Soviet press release on the talks. After the call, Warner felt obliged to brief the Western press in view of the pending Soviet press announcement. In the early afternoon, the first meeting between the two parties convened in a dacha at a military retreat in Barvikha, a site some twenty-eight kilometers southwest of the center of the Soviet capital.[4]

The Americans were escorted into the meeting room, a large, barren hall with a long table in the middle. The delegations sat at opposite sides of the table. After the introductions, Kasatonov proceeded with his opening speech — a business-like, polemic-free statement focusing on the desirability of practical measures to avoid incidents. The Soviet Navy deputy commander envisioned the talks as a means of working out "concrete proposals and recommendations for subsequent presentation to both governments." Stating that the U.S.S.R. was ready to fulfill obligations under "general norms and principles of international law, including the UN charter and the 1958 Geneva Convention on the High Seas," he further asserted that Soviet commanding officers were under strict instructions to obey international law. Stressing that the United States and other Western nations still violated international laws, Kasatonov said it would be impossible to overemphasize the danger of such actions. He noted that as a maritime nation the U.S.S.R. enjoyed high seas freedoms and would not accept actions infringing upon its sovereign rights carried out by warships of other nations in the waters near its shores. The Soviet admiral suggested that the International Rules of the Road form a basis for the talks. Kasatonov concluded by citing previous U.S.-Soviet cooperation during World War II and expressed hope that the talks would reduce the chance of armed conflict at sea and serve as a step toward improving the overall relationship between the two countries.[5]

Captain Congdon recalled, "It was as if we wrote his speech." The Warner team maintained their diplomatic poker faces as their leader then made his introductory remarks that emphasized past incidents should not be a focal point in the proceedings.[6] Kasatonov hailed Warner's remarks and then asked to table a proposed agenda. Upon receiving Warner's concurrence, the Soviet leader reached across the table to present the undersecretary with a paper typed in English. It read:

a. Conditions of mutual safe maneuvering of surface ships and submarines on the high seas and in restricted waters, and measures to avoid undesirable incidents.

b. Conditions to ensure mutual safety of aircraft in the air when they approach each other, and measures to prohibit low-altitude overflights of ships and vessels as unlawful actions.

c. Establishment of a procedure of mutual notifying of ships about operations on the high seas which constitute danger for navigation.

d. Procedures for documenting collision cases and damage caused in collisions.[7]

Warner analyzed the paper, which presented an agenda nearly identical to what he had brought, except that the Americans were not prepared to address air-to-air situations. More important, the Soviets did not bring up the subject of submarines maneuvering under the high seas. Warner called a short recess to talk with his delegation. "What do you think, Herb?"

"I say we go with it," recalled Okun.[8]

After this successful afternoon session, the delegation rushed back to prepare for a formal dinner to be given by the Soviet hosts. Based on the initial plenary meeting, the delegation felt upbeat, although still suspicious of their Soviet hosts. Some sensed that they still could be walking into a trap. However, fate continued to ride with them that night. During the dinner, news broke that President Nixon had accepted the Soviet invitation to attend a summit in Moscow the following spring. The announcement was exceptionally well received. Delegates clinked glasses and made toasts. Kasatonov welcomed the news "with pleasure" as a positive step toward "future normalization of Soviet-U.S. relations" and observed that the talks ought to produce understanding. Okun thought to himself at that moment, "Baby, we got a deal here, because the one thing you know is that leaders want to sign agreements at summits." Both sides left the formal dinner that night excited.[9]

For a portion of the American delegation, however, the night had just begun. A working group headed straight to the U.S. Embassy to prepare messages describing the day's events and negotiation expectations. Waiting for the group at the embassy was a message from the JCS drafted by Rear Admiral Doyle. Worried that the State Department and the White House would now want to push to have an agreement for agreement's sake, Doyle provided the delegation a strong reminder that they were not to give in on any fixed-distance proposals.[10]

During the next morning, the two sides established a routine that would be followed throughout the negotiations in Moscow. After a plenary session, the talks broke up into two working groups to discuss surface-to-surface and air-to-surface situations.[11]

Captain Rawlins's opposite number in the discussion of surface issues was Rear Adm. Alexander N. Motrokhov, Chief Navigator of the Navy. Born in 1919, Motrokhov graduated from the Naval School and Academy and was in his early twenties at the outbreak of the war. The two men quickly established a strong rapport, with both having backgrounds in submarines. During breaks in the talks, Motrokhov fondly recalled how, as a very young officer, he came to the United States in early 1945 to help man one of the Lend-Lease vessels given by the United States to the Soviet Union. He distinctly remembered that he had been in Washington, D.C., on the day President Roosevelt died and recalled the grief he felt over the loss of the great leader. In addition to being an outstanding technocrat who understood the subject at hand, Motrokhov came across as a truly warm individual who seemed to say the right things to allay suspicions. The flag officer fascinated Rawlins with his blunt confession that he had never held an afloat command. A flag officer with no afloat command experience![12]

(Congdon would later discover the secret behind this revelation.) Rawlins and Congdon made rapid progress working with the affable Motrokhov as the surface working group addressed interpreting naval vessels' obligations under the Rules of the Road, creating signals to inform intent, preventing disruptions of flight operations and unrep, defining what platforms were to be included in the agreement, and restricting the training of weapons and sensor systems upon opposing platforms.[13]

Assigned to discuss aircraft-related issues, Captain Day seemed not as fortunate in being paired up with Deputy Chief of Staff for Naval Aviation Gen. Maj. Nikolai I. Vishensky. Vishensky had served in Soviet naval aviation since 1940 and also participated in the Great Patriotic War. Having dealt with Vishensky during his Moscow tour as assistant naval attaché, now-retired Captain Manthorpe recalled, "In this exercise, he was a fish out of water. He was well versed in the party line and did not come across as a solid legal, military, or strategic thinker."[14]

The difficulty imposed by this unfortunate pairing was exacerbated by the American requirement to limit discussions of air-to-air situations and also by the tabling of some unrealistic Soviet proposals. One proposal tabled by Vishensky obligated each side to fly no closer than 1,500 meters from the other's warships. The Americans found this distance totally unacceptable due to the limitations it would place on American aircraft performing reconnaissance missions on Soviet surface warships. More significantly, such a distance limitation could give Soviet surface ships the capability to provide sanctuaries for Soviet submarines from low-flying American ASW aircraft. Another Soviet proposal even called for a twelve-hour warning before any mass launching of aircraft from aircraft carriers. Day quickly dismissed this overture.[15]

Commander Lynch noted frustration as the two men seemed to talk past each other. With little headway being made, Day decided to try a different tack. He opened one of the sessions by telling the story of how in the spring of 1968 he had the solemn task of returning the body of a dead Soviet naval aviator to an awaiting Soviet destroyer. The American concluded with a statement on the necessity of preventing such tragedies in the future. Becoming emotional, Vishensky informed Day that the body he had returned was that of his son.[16] Lynch noted that from that point on the two men talked to each other and achieved progress as the air working group focused on obligations of aircraft operating in the vicinity of opposing warships (such as eliminating simulated attacks), and establishing navigational and identification signals between opposing aircraft and ships operating in proximity.[17]

In mid-afternoon, the working groups returned to the main meeting room in the dacha and reported progress to Warner and Kasatonov. After the daily sessions, the Soviets usually had some late-afternoon sightseeing lined up for the visiting Americans. Every evening brought some entertainment for the two delegations. One evening at the Moscow Circus, Warner sat with Soviet Navy Commander in Chief Gorshkov watching the talented performers entertain the crowd and noted that about halfway through the performance the admiral was squirming. Warner suggested they excuse themselves to have a drink. Warner recalled going off and, through the interpreter, having a fascinating hour of conversation covering a whole range of subjects in history and philosophy, including Cicero and Plato. Gorshkov told Warner about his background and his experiences during the Great Patriotic War, noting that the Navy had played a relatively insignificant role. With most of the Soviet capital ships destroyed, Gorshkov spoke of being relegated to running a logistics supply operation in the coastal areas and on the inland waterway canals and rivers to supply the Red Army. Warner came away impressed: "To come from that background of naval power to become a Mahan of his own generation took an extraordinary human being."[18]

While Warner retired to the Rossiya each night after a long day of diplomatic and social activities, many in the delegation headed to the dilapidated structure that housed the U.S. Embassy. There they convened in a specially built "bug-proof" room to discuss Soviet proposals, review negotiating strategies, prepare and transmit daily situation reports to Washington, and receive and review feedback. If the Americans accepted a Soviet proposal or formulated a counterproposal, the draft agreement would be rewritten and retyped in both languages to reflect the change. After working most of the night, the Americans team took brief naps, woke up, showered and shaved, ate breakfast, and then hustled out to the dacha. By handing the Soviets revisions to the draft agreement that incorporated their own recommendations and by having solid counterproposals prepared, the Americans maintained the initiative and controlled the agenda. The Soviets stiffened somewhat during the second week as the surface and air working groups addressed some substantive issues. Still, a document that would form the basis for an agreement between the two superpowers was rapidly being created. In his subsequent report to the president, Warner speculated that the Soviet willingness to accept the American agenda was dictated by a desire to reach some sort of understanding, and by a belief that the Americans would address their chief concerns at a follow-on set of negotiations.[19]

On the weekend of 16–17 October, the American delegation received a respite from the negotiating table, for their hosts had arranged an excursion to Leningrad. Admiral Gorshkov made his personal aircraft available to the American delegation for this memorable trip. Rear Admiral Motrokhov served as the delegation's escort.[20]

Upon landing, the Americans were taken to the Leningrad Naval Base to allow Warner and Vice Admiral Harty to call on their Russian host in Leningrad, Adm. Ivan Ivanovich Baikov. A former submarine skipper, Baikov welcomed the two Americans. In a genial conversation, the Russian admiral expressed hope that he could soon see American warships visiting his city. After the call, Baikov arranged for Rear Adm. Ivan Mikhaylovich Kolchin to escort the delegation on a harbor tour using Baikov's personal barge. Afterwards, the Americans were whisked through standard tourist sights such as the Leningrad Naval Museum, the Hermitage, the historic cruiser *Aurora,* and the Peter and Paul fortress. On Saturday evening the delegation joined Admiral Baikov to attend a performance at the Maly Ballet-Operetta theater and then retired to the old Astoria Hotel, considered Leningrad's finest.[21] In a message to Washington, Warner described Baikov as "a dominant personality and in command of the situation."

At a luncheon reception at the Frunze Naval Academy, Baikov invited many of the current young ship skippers to mingle with the visitors.[22] During the meal Captain Congdon tried to converse with a young Soviet commander seated next to him. A senior Soviet captain provided translation. Amazed by how his inquiries intimidated this fellow, Congdon even noted that the Russian's hands were shaking. Toasts interrupted the conversation. Rear Admiral Kolchin toasted to peaceful U.S.-Soviet relations, stating that "when U.S. and Soviet ships meet at sea, it would always be under peaceful conditions and not as enemies." After the toasting, the interpreting captain pulled Congdon aside and asked him to excuse the shy behavior of the young officer. The interpreter explained that the Soviet Navy's rapid expansion into a powerful blue-water force had not been without difficulties. With the commissioning of the new ships, the Soviet Navy had to decide whether to retrain all the senior officers who grew up in the coastal defense and patrol craft navy, or to fleet up the young officers who were trained initially on these new weapon systems. The Soviet Navy chose the latter course and thus many ship skippers were only in their early thirties. The interpreter noted that Soviet naval leaders worried that some of these young officers did not possess the maturity or the ship-handling skills required for command, and this could lead to undesirable consequences. The interpreter concluded by telling Congdon that this underlying concern explained the Soviet decision to accept the long-standing American offer to implement some controls. The frank revelation stunned Congdon — but made sense. It certainly explained how someone like Motrokhov could make flag rank without a major sea command.[23]

Upon returning to Moscow, the two delegations worked hard to conclude a memorandum of understanding (MOU). The Soviets continued to push for the establishment of fixed distances between ship-ships and aircraft-ships. In aircraft-ship situations, the U.S. delegation countered the Soviet proposal with an offer that aircraft come no closer than 500 feet. The Soviets balked. Finally, on the morning of the twentieth, Kasatonov agreed to an American "general wording" formulation that exhorted commanding officers to use prudent judgment in meeting situations. The MOU identified thirteen points of mutual understanding. Nine of the points directly incorporated U.S. positions drafted by Okun's working group the previous March. Major U.S. concerns that were addressed included provisions that protected aircraft carriers conducting flight operations from harassing activities, obligated ships conducting surveillance to act prudently, and affirmed a commitment to operate to the letter and the spirit of the Rules of the Road. The MOU also incorporated U.S. objectives of ensuring proper use of international signals, and opening a navy-to-navy channel to exchange information on incidents at sea.[24]

On the afternoon of 20 October, the Soviets arranged for Warner to pay an official call on the Soviet Navy Commander in Chief. The undersecretary recalled walking into Gorshkov's office accompanied by Admiral Kasatonov,

Vice Admiral Harty, Captain Trost, and Okun. Only a huge globe sat in the corner for decor. Warner had arrived behind schedule for his appointment, and Gorshkov let him know about it, subjecting the undersecretary to a lecture on naval customs and the courtesy of being on time! For the next thirty-five minutes the men discussed the issues that had brought the delegations together. Ironically, Warner's tardiness may have played a factor in the negotiations. According to his public affairs officer, Capt. Herbert E. Hetu, Warner had a penchant for being late to meetings. Hetu claimed that Warner drove the Russians crazy with his tardiness and his constant reedits of proposals. Hetu concluded that "Warner's style simply wore them down, and nobody thought that was possible."[25]

In Washington, Secretaries Laird and Rogers closely followed the progress of the negotiations and notified Warner that the understandings achieved served the national interest. Having received the draft MOU late on 20 October, the Defense and State Department secretaries gave Warner authority to sign the MOU the following day. On 21 October Warner was ready to sign and depart; however, Soviet delegation members desired more time to fine-tune the draft and explain the MOU to their leadership. Throughout the twenty-first, Warner and Kasatonov met continuously with their advisors, putting in final form the language of the understanding. The MOU signing finally occurred on the following day at 1000.[26]

Warner emerged to hold a press conference and issue a press release stating that the delegations had reached an understanding to submit for consideration to their respective governments. The American delegation departed for the airport, where the Air Force C-118 waited to take them on the first leg of their journey home.

As Warner flew back to Washington, he and Okun began to work on the report to the president called for in NSDM 110. Warner wrote that he believed that three factors accounted for the success of his mission: the announcement of the upcoming summit, the fact that the Soviets were apparently under instructions to reach an understanding, and a Soviet willingness to defer consideration of some of their chief concerns. From Warner's perspective, the MOU was quite satisfactory as it incorporated the nine proposals submitted by Okun's group in response to NSSM 119. The undersecretary anticipated that the Soviets would expect another round of talks to focus on their concerns, and that they would expect the United

States to reach an accommodation. Warner wrote about how the negotiations had been conducted, concluding by recommending that the president direct a follow-on study to reassess the American position.[27] Warner's prediction of a Soviet desire for a second meeting proved accurate. Even before his aircraft touched down in Washington, *Pravda* carried a TASS announcement about the recently concluded meeting, saying, "It was deemed expedient to continue the talks at a time convenient to both sides."[28]

For the next few days, Warner and Okun made several calls and presentations on the recently completed trip, including an excursion to Brussels to brief representatives on the North Atlantic Council. Surprisingly, as Warner and Okun made the rounds they ran into some hardcore skepticism. Okun recalled that there were some in the Navy who were actually annoyed that an understanding had been reached with the Soviets.[29]

Issued by Kissinger in early November, NSSM 140 formed another interdepartmental working group to review the MOU. This time the Pentagon would be in charge. Tapped in mid-November to lead the new group, Deputy Assistant Secretary for OSD/ISA Lawrence Eagleburger received instructions to have a response back to the NSC Senior Review Group no later than 8 December.[30]

As Eagleburger's action officer who had sat at the negotiation table, Captain Congdon again teamed up with Captain Rawlins to undergo a most challenging and stressful month. The two naval officers spent many evenings and Saturdays researching and preparing the group's response to NSSM 140. Understanding that the MOU contained the "Essential Elements of Agreement" that the American government had sought prior to the October talks, the group focused on "what next?" Would it be to the U.S. advantage to attempt to complete the present agreement before continuing with the next round of talks with the Soviets? Since additional agenda items proposed for a second round of talks were all Soviet, the group had to determine whether there was a requirement to address these topics. Finally, the group had to recommend the U.S. negotiating position should a further round occur.[31]

Reviewing the October MOU, the working group found it acceptable as a basis for a formal agreement, with two slight clarifications involving understandings on how ships should maneuver when in proximity and requirements for pilots to display navigation lights at night. Looking at the Soviet proposals that had been put off at the October talks, Eagleburger expressed the opinion that some accommodation with the Soviets on establishing some fixed-distance regime seemed reasonable and he would have to be convinced otherwise. Opposing this viewpoint, Rear Admiral Doyle, now an active participant on this second panel, convincingly argued that any fixed-distance arrangements could impinge on the intelligence collection mission and set dangerous precedents limiting freedom of navigation. Strongly supported by the fleet and unified commanders, Doyle persuaded Eagleburger that a concession to any fixed-distance proposal would be unacceptable. The Air Force endorsed Doyle's no negotiation position regarding air-to-air and air-to-ship situations. Impressed, Eagleburger agreed to drop the previously adopted fallback fixed-distance positions over the objections of State Department representatives. Eagleburger's group recognized that adopting a hard line on fixed distances placed constraints on the future negotiating team. Thinking that a second round with the Soviets could be an exercise in futility, the working group proposed a "quick close," simply converting the October MOU into a formal agreement.[32]

On 4 January 1972 the Joint Chiefs approved the draft response to NSSM 140, and Admiral Moorer signed the memorandum sending the response to Laird. The Secretary of Defense sent it to the White House. Other agencies involved also submitted comments on the response. As the delegation head, Undersecretary Warner expressed concern over the lack of flexibility he would have in any future talks with the Soviets. To address Warner's concern, Captain Rawlins drafted a point paper that acknowledged that while a 200-foot minimum fixed distance between surface ships could be acceptable, it still was better to stay with a "general wording" formula to maintain consistency with the nonnegotiation position on air-to-air and air-to-surface situations. Rawlins concluded that it would be wrong to provide any negotiating flexibility that could harm U.S. security interests.[33]

As the NSC Senior Review Group reviewed the NSSM 140 response, Admiral Kasatonov waited in Moscow. Earlier, on 22 December 1971, at the Yugoslav Army Day celebration, he had pulled the U.S. Embassy representative aside to say that the Soviet side remained prepared, awaited further contact through diplomatic channels, and hoped that talks could be resumed in Washington during January or February. The admiral also noted with pleasure that no incidents had been recorded since the October talks. Kasatonov would continue to wait.[34]

Before departing on his trip to China, President Nixon reviewed the Eagleburger working group response to NSSM 140 and, with minor exceptions, approved the study. On 11 February 1972 Kissinger signed NSDM 150. The decision memorandum agreed to a second round of talks to address Soviet concerns if certain conditions were met. Ideally, such a meeting would take place after the two sides converted October's MOU into a formal agreement through an exchange of aides-memoire. The American side was willing to consider a second round of talks without having a formalized accord in hand, but it would be left to the Soviets to initiate this second round.[35]

On 23 February 1972, with Nixon attracting worldwide media attention in the People's Republic, Admiral Kasatonov, meeting with the U.S. defense attaché, complained that he had heard nothing from Warner and stated that the initiative for further talks rested with the United States. Ambassador Beam requested an update on the status of the talks.[36] After a short wait, Beam received a response directing him to seek an appointment with Admiral Gorshkov to present a proposal. On 7 March the American ambassador presented Gorshkov with a final version of the MOU. Gorshkov reviewed the proposed text and stated that his side might want to submit some "considerations" on the text and that the Soviet delegation deputy head, Adm. Vladimir N. Alekseyev, would be in touch with the American embassy within seven to ten days.[37]

Ten days later Alekseyev presented the Soviet response to the 7 March démarche. The Soviets accepted the proposed U.S. modifications to the MOU on aircraft navigation lights and the maneuvering of ships. The Soviets still desired a second round of talks in Washington, however. The Soviet admiral was told that a response would be forthcoming. The attempt for the quick close had failed. In the opinion of Ambassador Okun, "It didn't work because they wanted to visit Washington. It was that simple."[38]

As Alekseyev waited for the U.S. response, events were occurring that would put a chill in the warming U.S.-Soviet relations and jeopardize the planned May Moscow summit. On 31 March North Vietnam launched a massive offensive to conclude the conflict in Southeast Asia. A few days later, State Department spokesman Robert McCloskey noted that this invasion had been made possible by an influx of arms provided by the Soviet Union.[39]

Nonetheless, plans went forward to put in final form an agreement to prevent incidents at sea. On 5 April the U.S. Embassy in Moscow received directions to inform Admiral Alekseyev that the United States could now proceed with the second round as envisioned by the Soviets, who were extended an invitation to come to Washington at a time convenient to them. Two days later the U.S. naval attaché called on Alekseyev, who was joined by two other members of the October delegation: Igor D. Bubnov and Capt. First Rank Valentin A. Serkov. After receiving the invitation, Alekseyev stated that, as the host, the United States should suggest the meeting period. He hinted that a late April–early May date would be acceptable if it would not interfere with the American May Day celebrations. Stunned when told that May Day was not a holiday in America, the admiral was informed that a start date proposal would be forthcoming.[40]

As the admiral awaited the date proposal, conditions in South Vietnam deteriorated. On 6 April Kissinger called Ambassador Dobrynin to state that the situation was intolerable. As a hint of what the Soviets stood to lose if they were not more cooperative in Southeast Asia, Nixon's National Security Advisor went down the list of pending agreements to be signed at the summit. A few days later, he met with Helmut Sonnenfelt to discuss ways to exert pressure on the Soviet Union. Kissinger accepted some suggestions but rejected as unduly provocative deliberately harassing Soviet vessels en route to Cuba.[41]

While Kissinger pondered a course of action, planning for the incidents at sea talks continued with a Soviet arrival date of 3 May. The Soviets were informed that the nomination of John Warner to become Secretary of the Navy should not obligate them to raise the level of their head of delegation.[42]

On 27 April Ambassador Beam hosted a luncheon for the Soviet delegation in a relaxed and friendly atmosphere. Admiral Kasatonov made a gracious toast expressing hope that a second round would result in an overall agreement that would contribute to the propitious atmosphere of the upcoming Nixon visit. Several Soviet delegation members expressed an interest in arrival arrangements in New York and asked about sightseeing suggestions. Captain First Rank Serkov and others mentioned a desire to travel outside of Washington and asked about San Francisco. The ambassador telegraphed back to Washington that a travel program exposing the Soviets to American life could be useful. In Washington action was already being taken to accommodate this request. Anticipating their eventual arrival, Rear Admiral Small, shortly after the Moscow trip, submitted a memorandum to the CNO suggesting a list of visit possibilities ranging from historic sites to a car dealership. All of the suggested sites were within the Washington area. By the end of April, the plans extended to the West Coast, with the Commander of the First Fleet being tasked to host the Soviet delegation over the weekend of 12–14 May.[43]

Meanwhile, the Americans made final preparations for the second round of talks. To support the preparations, Admiral Zumwalt had accepted an offer from the Commander in Chief, U.S. Naval Forces Europe (CINCUSNAVEUR), Admiral Bringle for Capt. Robert P. Hilton Sr. to fly to Washington. Hilton would brief and show videotape to the negotiators about a recent Easter morning encounter between the USS *William V. Pratt* and USS *W. S. Sims* and Soviet warships in the Mediterranean.

The dramatic footage of Soviet shouldering tactics and near-collisions had first caught the attention of COMSIXTHFLT Vice Adm. Gerald "Jerry" E. Miller, who had been debriefed by Hilton on Miller's flagship USS *Springfield* on 7 April. Miller, who had been following the progress of the incidents at sea negotiations and was aware of the contentious fixed-distance issue, observed in a message to Bringle that the tapes "SHOW THE WEAKNESS OF TRYING TO PREVENT INCIDENTS BY DEFINING SPECIFIC DISTANCES IN THE RULES OF ENGAGEMENT."[44]

After a 13 April briefing by Hilton which included a screening of the video, Admiral Bringle came away similarly impressed. In a message to the CNO, he stated that the tapes demonstrated Soviet aggressiveness and illustrated how establishing a fixed-distance regime would create problems for surveillance operations.[45] Secretary Warner and Admiral Zumwalt had followed the progress of Hilton's "Bystander" operations in the Mediterranean and welcomed the opportunity to be personally briefed by the destroyer squadron commander.

On Monday, 1 May, Hilton met with the Secretary of the Navy. Warner asked Hilton several probing questions on the letter of instruction established for the Bystander shadowing operation and came away satisfied that the American guidelines had not been aggressive. To Warner, the video spoke louder than words. The tapes put the Navy's civilian leader on the bridge of one of his warships and gave him an appreciation of the situation faced daily by his skippers. One bit of footage, depicting a Kotlin-class destroyer steaming a mere thirty feet from the *Pratt* with its guns pointed at the American missile destroyer, caught his special attention. The tapes also demonstrated to Warner how unworkable a fixed-distance regime would be. If American ships had to stay a specific distance away, Soviet escort ships could theoretically edge them miles away from an intended surveillance target. Warner's attitude changed noticeably during the briefing. Hilton left with the impression that the young secretary would be a far tougher negotiator with the Soviets.[46]

On 3 May the Soviet delegation arrived and went to the Statler Hilton for their accommodations.[47] The two sides formally met the next day at Fort McNair's National War College. There were some new faces. Displacing Rawlins and Day as working group heads were Rear Admirals Dennis J. Downey and Thomas B. Hayward. The two former leading players reverted to supporting roles. Meanwhile, Capt. Robert E. Morris replaced Captain Congdon, who had departed from Washington for a new sea command. Commander Kurth, dropped from the official delegation, became the liaison officer for the Soviet delegation.

On 2 May, the day before the Soviet delegation's arrival, Kissinger returned to Washington from unsatisfactory talks in Paris with North Vietnam's Le Duc Tho. The situation in Southeast Asia was becoming desperate. Continuing their invasion launched on 31 March, North Vietnamese forces had captured Quang Tri City at the beginning of May and were advancing farther into the south. Tens of thousands of antiwar protesters prepared to descend on Washington. Kissinger met with the president to discuss possible options. Nixon expressed concern that any proposed American military actions could cause cancellation of the upcoming Moscow summit. Recalling the embarrassment that President Eisenhower had suffered at the Paris summit after the U-2 incident in May 1960, Nixon thought that if this summit were to be canceled, he should be the one to do it. Kissinger concurred. However, the next day at a White

House meeting, H. R. Haldeman expressed strong opposition. With his two key advisors at loggerheads, Nixon suggested to Kissinger and Haldeman that they sound out Secretary of the Treasury John Connally.

On 4 May, as the Soviet and American naval delegations reopened talks at Fort McNair, Kissinger and Haldeman sat down with the treasury secretary to discuss the cancellation proposal. Connally strongly supported Haldeman's view. An American cancellation gained the administration nothing domestically, and it subjected the United States to international charges of derailing East-West relations. Kissinger particularly appreciated one point that Connally made, namely that the United States should not be constrained in Southeast Asia for fear of Soviet reaction. After the meeting, Kissinger phoned CJCS Admiral Moorer to review plans for mining North Vietnamese harbors. Moorer was told not to inform Defense Secretary Laird of the planning. Kissinger then joined Nixon, Haldeman, and Col. Alexander Haig for a 1500 meeting that concluded with Nixon agreeing not to cancel the summit and to go ahead with the mining operation.[48]

As Nixon was consulting with his closest advisors, Admiral Moorer called in Admiral Zumwalt to discuss the phone call he had just received from the national security advisor. Because of the request to keep Defense Secretary Melvin Laird in the dark about the mining operation, Moorer felt uncomfortable to have his staff conduct the planning. The CNO gladly agreed to do the planning and gathered a team in his office that evening to draft plans to mine the North Vietnamese harbors.[49]

Peggy Rawlins, wife of American delegation member Captain Rawlins, was planning a less grandiose operation. Knowing her husband's fondness for his negotiating counterpart, Rear Admiral Motrokhov, Mrs. Rawlins thought it would be a delightful gesture to treat Motrokhov to a home-cooked meal served in a genuine American home. At one of the delegation's review sessions, Captain Rawlins mentioned his plans to extend this invitation to Motrokhov. Secretary Warner thought it was a wonderful idea. However, before Rawlins even hinted to Motrokhov about coming over for dinner, the invitation had to be cleared through the State Department bureaucracy. An elaborate plan emerged to host three home dinners on the evening of 8 May. Rawlins would host Motrokhov and some officials from the Soviet Embassy;[50] delegation lawyer Commander Lynch would host junior members of the Soviet delegation; and Warner would host the principal negotiators in his Georgetown townhouse: Admiral Kasatonov, Admiral Alekseyev, Major General Vishensky, and Mr. Bubnov of the Ministry of Foreign Affairs. The Secretary of the Navy also invited some of his own top brass, including Admirals Zumwalt and Hyman G. Rickover. The opportunity to meet Rickover greatly flattered the Soviets, because the father of America's nuclear navy was legendary even in the Soviet Union. The timing of the Monday, 8 May, dinner would also allow the Soviet delegation to share their impressions of their weekend adventure in New York City with their hosts.[51]

The New York visit was hosted partly by Vice Admiral Harty, now posted as a U.S. representative to the UN Military Council. From his quarters at the Brooklyn Navy Yard, Harty made his barge available to his guests to conduct a tour of the harbor. Okun, a native New Yorker, served as a guide while the Soviet delegation hit many of the tourist attractions after their voyage around Lower Manhattan. As the motorcade traveled through the streets of New York, Bubnov tried to keep his perspective by repeatedly pointing out the dirt, the poor people, and the pornography to Kasatonov, who was sharing the back seat with Okun. As Bubnov kept making his unpleasant observations, Okun received an earful from the admiral concerning Nixon's recent trip to China, with a warning to "watch the Chinese — you can't trust them — they are sneaky." Capt. Mark Flanigan, a Naval Reserve intelligence officer and New York native, also served to help escort the Russians. Flanigan vividly recalled his apprehension at watching Kasatonov peer out through an open portal on the top of the unfinished World Trade Center and thinking of the consequences if the number-two man in the Soviet Navy were to fall to the street below. Flanigan also recalled escorting the Russians through Macy's and to an evening ballet performance at Lincoln Center.[52]

When the incidents at sea talks resumed Monday morning at Fort McNair, another meeting convened in the White House. Admiral Moorer briefed the National Security Council on the mining operation slated to begin that evening. Flabbergasted, Secretary of Defense Laird pointed out that the North Vietnamese could still receive supplies by rail and still had reserve stocks. Laird believed that the less-costly solution would be to send more supplies to the South Vietnamese. However, President Nixon had already made his decision. The meeting broke up at 1220. After a short session with his closest advisors to evaluate the points made at the NSC meeting, Nixon signed the execute order for the operation.[53]

At about 1500 Secretary Laird returned to his office. Although there were instructions to keep the service secretaries from finding out about the pending operation and Nixon's televised announcement, Laird called Warner into his office to tell him of the pending operation. After finding out some of the specific details, Warner recalled stating, "Well, Mel, do you understand that I have got the deputy commander of the Soviet Navy here in my house tonight? We are making great progress on this thing, and it looks like we are going to achieve it. This is going to cause problems." Laird presented Warner with a rough draft of the speech and suggested he might want to cancel the dinner. He also reminded Warner that he had been given this information in strictest confidence. The Secretary of the Navy was not supposed to know about the impending operation.

Warner hurried back to his office and summoned Okun. When the deputy delegation head arrived in Warner's office, the secretary gave Okun the draft of the speech. As Okun read the text, Warner passed on Laird's suggestion about canceling the dinner. Okun disagreed, noting the summit was still a possibility. Deciding to go ahead with the dinner, Warner's next question was whether the Soviets should be invited to watch the speech. After weighing the pros and cons, the two men decided that it would be better to have the Soviets actually see the president make the announcement. Warner rushed back to his townhouse, where his wife was making final preparations for the evening dinner. Phone calls were made to the other two hosting homes.[54]

At Warner's townhouse, Admiral Zumwalt arrived a few minutes early to forewarn Warner about the contents of the president's speech. Warner feigned surprise. When the CNO suggested that they should allow the Soviets to view the speech, Warner wholeheartedly approved. The two men arranged the furniture to face the television set.

The guests arrived, and Admiral Kasatonov was invited to sit front and center before the television set. At the appointed hour, the set was turned on and the president of the United States addressed the American people. Okun and State Department interpreter Cyril Muromcew translated the speech verbatim to the elderly flag officer, who stared stoically at the image of the president. In the corner of the room, Mouza Zumwalt, the CNO's

Russian-born wife, translated to two other Soviets, adding her own commentary after each of the announced actions: "Khorosho!" ("Good!")[55]

With the speech completed, Warner turned the television set off and faced Admiral Kasatonov. "Admiral, I appreciate your coming to listen to our President. Is there anything further that I can elaborate?" All eyes in the now-silent room focused on Kasatonov: "No, it's perfectly clear. This is a serious matter; let the politicians decide. I think I'll have another drink. How about a bourbon?" Igor Bubnov did not take the speech as lightly. He began arguing with Zumwalt. Kasatonov turned toward the belligerent Bubnov and quietly instructed his comrade to "please be quiet — we are about to have a very nice dinner." As the group sat down to dinner, Okun called Helmut Sonnenfelt of the NSC to report the Soviet reaction. From this conversation, the White House received its first indication that the upcoming summit was not necessarily doomed. Commenting on the mild Soviet reaction to Nixon's speech, Okun concluded, "We were highball to highball, and they were first to clink."[56]

The talks continued the next day as if nothing had happened. Although the American press criticized the military action, the Soviet press seemed unconcerned. It quickly became apparent that the U.S.S.R. was going to overlook the American operation, even though it would restrict Soviet ability to support North Vietnam. The Soviet reaction had to be disconcerting in Hanoi, but Moscow had more important priorities. On 10 May Ambassador Dobrynin submitted a protest note over injuries and damage sustained by some Soviet merchant vessels that were in port when the raids began. The United States responded with a note of regret.[57]

As the summit appeared still to be "on," Rear Admiral Hayward approached Warner, explaining that the Soviets were still hung up on creating come-no-closer (fixed-distance) zones around ships and aircraft. Hayward, who went on to become CNO, reflected, "Warner told me to continue meeting even though it was a waste of time. I did, and it was."[58]

During a plenary session on the tenth, Rear Admiral Motrokhov suggested that the modifier "as a rule" could be applied to any agreement containing fixed-distance provisions for surface ships. Upon hearing this, Secretary Warner asked whether the same modifier could be applied to air situations. Major General Vishensky answered in the affirmative. Warner noted that this was the first time the Soviets had modified in any way their insistence on having fixed distances incorporated into the agreement.[59]

Still, NSDM 150 directed the use of the "general wording" formulation and forbade Warner to consider any agreement with fixed distances, even with an "as a rule" modifier. Consequently, Warner held off making a commitment. Meanwhile, the delegations continued work to agree on language for articles in the agreement, not including the contentious fixed-distance stipulation. Starting at 1800, deputy delegation heads Okun and Alekseyev and the legal experts began a marathon session that would last until 0230 the next morning.[60] Late that evening of 10 May, as the delegations worked, Kasatonov told Warner that he was obligated to send to Moscow — by midnight on 11 May — a cable reporting the status of the fixed-distance issue. The Soviet admiral then requested a meeting with Warner at 2000, four hours before this deadline, to determine whether there would be any flexibility in the American position.

Facing this pressure, Warner and Okun met at 1430 the following day with Admiral Moorer, Assistant Secretary of Defense for International Security Affairs Warren Nutter, Lawrence Eagleburger, and State Department representatives Richard Davies and Ronald Spiers. After discussing the progress of the negotiations, Warner announced his intent to tell Kasatonov that the United States would hold firm on the fixed-distance issue. Joint Chiefs Chairman Moorer supported Secretary Warner's stand. The State representatives withheld a commitment, wishing to defer directly to Secretary Rogers.

Shortly after the meeting broke up, Warner received a phone call from Rogers. Having just spoken with Nixon, Rogers relayed that he should seek to delay the U.S. response on the fixed-distance issue to the following week as the United States was continuing to study the issue. Rogers also told Warner that the Departments of State and Defense had been directed to submit memoranda to the White House over the weekend.[61]

At 2000 on 11 May Warner met with Admiral Kasatonov. Upon hearing Warner's explanation that the United States intended to study the fixed-distance issue further, Kasatonov began a lengthy monologue, repeatedly stating that his instructions, signed by Kosygin and in his pocket, enabled him to sign an agreement before he departed from Washington on 17 May.

Kasatonov exhorted Warner on the importance of an agreement to both navies, to future relations, and to world peace. Not displaying great disappointment with the American request for time, he offered to cancel the scheduled weekend West Coast sightseeing trip to facilitate movement on the issue. Although the clock approached 2100, Kasatonov requested that the talks reconvene "immediately," adding, "I am prepared to work all night if necessary." To show good faith, Warner gave in to the request to continue talks that night, but only after dissuading Kasatonov from holding any further discussions of the issue until the following Monday. Instead, when the delegations' senior members reconvened at 2230, the discussion focused on resolving the few other isolated areas of disagreement. One problem that arose was the American insistence that the agreement would apply to both warships and auxiliary vessels. Earlier, the two sides had agreed that AGIS qualified as auxiliary vessels. Not wanting the accord to apply to their spy trawlers, the Soviets sought to redefine the terminology. Seeking to curtail AGI harassment, the U.S. side refused to yield. Lasting until 0200, the session refined the areas of agreement and disagreement.[62]

Later on the morning of 12 May, the American and Soviet delegations met at the Soviet Embassy for a reception hosted by Ambassador Dobrynin. In a memorandum to Secretary Laird, Warner wrote:

> The atmosphere was cordial and the Soviets relaxed and affable. Ambassador Dobrynin informed me of his hope that we would reach an agreement during this Washington session. Rather directly, he metaphorically described the "cloud that is now hanging over our two countries," but that he had reason to believe that "in a few days" it would pass on. "We must continue to pursue our efforts to improve relations between our countries."
>
> Dobrynin has detailed knowledge of the issues of disagreement confronting the "Incidents at Sea" talks. He tried to draw me out on the issue of fixed distances and offered to "intercede" and "help" when I next meet with Kasatonov — on Monday. "I can evaluate, better than Kasatonov, the reaction of our superiors to the inclusion or absence of fixed distance provisions."
>
> Dobrynin advised me that Admiral Kasatonov filed a report with Moscow which stated that favorable progress was being made.[63]

At the reception's end, Admiral Kasatonov and his delegation departed for their West Coast trip. Meanwhile, work continued at the Pentagon and at

State on memoranda for presidential review. Warner had requested that ISA and CJCS collaborate on a memorandum for Secretary Laird to review for submission to the president. However, the response was more competitive than collaborative.

Apparently, word leaked out that the State Department memorandum recommended accommodating the Soviet fixed-distance proposals. When Law of the Sea expert Rear Admiral Doyle heard of the proposed accommodation, he strongly restated his opposition to any fixed-distance formula. His view was endorsed by his boss, JCS Plans and Policy Director Vice Admiral Weinel, and by JCS Chairman Admiral Moorer.

However, Defense Department proponents for changing the firm fixed-distance position worked to overcome CJCS opposition. Having been initially inclined to favor a more flexible position on fixed distances, Lawrence Eagleburger now sold his boss, Warren Nutter, on the idea of approaching Laird to overrule the Joint Chiefs. After learning of Nutter's pending approach, Doyle sat down and briefed his boss. Weinel reacted by phoning Laird's military assistant, Rear Adm. Daniel Murphy, to go over the issues at stake. Impressed with Weinel's argument that fixed-distance accommodation could undercut U.S. positions at the ongoing Law of the Sea–Freedom of Navigation talks, Murphy convinced Laird that the United States should stick to the "general wording" formula and continue to resist fixed-distance overtures even if doing so meant no agreement.[64]

As Laird signed off on the "no change" recommendation, the Soviet delegation became acquainted with California. Late on Friday, 12 May, the Soviets arrived at El Toro Marine Corps Base south of Los Angeles, where a motorcade awaited to take them to the Disneyland Hotel. After a Saturday morning visit to the Magic Kingdom, the Soviets headed south for a tour of the San Onofre nuclear power plant. After that, they continued on to San Diego, where on Sunday they met local naval commanders and visited the zoo. The Soviets returned to the nation's capital late Sunday night.[65]

On Monday, 15 May, Laird and Moorer had a breakfast meeting with Kissinger. Included on the agenda was a discussion of fixed distance versus a general-wording formula for the ongoing incidents at sea talks. Laird and Moorer convinced Kissinger that the United States could not give in on this issue. In addition, Laird sent a letter to President Nixon explaining his rationale for his decision. Later that day, when the two delegations reconvened, Warner advised his counterpart that the American position on fixed distances remained nonnegotiable at this time, but he offered a face-saving idea of a clause calling for consultations to be held within six months after the agreement signing to discuss fixed distances. Upon hearing this, Kasatonov agreed to initial the "Agreement Between the Government of the United States of America and the Government of the Union of Soviet Socialist Republics on the Prevention of Incidents On and Over the High Seas." The core of this document reflected the work completed in Moscow during the previous fall. Throughout the text, the two sides reaffirmed their commitment to abide by the International Regulation for the Prevention of Collisions at Sea. Provisions that prohibited the pointing of weapons and simulated attacks had also been brought forward from the October talks and refined. Soviet AGIS counted as auxiliaries and would have to abide by the agreement.[66]

On 17 May Warner and Kasatonov initialed the draft of the completed agreement at the National War College. The initialing signified agreement on a text that would be signed by appropriate officials at a later date. The Soviet delegation then departed Washington for Moscow. Warner would follow a week later as part of the Nixon entourage for the Moscow summit, where he would join Admiral Gorshkov to sign the implementing version of the accord.[67]

The agreement signed by Gorshkov and Warner contained ten articles that incorporated the eight proposals proposed by Okun's working group in the April 1971 NSSM 119 response. Article I spelled out definitions for *warship, aircraft,* and *formation.* Under the term *warship,* the American position prevailed to include unarmed naval auxiliaries such as AGIS. Article II directed both sides to remind their ship captains to abide by the established international regulations for preventing collisions at sea, commonly called the COLREGS, or Rules of the Road. However, a problem with the Rules of the Road is that one side could abuse the rules to harass the other side.[68] Article III instructed both sides to refrain from this practice, especially against ships engaged in unrep or aviation operations. Article III also ruled out other provocative behaviors, such as aiming weapons, launching objects, or pointing searchlights in the direction of the other party. While Article III satisfied many American concerns about surface ships, Article IV addressed Soviet concerns about "buzzings" by forbidding aircraft from performing simulated attacks or dropping objects in the vicinity of a surface ship. The latter occurred when American ASW aircraft dropped sonobuoys to detect submarines suspected of hiding beneath Soviet surface vessels. Article V discussed proper use of navigation lights, and Article VI directed each side to forewarn the other of danger by using flag, sound, or light signals. Eventually, the two sides developed a set of military-unique signals to augment the existing international code of signals. Article VII set up the navy-to-navy communication channel using naval attachés, Article VIII established the agreement renewal and termination mechanisms, Article IX instituted an annual implementation review meeting, and Article X established a committee to meet in six months to revisit the fixed-distance issue.

While Warner's and Gorshkov's signature of the agreement on 25 May marked the end of one process, it also assured the continuation of another process that had begun in conjunction with the negotiations. It also marked the beginning of a new phase in the relationship between the Soviet and U.S. Navies.

« 7 »

DÉTENTE

It was a glorious time for both men as they cruised on the Moscow River aboard Gorshkov's barge in late May 1972. For the Admiral of the Fleet of the U.S.S.R., the just-signed INCSEA agreement was an important milestone. The bilateral agreement with the world's most powerful navy signified that his fleet had come of age. Politically, it gave him and his service more leverage within the Politburo. His navy was now the only branch of the Soviet military that had established a direct communications link with its Western counterpart. For John W. Warner, the successful negotiations completed during the previous October certainly had not derailed his appointment to become Secretary of the U.S. Navy. The highly laudatory reports from the Moscow Embassy on the then-undersecretary's October performance could only have improved his standing within the Nixon administration. Kasatonov's last-minute acquiescence on fixed distances projected the image that Warner was no pushover, an image that would serve him well in his tour as SecNav and beyond.

During the sojourn, Gorshkov and guests Warner, Okun, and Rear Admiral Hayward consumed copious quantities of alcohol and had a frank conversation about the world and about their own backgrounds. Later, back at the hotel, Warner received a phone call from one of Gorshkov's aides explaining that the admiral wanted to show him personally one more thing before he left the Soviet Union and instructing Warner to show up at the airport with his party the next morning to board Gorshkov's airplane. The aide would not disclose the destination. So the next morning the American team showed up at the airport. Admiral Kasatonov arrived with Admiral Gorshkov's regrets that he was detained and would not be able to make the trip. With Warner, Okun, and Hayward seated on the plane, Kasatonov broke out the vodka. Warner recalled Kasatonov explaining that Admiral Gorshkov "wants you to leave understanding the heart and soul of Soviet thinking." A few hours later, they landed in Volgograd.

Throughout the day, the motorcade made its way through the industrial city, stopping at museums and sites detailing the struggle of the Great Patriotic War when the city was named Stalingrad. The Americans walked through the ruins of Flour Mill Number Four, left untouched as a testimony to the fighting. It seemed to Warner that the Soviets had left everything but the bodies! The tour concluded with a trip to Mamayev-Kurgan, the high promontory overlooking the city. At the top of the hill stood a 305-foot-tall concrete memorial statue that dominated the countryside for miles around. As Warner looked up at this female figure bearing a sword, Kasatonov pulled out a piece of paper containing a message from Gorshkov: "That sword points to the West because that is where the threat lies. We do not trust you today, nor tomorrow, nor in the distant future."[1]

Back in the United States, Secretary of Defense Melvin Laird had already initiated preparations for the forthcoming follow-up meeting called for in the agreement's Article X. On 22 May he sent a memorandum to the Chairman of the Joint Chiefs, the Secretary of the Navy, the Secretary of the Air Force, and the Assistant Secretary of Defense for International Security Affairs requesting nominees for a preparatory working group to be headed by Lawrence Eagleburger, as well as nominees for the delegation to go to Moscow to meet with the Soviets in November. Laird also sent to the State Department a letter inviting participation in both functions.[2]

With State having lost the mid-May showdown over the negotiation of fixed distances, Capt. Edward Day of State's Bureau of Political-Military (Pol-Mil) Affairs recommended to his boss, Thomas Pickering, that the department forego representation at the planned November discussions and in any working group formed to review the U.S. position, so long as the department could review the decided position before the fall Moscow meeting. He advocated that the department should continue to point out that the NSSM 140 response did not allow the U.S. delegation flexibility regarding fixed-distance questions. Day suggested for future annual review sessions that State needed to provide only two members of the delegation, with one serving as the deputy head. Okun concurred with this last point. Day's evaluation was accepted. On 2 June, the Pol-Mil director, Ronald I. Spiers, sent a letter to Assistant Secretary of Defense Warren Nutter declining the offer of State participation.[3]

In his 22 May memorandum Laird had directed the Chairman of the Joint Chiefs to nominate a vice admiral to head the November delegation. Consequently, Plans and Policy Director (J-5) Vice Admiral Weinel received orders to lead the team to Moscow. Rear Admiral Hayward, Air Force Brig. Gen. Harry M. Chapman, and three Navy captains joined Weinel on the U.S. team. In mid-June the State Department informally notified the Soviets of the delegation's composition. On 4 July Marshal Grechko received a message from Laird formally notifying him of the composition of the six-man U.S. military delegation.[4]

The Eagleburger-led working group held its inaugural meeting at 0930 on 7 July in Room 4D746 of the Pentagon. Then, and later, the group reviewed the fixed-distance issue and continued to find any fixed-distance regimen unworkable. The group also reviewed the implementation of an experimental special signal system that had been worked on at the May negotiations and considered whether third countries should be asked to adhere to the accord.[5]

One factor contributing to the continuing "no change" position was the positive reports coming in from the fleet. Back in the Mediterranean, two days after the accord was signed, Rear Admiral (Select) Hilton, again embarked in uss W. S. Sims, met a flotilla of Soviet submarines and surface ships entering the Mediterranean through the Strait of Gibraltar. Hilton welcomed the inbound vessels with the flashing light greeting (in Russian) "GOOD DAY, WELCOME TO THE MEDITERRANEAN." The message elicited responses from several of the Soviet ships, including a comeback from a Juliett-class submarine stating, "WE WILL LIVE COMPLETELY BY AGREEMENTS ON NAVIGATION." Hilton observed that since his ships had intercepted the Soviet flotilla, behavior on both sides had been impeccable.[6] On 8 June Kissinger had directed the NSC Under Secretaries Committee to provide President Nixon quarterly reports on agreements signed at the May Moscow summit. The first report, submitted on 28 July, reported no Soviet violations of the

INCSEA agreement.⁷ The Soviets also seemed pleased with the implementation of the accord. In an early July interview in *Izvestiya*, Gorshkov lauded the recently signed agreement and emphasized that it was being studied and implemented within the Soviet Navy from himself "down to the lowest watch officer." He also stressed the practicality of concrete fixed distances.⁸

By mid-September, the Eagleburger-led working group had finished work on the negotiating team position paper. After reading the paper, Secretary Warner recommended that the White House be forewarned that the American obstinacy on the fixed-distance issue could cause the discussions to be broken off. Acting Assistant Secretary of Defense for International Security Affairs Armistead I. Selden Jr. responded by stating that there was no need to raise unnecessary apprehension at the White House since, in his view, the Soviets would now have little to gain in breaking off discussions.⁹ Warner's concern that the Soviets might break off the talks proved unwarranted. Despite the fact that Weinel traveled to the Soviet Union with a mandate not to negotiate on fixed distances, the series of meetings in Moscow that began on 13 November still yielded some positive accomplishments.¹⁰

Across the negotiation table from Weinel sat First Deputy Chief of the Main Naval Staff Adm. Vladimir N. Alekseyev. Having served in this post since 1966, this Hero of the Soviet Union had served as Kasatonov's military deputy head during the two previous negotiating sessions. Alekseyev initially gained experience in submarines and torpedo boats. With the latter vessels, he distinguished himself during the Great Patriotic War. After the war Alekseyev rose through the ranks to command several naval bases and serve as chief of staff of the Baltic Fleet.¹¹ In addition to the experienced Alekseyev, Rear Admiral Motrokhov and General-Major Vishensky returned to head up the Soviet surface and air working groups.

Alekseyev presented his fixed-distance proposals, including recommendations that ships come no closer than two miles during the day and three miles at night or in low visibility. Alekseyev also added the "as a rule" modifier to mollify Weinel. Weinel responded that he would happily take these proposals back to America for review. While Weinel successfully sidestepped that issue, the two sides progressed on the issue of incorporating a protocol to expand the agreement to include merchant ships. The

American side had not come prepared to address this Soviet proposal but agreed to consider it upon return to the United States. The two sides also refined the special flaghoist signal system being developed for fleet communications. Concluding the discussions on 18 November, Weinel advised Ambassador Beam that the talks had been generally successful.[12]

President Nixon's landslide reelection probably helped Weinel during his Moscow visit. Perhaps the Soviets did not desire to send the wrong signal to an administration they expected to deal with for the next four years by being adamant on fixed distances. The personalities involved also contributed to Weinel's success. Despite the differing positions, the two delegation heads got along fine. Weinel later reflected, "There is something that binds seafaring men together. I don't know what it is — it's there. You meet seafaring people from any country in the world, and there will be an immediate attraction between the two of them."[13]

In his post-trip report, Weinel recommended expanding the working group that had developed the U.S. negotiating position to include a State Department representative and an expert on merchant marine affairs. He added that this group should continue to oppose any fixed-distance proposals but could examine the Soviet proposal to expand the accord to incorporate merchant shipping.[14]

After being briefed on the Moscow talks on 1 December, Admiral Zumwalt sent a message to his fleet commanders discussing the November meeting and the Soviet positions and requesting feedback. Commander Carrier Division Four, Rear Adm. Donald D. Engen, wrote the CNO that:

> As a tactical commander, one point I would like to make is that any distance agreements between ship to ship or aircraft to aircraft could be tactically limiting and not always in the best interest of both parties. There could be situations in which specified distances would create the misunderstanding that we seek to avoid. I would hope that we avoid writing these distances into our agreements.

Engen also noted that the agreement had been salutary with regard to U.S.-Soviet relations at sea: "We have achieved a mutual understanding that has enhanced safety and taken 'the heat' out of encounters at sea." In his response, Zumwalt noted that Engen's comments reflected those of many of his fellow commanders. He also added that he didn't anticipate any change on the fixed-distance issue.[15]

Shortly after the CNO sent this response, on 9 January 1973, now Acting Assistant Secretary of Defense for International Security Affairs Lawrence Eagleburger reconvened his team to review the results of the November meeting. Responding to a DoD request generated by Weinel's report, Undersecretary of State U. Alexis Johnson provided two State representatives to the working group. In addition, a technical expert on merchant marine matters joined the group. After rejecting the latest Soviet fixed-distance proposal, the Eagleburger group again recommended that the United States continue to support the "general wording" formulation.[16] The group did agree with the Soviet proposal to extend the agreement to provide for the safety of nonmilitary ships.

With the signing of the Paris Peace Accords in January 1973, America finally could withdraw from the national nightmare that was Vietnam. With this sore spot removed, Soviet-American relations promised to make further advances. In Moscow détente was reflected by Soviet flag officers being more accessible to America's resident naval attaché contingent. On various occasions, Admirals Kasatonov and Alekseyev held extended conversations with the U.S. Navy representatives. At a 26 February reception at the naval attaché's flat, Alekseyev said that he looked forward to receiving the official invitation for the first annual review in Washington and hoped he would be slated to go.[17] Throughout March in Washington, Navy officials arranged for facilities, selected delegation members, and informed allies. Finally, on 6 April, the United States sent an invitation to the Soviets to attend talks starting on 14 May.[18]

Again heading the American delegation, Vice Admiral Weinel wanted to build on the personal relationships already established. Throughout April and early May, staff officers assembled a social itinerary that included lunch with Admiral Zumwalt, a National Symphony performance at the Kennedy Center, a visit to the Naval Academy, and a sightseeing trip to Florida. The American defense attaché in Moscow attempted to clear the proposed social itinerary with the Soviets but was rebuffed. The Soviets felt that settlement of the social itinerary should be left to the initial meeting of the delegations. Responding to a question about appropriate gifts, the defense attaché telegraphed: "We believe that inquiry regarding gifts, however informal, is highly inappropriate. It is the Russian way to present gifts in a mood of spontaneity, though contrived it may be."[19]

Shortly before the Soviet visit, Weinel huddled with his team for the review preview. Over the previous year there had been a significant turnover in delegation membership. Only Captain Rawlins remained from the team that went to Moscow in October 1971. After going over the position papers, Weinel emphasized certain rules of behavior:

> No posturing, no bragging, and no looking down our noses at the Russians. Take no interest whatsoever in any kinds of secrets. Don't even *act* like you're trying to find out anything, because we are not on any intelligence missions. I don't give a damn if they were building seventeen aircraft carriers. That's not what we are here for. Establish give and take with your counterparts. Don't make it one way. Be able to listen as much as you talk. Admit to yourselves that the Russians could be right and have a better mousetrap than we have. Always focus on the bottom line, which is we both see the foolishness of the games of chicken and we need to agree to knock it off. And finally: Be absolutely, completely honest with them![20]

With that last thought in mind, retired Admiral Weinel recalled that the Soviet delegation had flown to Washington from New York's Kennedy Airport on National Airlines. Somewhere en route, National lost their luggage. When Weinel went to greet the Soviets the next morning at the Hilton, he noticed that Alekseyev was somewhat heated:

> First thing he said was: "Where the hell is my luggage?" For some reason — I don't know why to this day I said it — I said, "Well, Admiral Alekseyev. We didn't realize you had as much luggage as you had. We haven't finished searching through your luggage yet, but we should be done about ten o'clock this morning." Alekseyev then calmly turned to the interpreter and said: "Well, I'm going to have ham, eggs, potatoes, and a pot of coffee." Didn't bat an eye, and after that whenever he had an opportunity, he would tell his listener: "What an honest man Admiral Weinel is. I can completely trust him!"

Shortly after the convening of one of the early sessions at Fort McNair, the two leaders slipped away with a Soviet interpreter. Driving over to the nearby Washington Navy Yard, Weinel invited the Soviet admiral into his quarters for a drink and an one-on-one discussion. Weinel recounted the conversation. On the coffee-table before him were spread a bunch of the secret position papers. The American vice admiral pointed to them. "You know, you could have the position papers — all of them. You don't have to read them now. You can take them with you and have your staff go over them."

Alekseyev didn't even glance at the classified documents. Weinel recalled saying, "I don't have any give. My Air Force, my Navy, and the Joint Chiefs of Staff all insist that we should just stick with the Rules of the Road."

Alekseyev responded, "Ah, but I've got a problem, because my Navy is interested in fixing the distances, because that solves the problem. If we can't come within 2,000 yards of each other, then we can't have an accident."

Weinel countered: "I agree with you. In fact, if I were in your shoes or had my way with the Americans, I'd make it 10,000 yards! I'd make it so goddamn far out that it would be ludicrous — you would never have a problem. Unfortunately, that is not where my country is coming from, but I see your point." He argued that there had to be a way to do this so that both sides could be satisfied and then suggested, "For the time being we go with the Rules of the Road, but I am perfectly willing to stipulate right now that fixed distances remain an open agenda item, and at the first review we have where this is not going right, then we bring the subject of fixed distances back on board."

Alekseyev thought about it and agreed. Weinel did have some good news for Alekseyev. On 15 May President Nixon approved a position paper that recommended acceding to the protocol proposed by the Soviets to extend INCSEA to cover merchant ships.

Having agreed to the outcome of the talks shortly after the onset, the two men then walked through the historic shipyard to the Officers' Club for lunch. Alekseyev glanced around and asked, "What is this place?"

Weinel answered, "This is the Washington Navy Yard, but it really doesn't function as an active navy yard. A Russian spy wouldn't give five dollars for all the blueprints and information stored here."

Alekseyev retorted, "Is that because it's not worth five dollars or that we already have it?"[21]

Returning to Fort McNair, Weinel never mentioned to his team that he had already reached an understanding. Captain Rawlins would later comment that he thought it somewhat strange how the Soviets would immediately drop an issue if rebuffed. The interaction between the working groups was smooth. At the plenary sessions, Weinel took every opportunity to praise Alekseyev. Overall, the negotiations turned out to be a pleasant experience. Subsequently, on 22 May 1973, the two sides added a protocol that mandated merchant vessels of the two nations to be covered under the 1972 agreement.[22] In addition, work continued on a special table of flag signals so that the two navies could communicate military situations that were difficult to convey with the standard international flag signals.

With the protocol concluded, the Soviets hosted a reception at the So-viet Embassy retreat on Maryland's Eastern Shore featuring the "spon-taneous" exchange of gifts. Vice Admiral Weinel had taken great care to find something appropriate for his opposite number. Consulting with the Soviet staff, Weinel found out that Alekseyev had a little dacha just outside of Moscow where he enjoyed tinkering and building little things. One aide mentioned that Alekseyev could always use some good tools because they were hard to come by. Weinel obtained a super toolbox. Then Weinel asked the aide, what did this man really love in life — what turned him on? The answer was his grandson. Weinel found a windup Victrola and some records. When the gift-giving time came, Alekseyev was deeply touched by the toolbox. Then Weinel presented him the Victrola for his grandson. The grandfather's eyes welled with tears. He didn't expect this. The Soviet admiral then expressed a hope that someday his grandchild and Weinel's could live on this planet as friends.[23]

The friendly Soviet disposition extended to the other side of the world as the USS La Salle joined with ships from Great Britain, India, Italy, Iran, Norway, the Netherlands, and the Soviet Union to celebrate the annual Imperial Ethiopian Navy Days. In previous years there had been some tension at events attended by the Soviet and American flag officers. However, when Rear Adm. Robert J. Hanks arrived for a luncheon on board the French frigate Protet, he was seated directly across from his counterpart, Rear Admiral Krugliakov.

Speaking through a translator, the Soviet flag officer complimented Hanks on the professionalism exhibited by the USS Sellers when that Middle East Force destroyer passed through the Soviet Navy anchorages off Somalia's Cape Guardafui and South Yemen's island of Socotra. Krugliakov noted that the *Sellers* skipper, Comdr. Robert Rumney, had scrupulously observed the 1972 INCSEA agreement and added, "Your captain saw that there was an admiral on the *Senyavin* [his cruiser flagship] and asked permission to enter the anchorage. I answered he could steam anywhere he wished." However, Krugliakov added, "He's not like some American captains who act like boys on motorcycles — as did your destroyer captain who caused a collision in 1967."

Hanks responded, "I'm sure you'll understand we viewed that event rather differently. Your skipper was guilty of bad manners and worse seamanship when, without even seeking permission, as *Sellers'* skipper did, he elbowed his way into the middle of a U.S. carrier task force and, in clear violation of the International Rules of the Road, caused the collision." Having made his retort, Hanks added that he appreciated the compliment about the *Sellers* and noted that many of the AGIS that had tailed his ships in the Gulf of Tonkin were responsibly handled. As the exchange between the two officers became more upbeat, Krugliakov extended an invitation to Hanks to allow crewmembers from the *La Salle* to tour the destroyer *Skrytnii*. Hanks recalled that "throughout that 1973 Imperial Ethiopian Navy Days, Soviet representatives made a concerted effort to be friendly, open, and hospitable."

In Washington and Massawa, the personalities and the nautical backgrounds of the individuals involved facilitated cooperation. Orders to comply with the accord were obviously passed down to ships on both sides. Still, the joviality and toasting represented a veneer. Despite détente, basic ideological differences and conflicting national objectives remained. On board the *Skrytnii*, Rear Admiral Krugliakov approached an American sailor and asked his father's occupation. The admiral expressed puzzlement and distaste when the sailor responded that his dad was a real estate agent. "That's terrible! In the Soviet Union, all land belongs to the people!" Moving to the next sailor Krugliakov asked the same question. With a straight face the sailor responded that his father was "a worker." After translation, the Soviet flag officer grinned, slapped the sailor on the back, and stated, "That's fine, son — say hello to your father for me!"[24]

Within months of these May 1973 meetings, the INCSEA agreement would receive its first big test.

THE 1970s

The implementation of the INCSEA agreement and the subsequent protocol occurred at a time when the navies of the two superpowers appeared to be heading in opposite directions. For the U.S. Navy, the early 1970s represented a period of retrenchment as hundreds of World War II–vintage ships reached the end of their service lives. Programs to replace these ships systematically had not been funded during the 1960s because of other priorities, such as America's efforts in Southeast Asia. As the Navy decommissioned old ships to free up funds for new ship classes, Admiral Zumwalt grew increasingly pessimistic over prospects in a conflict with the Soviets. In 1970 the CNO estimated that the U.S. Navy had a 55 percent chance of winning in a conventional fight with the Soviets. A year later he told Navy Secretary John Chafee that the Soviets now maintained a 65-to-35 percent edge.[1]

One factor influencing Zumwalt's thinking was a study called the Middle East Power Equation (MEPEQ). The study projected what could have happened if Soviet and American naval forces in place at the time of the Jordanian crisis had fought. With the support of computer programs, analysts repeatedly ran the scenario and came to the same bleak conclusion: if the Soviets launched a preemptive strike, the United States could be expected to lose two of three aircraft carriers.[2]

Soviet submarines remained a major concern to the Americans three decades after the struggle in the North Atlantic against German U-boats.

The Soviets had always maintained a large undersea fleet. During the early 1970s, that fleet was composed of both conventional diesel-electric and nuclear-propelled classes. In addition to launching torpedoes, many of the newer Soviet submarines could fire missiles at surface ships. While some, such as the Juliett and Echo II classes, had to surface to fire their missile salvos, the Charlie class could launch its antiship missiles from below the surface.[3] Newer classes of surface warships entering the Soviet naval inventory compounded the problem. The Kresta and Kara classes, typifying the new-construction Soviet warships bristling with weapons and electronic sensors, were increasingly seen on the world's oceans. Meanwhile, shore-based Soviet naval aviation aircraft carrying long-range air-to-ship missiles posed another threat.

Against this array of Soviet Navy platforms, the U.S. Navy's ability to perform one of its primary missions — keeping the North Atlantic sea lanes open to allow the transport of supplies and reinforcements to Europe in the event of war — seemed doubtful. In 1974 Zumwalt told a Senate subcommittee that the odds were against being able to protect NATO's flanks and the sea lanes adequately.[4]

Not everyone shared Zumwalt's pessimism. Training and equipment reliability had to be considered in the power balance. In contrast to the Soviets, who spent much time in port or anchored while deployed, the U.S. Navy steamed and regularly exercised its weapon systems. Former COMSIXTHFLT Vice Adm. Jerry Miller had little respect for Soviet seamanship and warfighting ability: "Hell, these guys are a bunch of amateurs. They haven't gotten around to the first phase of professionalism in warfare."[5] In a scrap with the Soviet Union, the United States could also count on the resources of many allied nations, such as Great Britain and Japan, with long maritime traditions. Finally, when the MEPEQ study results were further scrutinized, analysts who placed themselves in Soviet shoes realized that a surprise first strike on American forces in one area of the world would set up the Soviet naval units positioned in other parts of the world for nearly instant annihilation.[6] Still, American confidence in the U.S. and allies' ability to maintain maritime supremacy became quite tenuous. The events of October 1973 did little to alleviate the concerns of Zumwalt and other American naval leaders.

When the Arab armies moved against Israel on Saturday afternoon, 6

October 1973, forty-eight American warships were in the Mediterranean. Most were centered on the two aircraft carriers: the uss *Independence,* at anchor with her escorts in Athens, and the uss *Franklin D. Roosevelt* and her escorts enjoying liberty in various Spanish ports. In addition, a ten-ship amphibious task force centered on the uss *Guadalcanal* was scattered among several Greek ports, and the Sixth Fleet flagship, uss *Little Rock,* was steaming at sea south of Crete. On board the *Little Rock,* former SecDef assistant and now comsixthflt Vice Adm. Daniel Murphy was receiving frequent updates on the breaking hostilities in the Middle East and the movements of the Soviet Mediterranean squadron: the Fifth Eskadra. On 6 October the Soviet forces appeared formidable. Murphy's intelligence people plotted fifty-seven Soviet warships in the Mediterranean, including a Kynda-class antiship missile cruiser, an older *Sverdlov*-class gun cruiser, three Kashin-class and two "Mod" Kotlin-class missile destroyers, two "guns-only" Kotlins, nine frigates and corvettes of various classes, two amphibious vessels, two minesweepers, and several auxiliary ships. Most of the ships were at anchorages off Crete or Egypt.

Reacting to the outbreak of hostilities, the Americans canceled shore leave and the *Independence* group left from Athens on 7 October, proceeding to an area south of Crete to join *Little Rock* the following day. As the *Independence* left Athens, lookouts reported the presence of a Soviet tattletale destroyer. During the first week of the Arab-Israeli war, Murphy's flag plot noted no overt moves by the Soviet flotilla against the task group. However, on 9 October, the Kynda-class cruiser and the submarine tender that served as the Soviet flagship joined the destroyer tagging behind the *Independence–Little Rock* formation. Meanwhile, the amphibious force had moved to Souda Bay, Crete, where it would remain on the sidelines through 25 October. The Soviets posted an agi to watch these forces.

As the fighting continued, more Soviet Navy units augmented the Fifth Eskadra. Foxtrot submarines in the process of being relieved were held on station. Black Sea Fleet vessels made their way toward the Dardenelles. As opposition forces grew, Washington restricted Murphy's ability to deploy his forces as he saw fit. The *Independence* was to stay south of Crete while the *Franklin D. Roosevelt* group was to remain in the western Mediterranean. The Sixth Fleet's defensive posture was further weakened when the United States began its resupply airlift to Israel a week into the conflict. Because of the denial of overflight rights by many of America's allies, Murphy had to set up a line of picket ships to support the Mediterranean air-bridge route.[7]

Assured of resupply, the Israeli Defense Forces began offensive operations that turned the tide of the war. Syrian forces were routed, so that Damascus came within range of Israeli artillery, and Egyptian gains in the Sinai were erased, with Israeli armored units operating east of the Suez Canal and executing a masterful pincer movement that would trap the Egyptian Third Army.

With this reversal of fortune for its Middle East client-states, the Soviet Union increased its military activity in the region. On 16 October Murphy's lookouts reported the presence of another Soviet cruiser and destroyer, which had arrived to relieve the cruiser and destroyer that had been tracking the Americans. The relieved ships withdrew over the horizon to join an ever-growing Soviet Mediterranean fleet. By 24 October the number of Red ships tracked in Murphy's flag plot had increased to eighty, of which twenty-six were surface combatants. Below the surface, ten American SSNs strove to keep tabs on the growing number of Soviet submarines crowding the Mediterranean basin.

In the event of hostilities, the Soviets had the capability to launch a coordinated salvo of forty surface-to-surface missiles. Murphy's objective — to prevent the Soviets from positioning to launch such a devastating blow — led to an increasingly tense game of shadowing the shadowers and their comrades over the horizon. American destroyers and cruisers positioned themselves within gun range of tailing Soviet missile ships, ready to fire at the first hint of a missile launch. On the *Little Rock*, "white birds" were run out onto the rails, surface-to-air missiles ready to fire at a moment's notice. Over the horizon, armed American attack aircraft constantly circled the Soviet missile ships. As the fighting continued on land, the two superpower fleets jockeyed for tactical advantage at sea.[8]

By 22 October the crisis that had created the intense naval standoff seemed on its way to a peaceful resolution. However, a UN Security Council–brokered cease-fire that went into effect that afternoon was broken, and the Israelis moved on and reached Suez City on the morning of 24 October, when the next cease-fire again took hold. At that time, Vice Admiral Murphy felt confident that the diplomats were in command and that his fleet could soon return to normal operations.

It was not to be. On the day before the cease-fire, Soviet Premier Leonid Brezhnev sent a hotline message to the White House desiring immediate and decisive action in light of alleged gross Israeli violations of the first cease-fire. On the twenty-fourth Admiral Zumwalt received a memorandum from one of his top Sovietologists warning of possible Soviet ground-force intervention. That night the CNO returned to the Pentagon as the National Security Council met at the White House.

Zumwalt kept track as the White House reacted to a Soviet proposal to send troops into the region unilaterally. At 0025 on 25 October, the United States raised its defensive posture to Defense Condition (DEFCON) Three. Immediate actions included ordering additional warships to the Mediterranean and placing the 82nd Airborne Division on alert.[9] American strategic forces also assumed a higher readiness posture. B-52s stationed on Guam were ordered to the continental United States for refitting and redeploying. Navy Secretary Warner and Herbert Okun, in Scotland on a fence-mending mission, somberly watched U.S. SSBNs deploy out of Holy Loch.[10]

Although the Soviets did not introduce troops into the region, tensions increased in the Mediterranean as the Soviets, on 26 October, began six days of large-scale anticarrier warfare exercises involving both surface and submarine units. While submarines, destroyers, cruisers, and missile boats staged mock attacks, additional Soviet warships entered the Mediterranean. Murphy recalled, "By 31 October, SOVMEDFLT strength had increased to 95 units, including 34 surface combatants and 23 submarines, possessing a first launch capability of 88 SSMs, 348 torpedoes, 46 SAMs."[11]

On 30 October Murphy moved his forces westward and the tension began to subside. The Soviets started dispersing their forces on 3 November. Although the crisis had passed its climax, the Sixth Fleet remained in heightened readiness until 18 November. Reflecting what had occurred in the eastern Mediterranean during that period, Admiral Zumwalt wrote, "I doubt that major units of the U.S. Navy were ever in a tenser situation since World War II ended than the Sixth Fleet in the Mediterranean was for the week after the alert was declared."[12]

Seven months after the showdown, Admiral Alekseyev greeted Vice Admiral Weinel as he stepped off the airplane upon his arrival in Moscow. As the two men exchanged pleasantries, Weinel could not help but notice that nearly everyone within the Soviet reception committee kept peeking at their watches. Then, "in some phenomenally short time like four minutes sixteen seconds," the luggage was brought up and Alekseyev proudly announced, "You can pick up your luggage now!"[13] Frocked Vice Adm. Harry S. Train II joined Weinel. As the new director of the Joint Staff, Train had just put on his third star. After attending the initial 1974 annual INCSEA review plenary session, Weinel turned the helm over to his Joint Staff colleague and returned to Washington.

Returning to lead the Soviet side, Admiral Kasatonov joined the veterans Motrokhov, Vishensky, and Captain First Rank Serkov to face the American delegation. Defense Intelligence Agency analysts speculated that the return of Kasatonov to head the Soviet delegation signaled a harder line, believing that Alekseyev had been too friendly and amenable to compromise. Or perhaps the return of the number-two man in the Soviet Navy signaled a renewed commitment to the accord, in anticipation of possible negative attitudes on the American side in light of the previous fall's naval showdown.[14]

With Weinel gone, Train recalled how stressful it was for him to sit across from his Soviet counterpart: "Kasatonov really was a dominating figure, a daunting figure." The newly minted 46-year-old vice admiral added, "He made admiral four years before I entered the Naval Academy. He would call me 'my boy,' and 'young man.'" Again the Soviets brought up the issue of fixed distances, which Train successfully deflected. Kasatonov also tabled a proposal to expand the agreement to cover civilian aircraft, which the American side was not prepared to address. Train succeeded in getting the Soviets to concede that tracking aircraft with fire-control radar was not in the spirit of the agreement.[15]

Regarding the events of the previous fall, Train recalled, "The '73 October War had no impact on the '74 meeting. It was never discussed to my recollection."[16] Despite the influx of more than 150 warships into a relatively small body of water, and constant maneuvering to gain tactical advantage, there were few violations of the agreement signed in Moscow in May 1972. Despite the confrontation in the Mediterranean, the number of alleged Soviet violations of the accord dropped from twenty-four the first year to seven. The Soviets alleged five American violations. There were no collisions or instances of harassing close-quarter maneuvering. The accusations against the Soviets focused on weapon pointings, flare shootings, and searchlight shinings. Compliance with the agreement by the vast majority of the units obviously prevented a tense situation from becoming more tense. Soviet ships avoided interfering with the carrier task group formations, and both sides used the new flag signals agreed on for enhancing communications.[17]

Experience with exchanging the experimental special signals gained during the October War and other encounters during the previous year allowed Train and Kasatonov to propose that the signals be made permanent. Early in 1975, the Inter-Governmental Maritime Consultative Organization (IMCO) would receive a letter from both parties detailing the agreed-on signals.[18] At the conclusion of the review, Train reported that the results were "in consonance with the U.S. position paper."[19]

At the 1974 annual INCSEA review, Train and Kasatonov solidified a pattern of professional and social interactions that had been initiated with the first set of negotiations in October 1971. These patterns would remain in place for the next five years despite a general decline in U.S.-Soviet relations.

The format of an annual review session then included an initial informal meeting between the delegation heads to agree on a social itinerary. The first formal plenary session consisted, as Naval Reserve Comdr. Richard Massey called it, of a scripted "kabuki dance." The host delegation head's welcoming statement discussed the importance of the work to be done, referred to other bilateral cooperative efforts in the past and present, and introduced his delegation. The visiting delegation head echoed the host's comments on the importance of the proceedings, commented on the warm hospitality shown so far, and introduced his delegation. The visiting delegation head then tabled the proposed agenda. The agenda usually contained the Soviet proposal to discuss fixed distances, always called for reviewing the accord's implementation and the effectiveness of communications, and concluded with discussion to set the date for the next meeting, usually the following May or June. If there was no further discussion, the hosting delegation head would then charge the surface and air working-group heads to begin meetings to act on the agenda.

As the working groups consulted, the host delegation head kept the visiting delegation head occupied with formal calls or trips to cultural events. There usually was a social event every evening. Early in the review, the hosting navy would sponsor a welcoming reception. Late in the review, the visiting party would host a reception at its embassy. After the two delegation heads had received briefings from their working-group heads, they sat down at a final plenary session to review and record areas of agreement and disagreement. Afterwards, there usually was a two-day trip away from the capital city. Upon return the two delegation heads signed a "Results of Consultations" document; the signing would be followed by drinks and an exchange of toasts.[20]

At both surface and air working-group sessions, the Soviets always tabled fixed-distance proposals, and the Americans countered with well-rehearsed arguments on why such an arrangement would be counterproductive. Occasionally, the Soviets cited incidents to illustrate their case. Incidents did continue to occur after the accord was signed in 1972, and the working groups spent much time analyzing them, not so much to fix blame as to see whether measures could be implemented to prevent further occurrences. The review was not the time for either side to present complaints of agreement violations. Addressing these was an ongoing process handled through the communication mechanism put in place under Article VII. For example, if an American ship allegedly violated the accord, the Soviets would contact the American naval attaché in Moscow, who would relay the report to OpNav in Washington, where an investigation was initiated. Thus, if one side referred to an incident at the review, the other side had plots, deck logs, and photographs on hand for analysis. Together, the two sides could reconstruct the event. The system didn't always work this way. During the 1974 review the American delegation expressed annoyance that in two cases the Soviets had complained of U.S. actions using normal diplomatic channels instead of the navy-to-navy channel.[21]

As for the number and types of incidents discussed, the mid-1970s marked a period of strict compliance by both sides. The Soviets alleged three American violations during the accord's first year, five during the second, two during the third, four during the fourth, two during the fifth, and two during the twelve months from May 1977 to May 1978. Alleged Soviet violations plummeted from twenty-four instances occurring between May 1972 and May 1973 to five and then three in successive years. In the period

May 1976 to May 1977, the number of alleged violations climbed to twenty-four, and there were twenty-two alleged Soviet violations reported prior to the 1978 talks.[22]

Soviet complaints focused on perceived aggressive maneuvers of American aircraft in proximity to Soviet ships and aircraft. One Soviet protest involved contact between a U.S. Navy F-4 Phantom and a Soviet Tu-16 Badger over the Norwegian Sea that occurred on 4 October 1973. Later, the Soviets produced photographs of the damaged Badger to reinforce their claim. Soviet complaints against U.S. surface-ship activities were rare. One notable exception — the Soviets claimed that on 29 March 1978 the cruiser USS *South Carolina* performed dangerous maneuvers close to Soviet vessels conducting unrep.[23] The sudden increase in the number of U.S. complaints of Soviet violations during the 1976–77 and 1977–78 periods is deceiving. With few exceptions, the Soviets strictly complied with the terms of the accord. Many of the American complaints were of Soviets directing weapons and fire-control radar at U.S. ships and aircraft. While the agreement addressed only the pointing of such systems at ships, Admiral Kasatonov had conceded to Vice Admiral Train that directing weapon systems at aircraft was a violation of the spirit of the agreement. Still, Soviet ships continued to point weapons and occasionally shoot flares at what they perceived as harassing aircraft. At the 1976 annual review Vice Admiral Train told his counterpart that the United States would treat all such future instances as violations of the accord. Hence the subsequent rise. Otherwise, most U.S. allegations involved Soviet surface ships that either had maneuvered recklessly or had pointed weapons at nearby U.S. Navy ships. In the summer of 1977 close American surveillance of Soviet flagships apparently provoked the Soviets to act aggressively. Three instances involved hazardous maneuvering by Soviet warships to drive a U.S. Navy cruiser away from closely observing the new Soviet antisubmarine cruiser *Kiev* during sea trials. In a message to his boss, the Sixth Fleet commander confessed, "We got under their skin (if not in their way) during the *Kiev* transit" and noted that the agreement had been observed by both sides.[24]

The ramming of the frigate USS *Voge* by an Echo II–class submarine in the Ionian Sea on the afternoon of 28 August 1976 was not discussed under the accord's auspices. Submerged except for a portion of her sail area, the Soviet submarine had turned into and broadsided the American frigate near the stern. Aboard the *Voge*, water poured into the after steering compartment, and part of a propeller was sheared off. One sailor was injured when he was tossed from the 01 level onto the main deck. The prognosis for the Echo II was more uncertain as she failed to surface. Vice Admiral Train had just assumed command of the Sixth Fleet and was at his home ashore in Gaeta, Italy, when the "Flash" message report from *Voge* arrived. Train, through his chief of staff on the flagship, relayed a message to the frigate USS *Koelsch* stationed off Greece near the Fifth Eskadra flagship, to inform Admiral Akimov of the collision. Akimov responded, "Thank you very much," and dispatched a ship to the scene.[25]

Eventually the Echo II did surface. The whole front of her sail was crushed. In this case, the United States counterprotested a 1 September Soviet protest using standard diplomatic channels rather than the navy-to-navy channel established under INCSEA. In this case both sides agreed that submerged submarines, obligated to stay out of the way of surface ships, were not covered by the accord.[26]

For the annual review sessions, both sides strove to maintain continuity within their delegations to preserve corporate knowledge of previous discussions of contentious issues. Maintaining delegation continuity also helped establish a personal rapport between opposing members that often worked to ameliorate potentially heated disputes.

Unfortunately for the American side, the two-to-three-year rotation schedule for tours of duty for American naval officers forced a constant turnover on the American side. From the original American INCSEA team that first went to Moscow in October 1971, only Captain Rawlins remained on board until 1974. Comdr. Ronald Kurth, a member of the 1971 delegation, would later return to serve on several American delegations during the 1980s and early 1990s. Beginning in 1975, Comdr. Edward J. Melanson became the OSD/ISA representative on the delegation. Because he served in various billets within OSD for the next dozen years, Melanson remained with the U.S. delegation through 1986. George Fedoroff, an analyst specializing in the Soviet Navy, joined the delegation in 1977 and remained through the end of the Cold War and beyond. At the top, Train took over leadership of the American delegation from Weinel in 1974 and held that position through 1976. Vice Adm. Patrick J. Hannifin of the Joint Staff joined the delegation as Train's deputy in 1975 and assumed command of the delegation for two years beginning in 1977. In 1979 Vice Adm. William J. Crowe assumed head-of-delegation duties.

Crowe's one-year tenure as the head of the delegation represented an internal change on the American side. Although INCSEA was touted as a navy-to-navy accord, the American head of delegation had been detailed from the JCS, and OSD/ISA closely monitored the process. For the first few years OSD/ISA submitted quarterly progress reports to the president. Pres. Gerald Ford personally reviewed and approved the U.S. delegation position paper. During the Carter years, National Security Advisor Zbigniew Brzezinski performed this role.[27] As the Navy's DCNO for Plans and Policy (OP 06), Crowe represented a change to more direct Navy control of the process. In the successive years, OpNav selected the head of the U.S. delegation.

The Soviet side maintained much greater continuity. After Train met with Kasatonov in 1974, he sat across from Vice Adm. Igor A. Sornev in 1975, and then Vice Adm. Petr N. Navoytsev in 1976. Navoytsev would go on to head the Soviet team through 1987. From the original team that negotiated INCSEA for the Soviets, Motrokhov remained until 1975, and Vishensky stayed through 1980. Another October 1971 veteran, Capt. First Rank Valentin A. Serkov, would remain with the Soviet delegation through 1991.

To many on the American side, Serkov was the power behind the power. "That man had more *vlast* [power] than any four-striper I've run into," recalled one intelligence officer.[28] In later years, retired Rear Admiral Kurth, the veteran of a dozen U.S. delegations, reflected:

> Well, Captain Serkov was a naval lawyer. He had started out at sea, but early in his career he had gone to an international maritime law school. At first he comes across with many stereotypical Russian characteristics. Serkov was the deputy head of the delegation, but he was only a navy captain, and there were at least two Soviet admirals on the delegation, and he had precedence over both of them. That initially created a very serious problem for the U.S. delegation. I remember one time well. Adm. "Blackie" Weinel was the head of the U.S. delegation, and he had invited to a social occasion the Soviet admirals but not Serkov, and Serkov got his nose severely bent. He came to me, as I was assigned as the senior liaison officer, to point out that he was the deputy head of the delegation and that he was offended. Therefore we quickly uncovered a sort of professional cultural difference in that in the United States you would

generally never give a junior a position of authority over a senior. In the Soviet delegation, it became obvious that function overrides rank.[29]

William Manthorpe and Steve Kime were assistant naval attachés attached to the U.S. Embassy in Moscow during this period and had frequent contacts with Serkov. Reflecting Kurth's observation of stereotypical characteristics, Manthorpe commented that "he had no personality whatsoever," and he recalled that there was speculation that Serkov was either a KGB or GRU watchdog. Kime observed that between the annual meetings Serkov was the effective head of the Soviet side. Kime had high regard for Serkov's professionalism, although he too speculated that Serkov might have held a watchdog role.[30]

Retired Rear Admiral Hilton, a veteran of four delegations, added:

He was in charge of getting this thing done and he was deadly serious — didn't have any sense of humor — very competent. He got things done. Serkov organized their side, and he liked to shepherd. I've seen him tell three stars to avoid some of the social things. For eleven years Ed Melanson and Serkov would sit down and draw up the agreed minutes and I always thought it was interesting that they did it so well, as Melanson didn't really speak Russian and Serkov really didn't speak English. He understood more than he let on.[31]

As later events would demonstrate, Serkov's presence on the Soviet delegation was to contribute to the survival of the accord through the end of the Cold War.

Beginning with the October 1971 talks, social events played an important role in the process as the events provided the participants an opportunity to further understand each other's cultural and social values. The custom (initiated by the Soviets in October 1971) of sponsoring an orientation trip outside each national capital provided insights for members on both delegations. Retired Captain Melanson recalled, "The idea of having them see more of the country than just Washington was very popular with them, because it gave them more credentials to talk about the U.S. back home in contrast with their defense counterparts."[32] The same could be said for the Americans, as illustrated by the lasting impression made on Secretary Warner by his May 1972 trip to Volgograd.

The Soviets insisted that the social regimen be agreed on as the first item of business when the two delegation heads first met informally at the beginning of the talks. The Soviets believed that, by adopting this custom, a positive mood could be set for discussing the more substantial issues at the later, formal sessions. In 1973 this strategy backfired. Prior to the Soviet arrival, Weinel walked the Pentagon corridors selling the idea of taking the Soviet delegation out to sea aboard an aircraft carrier with a full air wing for a full-blown firepower demonstration. Although some opposed the idea, many agreed that it could be useful for the Soviets to see first-hand the capabilities of the U.S. Navy. Weinel received permission to make the arrangements.[33] Attempts to sound the Soviets out on the activities proposed by Weinel failed because the U.S. defense attaché reported back that Captain First Rank Serkov had insisted that discussion and approval of the social program should await their arrival in Washington, in accordance with the Soviet practice of discussing the entertainment program as part of the agenda. Consequently, when the Soviets arrived, Vice Admiral Weinel joyfully told Alekseyev about the wonderful sea-power demonstration he had arranged. The Soviet leader didn't think twice. He said, "Nyet!" Serkov later explained that if they accepted, they would have to extend a reciprocal invitation. Weinel recalled responding, "Wait a second! You haven't got any aircraft carriers. How the hell can you reciprocate? You don't have to reciprocate! I'll give it to you in writing — it's not necessary!" Serkov said no; it was the principle.[34] So, instead, the Soviets were taken to Williamsburg, the Naval Academy at Annapolis, and the Kennedy Space Center.[35]

Two years later, the Soviets did get on board an aircraft carrier. Captain Ronald Kurth, while preparing to take on his new assignment as Naval Attaché Moscow, again served as the senior liaison officer for the Soviet delegation, keeping the visitors busy. Arriving on a Friday with Vice Admiral Sornev heading the Soviet delegation, the Soviets were given a weekend tour of the nation's capital and took a helicopter ride to Williamsburg. During the long following weekend, which began on Thursday morning, the Americans flew their guests to Corpus Christi, Texas, to visit the naval air station and catch a flight out to the training carrier USS *Lexington* off the coast in the Gulf of Mexico. Apparently the *Lexington* visit caused some bewilderment to the Soviets as they arrived during the filming of the Hollywood production of *Midway*. One of the Soviet officers noted the striking resemblance of one of *Lexington*'s officers to Charlton Heston

whom he had seen in *Ben Hur.* Returning to Corpus Christi, the party then
flew on to New Orleans to experience Creole culture for a few days.[36]

When the Soviets returned in 1977 under the leadership of Vice Admiral
Navoytsev, they were treated to a West Coast excursion that included San
Francisco and environs — Treasure Island, Sausalito, Muir Woods, and
Fisherman's Wharf — as well as a side trip to Disneyland on the return
swing.[37] The Soviet visit of 1979 proved to be the last to incorporate an
extensive social regime for years to come. While in New York the Soviets
were treated to a harbor tour aboard Malcolm Forbes's *Highlander,* dined at
the Windows of the World at the top of the World Trade Center, and toured
New York's other famous skyscraper. After seeing the Empire State Building,
the visiting officers were hustled to the Stork Club and the Playboy Club
before retiring to the Lincoln Center for a ballet performance. Everyone
assumed that the Soviet officers would love ballet; however, after serving on
the American delegation for nearly two decades, analyst George Fedoroff
has concluded that "the typical Russian naval officer is probably as thrilled
at the prospect of going to the ballet as the typical American naval officer."[38]

With Vice Admiral Crowe returning to Washington, Melanson and
Fedoroff took over the chaperoning duties as a tour bus picked up the 1979
Soviet delegation and drove up Interstate 95 to Newport, Rhode Island. The
Newport itinerary included an afloat harbor tour followed by a tremendous
reception hosted by the Naval War College president, Vice Adm. James
Stockdale. After exchanging pleasantries, Stockdale immediately asked the
visiting Navoytsev whether he had ever been a prisoner of war. Fedoroff
thought to himself as he translated that "this was going to be a real short
conversation." However, Navoytsev quickly said that he hadn't. Stockdale
responded that this was good "because I would not wish that on my worst
enemy." Fedoroff noted that struck a chord with the Soviet vice admiral. The
two men went on to discuss educational curriculum. Stockdale noted that
the Naval War College's reading list was quite comprehensive, starting with
Plato and Aristotle and including even Marx and Lenin. Stockdale pointed
out that the challenge for the students was to boil down the various
philosophies offered and to develop their own outlook. Navoytsev
responded that the Soviets also offered courses with similar reading lists but
that the students were provided interpretation. Fedoroff continued to
translate and later recalled Navoytsev's comment about the American

practice: "I don't think it is productive or useful, because a house built on sand does not have a firm foundation. We instruct our people to the correct approach versus the incorrect approach." Fedoroff translated and recalled Stockdale's comeback: "Well, I would question who gets to judge which is the correct and the incorrect interpretation, which is why we have faith in our students to take all the material and come to their own judgments."[39]

The next morning the Soviets toured the Naval War College and visited some of the mansions that were open for public viewing. The group then returned to Washington.

As illustrated by some of the experiences with the visitors, the hosts learned much about Soviet customs and thinking. No doubt the visiting Soviets also learned much about the United States, its people, and the ways and thinking of their naval counterparts. George Fedoroff closely observed the visiting Soviet delegations and noted that they sometimes seemed to have a problem with accepting what they were seeing in contrast to what they had been told to expect:

> You could see the contradictions in their minds. They would always state that they had the same thing in the Soviet Union only "a little different." Gorky Park is not Disneyland. Nonetheless, what people see with their own eyes becomes inescapable fact. These are the first-hand impressions. No longer are you being told how it is: you are being confronted on how you see it is! So you have to determine whether you are seeing potemkin villages. However, once you see many different places and see the same supermarkets again and again, you must face the fact that "we ain't putting you on." This is us. This is the way it is. This is what America is![40]

During this period, three of the annual reviews were held in the Soviet Union. Like the visiting Soviets, the Americans learned much about their counterparts' culture and customs. However, few preconceived notions were dispelled. Train recalled, "Moscow was the most depressing city I have ever visited in my life, and ten days was about as much as you could take." Other than the subway system, which he admired, "it was really grimsville."[41] However, any expectations of overt hostility were often quickly dispelled. The Americans usually found their hosts friendly and willing to socialize. As Warner and the visiting Americans had learned in 1971 and

1972, alcohol was an important ingredient in almost any social activity. In 1974 Kasatonov took Train's delegation to visit Odessa. Train recalled that the time spent in Odessa was relaxing, with lots of food. On the way back on a Soviet naval aviation aircraft, as Train recalled, four of them sitting around a table began negotiations with toasts. Kasatonov proposed, "Here's to the principle of fixed distances." Train countered, "Here's to the principle of freedom of the seas." "And for three hours we went through this, and finally his eyes crossed and he fell right out into the aisle. They picked him up and laid him on the settee across from the table," added Train. The young vice admiral didn't feel a thing: "My adrenaline was pumping so hard I was burning that alcohol up before it got in my system." Train added that another person sat in Kasatonov's chair, and "the four of us drank three-and-a-half bottles of vodka — we ran out — and then a bottle of cognac." Train recalled that they landed in Moscow in a blizzard and, a year later when he recalled to the deputy head of their delegation how bad the weather was, the deputy responded, "Yes, but we weren't cold."[42] Two years later the Soviets took Train and the American delegation to Leningrad. Train recalled that he and the Soviet Army captain assigned to interpret shared a passion for fly-fishing. Listening to an ideological lecture about the *Aurora*, the captain turned to Train and said, "Now this is a bunch of crap — why don't I let him talk for a while, then we'll talk about fly-fishing, and then we'll let him talk on for a while."[43]

Vice Admiral Hannifin led the American team into Moscow in 1978 not knowing what to expect regarding social activities. In Moscow the delegations went to the Bolshoi and, as Hilton described it, "some singing thing with country folk songs in the Palace of the Congresses in the Kremlin that was so boring that even the Russians were going to sleep next to us."[44]

Rear Admiral Hilton hoped to visit Leningrad, having heard wonderful things about Peter the Great's city from prior delegation members. However, when the excursion plane lifted off from Moscow, it headed south instead. The first stop was Volgograd. Following the footsteps of Secretary Warner, Hilton recalled that the American delegation "had to see the hill topped with that huge statue of a woman holding a sword." The tour bus went on to a power plant, "and they took us out and marched us through this power plant and explained this power plant." The group ate lunch at an officers' club and then reboarded the airplane and flew on to Sochi. The group arrived at the Black Sea city in time for dinner and checked into their new home — a military sanitarium with restrictions against drinking and smoking. Still, one of the team members smuggled in a bottle of vodka, so a group formed in one of the rooms to share the forbidden drink, and a few cigarettes were lit. Hilton recalled, "Suddenly, this nurse came in who looked like she could play for the Redskins, screaming 'Nyet, nyet! Don't smoke! It's forbidden!'"[45] With the party broken up, the Americans retired to their rooms. To soothe the guests to sleep, music played from speakers in the corridors. George Fedoroff recognized the music as Schubert's "Ave Maria."

Upon returning to Moscow, Hannifin and Navoytsev signed the results paper drafted by Serkov and Melanson, and the two delegations exchanged farewell pleasantries. Navoytsev respected Hannifin, a fellow World War II veteran who also had spent a career in submarines, and presented the American vice admiral with a Soviet submarine command pin as a parting gift.[46]

One variable that remained constant on both sides was a deliberate effort to keep the delegations away from public attention. On the American side at the onset there was a security concern. There were no press releases associated with the May 1972 trips to New York and California. The Soviets donned civilian attire to appear inconspicuous. One of the escorts for the New York trip, Naval Reserve Capt. Mark Flanigan, recalled that there was some concern that the Jewish Defense League or another anti-Soviet group might act against the visitors.[47]

Another reason for the low-publicity approach was concern that some conservatives might be horrified to find a social regimen that involved wining and dining naval officers of the hated Soviet Union. Even those who weren't avowed anticommunists might see the social expenses as another Pentagon boondoggle, not understanding the underlying value of the regimen. For example, in 1975, a month after the Soviet delegation departed, Secretary of the Navy J. William Middendorf III received a forceful letter from Congressman Larry P. McDonald communicating his distress that Soviet naval officers had been permitted aboard *Lexington*. The Georgia congressman, who later would be killed on KAL 007, demanded an explanation. The secretary's response apparently satisfied McDonald.[48]

However, it was the process itself — the navy-to-navy contact — that naval leaders on both sides saw as vulnerable. Because the contacts led to frank and productive discussions, both navies became protective of the accord. Train noted that "the cowboy mentality started to go away after John Warner signed that agreement."[49] Yet, in October 1975, Congressman Edward J. Derwinski challenged the agreement's effectiveness. In a letter to Thomas R. Morgan, chairman of the Committee on International Relations, the Illinois Republican stated that he had heard that in the Ionian Sea near Crete, a Kresta II missile cruiser had made "belligerent threats against the *John F. Kennedy.*" Derwinski believed that the incident violated the INCSEA agreement and wanted to know what action had been taken. Morgan forwarded Derwinski's letter to Secretary of State Kissinger.[50]

On 24 November Robert J. McCloskey of the State Department responded that a Kresta-class cruiser had indeed trained its missile launchers on the *John F. Kennedy* on 12 September, and that the Navy had called in the Soviet naval attaché to discuss the incident. McCloskey noted that the Navy had yet to receive a response from the Soviets. He further explained the unique nature of the accord, which placed communications at a "service to service level rather than a diplomatic level," although McCloskey stressed that the State Department was kept informed. McCloskey concluded by stating that there had been a marked decrease in incidents since the signing of the accord in 1972.[51]

Congressman Morgan passed this response to Derwinski. Not satisfied, in mid-December Derwinski wrote directly to Kissinger questioning why the State Department had not issued a proper protest, worrying that the department was conducting only minimal follow-up to obtain Soviet cooperation with the 1972 agreement.[52] Clearly Derwinski did not appreciate the unique aspect of the accord that established the direct navy-to-navy communications channel. While the Soviet naval attaché may not have provided a direct response to the complaint he had received, the Soviet Navy had been alerted that this incident would probably be discussed at the 1976 annual review and thus steps had to be taken to investigate the complaint.

During the 1970s the two sides standardized arrangements under INCSEA which served the interests of both nations, especially during the Middle East crisis of October 1973, when a slight miscalculation by naval commanders on either side could have had dire consequences. The maintenance by both sides of a low profile for INCSEA, combined with accord compliance, an effective bilateral communications mechanism, and growing cultural understanding, contributed to continuing the accord and maintaining the bilateral navy-to-navy relationship. These established arrangements would serve both sides well during the tenser times that lay ahead.

P2V Neptunes flying reconnaissance over the western Pacific and Sea of Japan frequently drew Soviet attention. Three were shot down during the 1950s. *Courtesy of U.S. Naval Institute.*

Beginning in the early 1960s, AGIs became a frequent sight off allied naval bases and steamed within allied task groups. *Courtesy of U.S. Naval Institute.*

The U.S. Navy's ability to control the seas gave the United States leverage during the Cuban missile crisis. *Courtesy of U.S. Naval Institute.*

Under Admiral of the Fleet Sergei G. Gorshkov's leadership, the Soviet Union built a blue-water navy that would challenge the Western alliance. *Courtesy of U.S. Naval Institute.*

A Tu-16 Badger being escorted past the USS *Kitty Hawk* in the North Pacific in January 1963. *Courtesy of U.S. Naval Institute.*

On 10–11 May 1967, the *Walker* collisions with Soviet warships in the Sea of Japan bring public focus to a problem area in U.S.-Soviet relations. *Courtesy of U.S. Naval Institute.*

INCSEA negotiations in May 1972 at the National War College (*left to right*): Igor Bubnov, Adm. V. A. Alekseyev, Adm. Vladimir Kasatonov, Secretary of the Navy John W. Warner, Herbert Okun, and Vice Adm. Harry L. Harty Jr. *Courtesy of Sen. John W. Warner.*

INCSEA negotiations in May 1972. *Courtesy of Sen. John W. Warner.*

Admirals Kasatonov and Alekseyev visit the Magic Kingdom, May 1972. *Courtesy of The Walt Disney Company.*

Signing of the Memorandum of Understanding in Washington, D.C., which formed the basis of the 1972 Incidents at Sea Agreement. *Courtesy of Sen. John W. Warner.*

Admiral Alekseyev and Vice Adm. John P. "Blackie" Weinel Jr. sign the protocol to the INCSEA agreement in May 1973. *Courtesy of Sen. John W. Warner.*

In the Sea of Japan on 13 March 1980. An Il-38 May as seen from a P-3 Orion. The United States protested after this Soviet aircraft turned toward the American plane, forcing evasive action. *Courtesy of Naval Historical Center.*

In extremis! USS *Harlan County* received close scrutiny by Soviet naval and air forces in April 1980. Here a patrol frigate blocks the LST's path. *Courtesy of Naval Historical Center.*

Collision, Arabian Sea, 17 November 1983. The *Razyashehy* comes alongside the USS *Fife*. *Courtesy of Naval Historical Center.*

Black Sea incidents, February 1988. *Bezzavenny* comes alongside USS *Yorktown*. Note the Soviet warship's starboard anchor. *Courtesy of Naval Historical Center.*

Black Sea incidents, February 1988. Mirka patrol frigate SKR 6 nudges the stern of the USS *Caron*. *Courtesy of Naval Historical Center.*

Black Sea incidents, February 1988. Damage to Soviet and American warships.

Courtesy of Naval Historical Center.

« **9** »

THE AGE OF THE
EVIL EMPIRE

During the later years of the Carter administration, events and initiatives integrated the Navy into a more assertive U.S. foreign policy that placed fleet units in closer proximity to their Soviet counterparts. For example, the fall of the shah of Iran and the Soviet invasion of Afghanistan led Pres. Jimmy Carter to order Navy carrier battle groups into the Arabian Sea to bolster America's presence and add military muscle to the region. During this period, he also directed an expansion of the Freedom of Navigation (FON) program, sending Navy warships to contest territorial claims of littoral states. Some American initiatives had their impetus at the fleet commander and Navy Department levels, reflecting changes of strategic thought on both the Soviet and American sides regarding how navies were to be used in warfare.[1] The cumulative effect of these events and initiatives during the Carter and early Reagan presidencies would lead to an increase in the number of serious incidents reported between U.S. and Soviet naval forces. From mid-1980 through mid-1982, the Americans alleged an average of five Soviet violations per annum. This number jumped to nineteen during the following two years. The number of alleged U.S. Navy violations of the INCSEA accord reported by the Soviets also rose.[2]

In January 1979 an Islamic revolution forced the shah of Iran into exile, and the following November young Iranian militants stormed the U.S. Embassy in Tehran and eventually held fifty-two Americans hostage. In December the Soviet Army invaded Afghanistan. Consequently, the United

States pressed its fleet to perform additional overseas service. In contrast to 1978, when the combined total for months overseas by U.S. carrier battle groups came to forty-four, in 1979 and 1980 this number jumped to an annual average of fifty-six. Many of these months were spent in the Indian Ocean, where the American ships found themselves in the presence of Soviet Navy ships.[3]

For both navies Indian Ocean deployments were a relatively new phenomenon. For decades the Indian Ocean had been the preserve of the Royal Navy, augmented by a substantial presence of French and Dutch naval vessels. However, with the dissolution of the British, French, and Dutch colonial empires, the European presence in the Indian Ocean and the Persian Gulf region declined. In January 1968 the Labour government in London announced its intent to withdraw Britain's military forces from east of Suez. The Soviets quickly moved to fill the void. Two months after the British announcement, a squadron consisting of a *Sverdlov*-class cruiser, a Kashin-class guided missile destroyer, a Krupnyy-class destroyer, a nuclear submarine, and a tanker slipped into the region to call on various ports along the South Asia and East African littoral. Eventually, the Soviets established a facility at Berbera, Somalia, to provide logistical support.[4]

Since the late 1940s the Middle East Force, usually centered on an old seaplane tender and one or two pairs of destroyers, represented the Stars and Stripes in this region. A small Naval Control of Shipping Office located within a Royal Navy base in Bahrain provided logistical support to these few visiting U.S. Navy ships. When the British departed Bahrain, the Americans were able to continue operations through leasing a portion of the former Royal Navy base. Occasionally, the United States augmented its presence. To demonstrate support for Pakistan during the Indo-Pakistani War of December 1971, the United States deployed Task Force 74, consisting of the USS *Enterprise* and escorting combatant and support ships. To show support for India, the Soviets sent two groups of warships, each centered on a missile cruiser.[5]

For the next six years, the Soviets maintained a steady regional presence, usually consisting of a missile cruiser, several destroyers, some frigates, and support ships. The Soviets temporarily reduced their presence in 1978 after being evicted from their Somali base in late 1977. The U.S. Navy continued to maintain a presence based on its limited presence in the Persian Gulf and periodic deployments of carrier task forces into the region. With the departure of the British, the United States pursued a "Twin Pillars" strategy centered on building the military capacities of Iran and Saudi Arabia. With regards to Iran, the United States provided the Iranian military with modern armaments, including F-14 Tomcat fighters and P-3 Orion maritime patrol planes, and was preparing to deliver four upgraded *Spruance*-class destroyers.

The fall of the shah and the subsequent rise of a vehemently anti-American regime ruined the American strategy for the region. The Iranian crisis and the Soviet invasion of Afghanistan led to a permanent U.S. Navy presence, to be supported by a base acquired from the British at Diego Garcia.[6] Consequently, during the 1980s, the Indian Ocean became one more area of the globe where U.S. and Soviet ships came into frequent contact.

U.S. ships also found themselves operating closer to Soviet territorial waters during the 1980s. One contributory impetus for this pattern occurred in 1979 when President Carter initiated an aggressive FON program to further assert high-seas navigation rights. The pressure to implement the program stemmed from ongoing Law of the Sea Treaty negotiations having a potential result of allowing littoral states to claim as territorial waters thousands of square miles of oceans and seas formerly recognized as high seas. The new rules had complex provisions to keep straits open to international commerce. The Carter administration wanted to prevent any attempts by littoral states to misinterpret the new rules and close off waters to free passage.[7]

The FON program that the Carter administration put into place merely formalized a process that had been ongoing. The United States, as a maritime nation, has advocated the freedom to navigate on the high seas since its earliest days, and a mission of the U.S. Navy has been to ensure the free passage of American ships on the high seas. Besides fighting pirates and privateers, the Navy has challenged foreign efforts to lay territorial claim to adjacent open bodies of water. With international law often based on behavioral norms, acquiescence of maritime nations to excessive territorial claims made by certain littoral nations might lead to those claims being accepted by the international community.[8] While U.S. Navy FON operations contesting Soviet and Libyan claims sometimes attracted media attention, the FON program applied to friends as well. American ships disputed Italian claims to sovereignty within the Gulf of Taranto as well as Libyan claims to the Gulf of Sidra. From 1979 through 1992, under the Carter FON program, the United States annually issued an average of 110 diplomatic protests and annually conducted some thirty-five to forty operations to challenge excessive coastal claims.

The Black Sea was one of the areas receiving additional FON attention. U.S. ships had long entered this enclosed body of water in what were dubbed "Silver Fox" operations, usually once each quarter. In the Silver Fox operations order, two Sixth Fleet vessels would steam into the Black Sea to demonstrate their right to navigate these waters freely and avail themselves of intelligence collection opportunities that occurred when they stumbled across newly constructed vessels or Soviet forces conducting war games. Before INCSEA, as illustrated by the cases of Captain Zumwalt on the USS *Dewey* in the Baltic in 1962, and Lieutenant Bishop on the USS *Banner* in the Sea of Japan in 1965, these American ships could almost always anticipate Soviet harassment.

Implementing INCSEA made a difference in the treatment American ships could expect. A briefing report of a Silver Fox operation conducted by the USS *Josephus Daniels* and the USS *Mitscher* from 8 to 14 May 1973 stated that the Soviet reaction "throughout the mission appeared more restrained." Soviet reconnaissance aircraft took care not to fly directly overhead, and the two American ships exchanged pleasantries and INCSEA flaghoist signals with the trailing Kotlin-class destroyer.[9]

Seven years later, this pattern of behavior was still holding. During the winter of 1980–81, the guided missile destroyer USS *Coontz* and an accompanying frigate entered a stormy Black Sea. As Capt. Joseph "Paul" Reason maneuvered *Coontz* out of the straits, a Soviet Krivak-class frigate awaited him. The DESRON commander, Capt. Jeremy "Mike" Boorda, joined Reason to observe the Black Sea patrol. After three days of rolling and pitching in the high seas, the impatient skipper of the Krivak sent a flashing-light message to the Americans: "ARE YOU LEAVING NOW?" The American response was, "WE LIKE IT HERE SO MUCH WE MAY STAY TWO MORE DAYS." The Soviet skipper may not have been amused by the response, but Boorda thought it would be a nice gesture to send him a care package. Accordingly, a suitable box was found, plastered with *Coontz* bumper stickers, filled with some Cokes and a few girlie magazines, sealed with chemical lights and flotation balloons attached, and then dropped over the side. The navigator sent a flashing-light message in Russian stating, "BOX IN THE WATER IS GIFT FOR YOU." The Krivak slowed down and turned her deck lights on to retrieve the floating object. A few minutes after the recovery was made, a flashing-light message came back: "THANK YOU." The Americans eventually departed.[10]

While the aggressive FON program did not in itself adversely affect U.S.-Soviet naval interactions on the high seas, when combined with other fleet activities along the Soviet periphery the program eventually contributed to increased tension between the two sides during the Reagan administration. While Carter was willing to use the fleet assertively to protect the rights of free passage, his vision for the fleet in wartime focused on maintaining the sea lanes of communication (SLOCs) across the Atlantic to assure the transport of reinforcements to the Central European battlefield.[11]

U.S. naval leaders agreed that maintaining the North Atlantic SLOCs was a critical mission and practiced for that contingency in exercises such as "Northern Wedding." However, they thought that the Navy could do more than reenact World War II's Battle of the North Atlantic to help stem the Red Army push in Central Europe. Besides, there were indicators that the Soviet naval strategy was shifting away from the sea-denial mission that the Nazis had pursued three decades earlier.

With the commissioning of Delta-class ballistic-missile submarines in the 1970s with 4,000-mile-range SS-N-8 ballistic missiles, the Soviet strategic submarine force did not need to venture past the ASW chokepoints constructed by the United States and its allies along the northeastern rim of the Atlantic and the northwestern rim of the Pacific. Since the Deltas could launch ballistic-missile attacks from the Barents Sea or the Sea of Okhotsk, Western analysts speculated that the Soviets were configuring their fleet to complement a strategy that would establish and protect Soviet SSBN bastions.[12]

In retrospect, the indicators were obvious. Whereas Soviet ships built in the 1960s such as the Kynda, Kresta I, and Kashin classes featured antiship missiles as a component of their main batteries, the Kresta II, Kara, Krivak, and Kiev classes of the 1970s were armed with antisubmarine missiles for use against American subs.[13] Analysts did not immediately recognize the

Soviet shift because of an intelligence blunder that classified the main missile carried by Kresta II– and Kara-class cruisers and Krivak-class destroyers as an antiship missile. One intelligence officer noted that the Soviets had classified the Kresta II as a large ASW ship, "but we simply did not believe them."[14] By 1975 Western intelligence analysts had finally begun to conclude that the Kresta II, Kara, and Krivak classes indeed had an ASW mission. The same was true of the *Kiev* when this ship became operational in 1976. The largest Soviet surface warship built to date, featuring an angled flight deck that could operate vertical/short takeoff and landing (VSTOL) jet aircraft, the *Kiev* was seen by Western naval analysts as a first step in challenging Western carrier and air-power dominance on the high seas. When the Soviets declared that the ship was a "large ASW cruiser," analysts simply saw that as a ploy to get her legally through the Dardanelles to conform to the Montreux Convention, which forbade the transit of aircraft carriers through the strait. However, with her complement of KA-25 Hormone helicopters and assorted ASW weaponry, the *Kiev* indeed did have an ASW mission.[15]

After 1975 the Soviets conducted no more Okean global fleet exercises to practice delivering a crippling blow to Western naval forces in a co-ordinated, devastating strike. By the late 1970s analysts had begun speculating about a new Soviet bastion strategy, and U.S. naval leaders had to account for this trend in their calculus on how to use the fleet if war broke out.[16] U.S. Navy operational commanders reacted. In the Pacific, during his tenure as CINCPACFLT from 1977 to 1978, Adm. Thomas B. Hayward developed a "Sea Strike Project" that envisioned Pacific Fleet units conducting offensive actions against the eastern Soviet Union. Meanwhile, in the Mediterranean, COMSIXTHFLT Vice Adm. William N. Small revised a long-standing war plan that had American carriers withdrawing to the western Mediterranean until Soviet fleet units were eliminated. Instead, the carriers would assume a forward posture in the eastern Mediterranean to provide air power for NATO forces operating along the southern flank.[17]

In Washington, the offensive vision of the fleet commanders was reflected in "Seaplan 2000." Initiated at the secretariat level, Seaplan 2000, as envisioned by Navy Secretary Graham Claytor, Undersecretary James Woolsey, and CNO Admiral Holloway, emphasized superiority at sea against the Soviets and saw forward offensive operations as the most effective way to attain the national military objectives. The selection of Admiral Hayward to replace Admiral Holloway as CNO accelerated the strategic-thinking process in Washington, D.C., and at the Naval War College in Newport. However, the process of implementing any new strategic concepts had to be placed on hold while the Navy responded to international crises.[18]

Although the U.S. Navy activities focused on the Persian Gulf region during this period, Naval Intelligence still monitored Soviet Navy activities closer to the homeland as the Soviets implemented their bastion strategy. Sent to observe Soviet ASW exercises in the Barents Sea, the USS *Harlan County* attracted much undesired attention. The United States claimed that Soviet ships and aircraft violated the provisions of the INCSEA accord on six occasions between 11 and 18 April 1980. In Washington, Navy officials protested to Soviet Naval Attaché Rear Admiral Sakulkin. After two additional incidents on 20 and 26 April, Admiral Hayward contemplated postponing the planned annual review, scheduled in Moscow on 12 May. In the wake of Afghanistan, OSD/ISA had already contemplated postponement or moving the review to a neutral site such as Vienna. Then, on 29 April, Vice Adm. S. R. Foley Jr. sent a letter to Assistant Secretary of Defense for International Security Affairs McGiffert recommending OSD approval should Hayward desire a ninety-day postponement of the annual review. OSD approval was not forthcoming. Legal Advisor M. J. Cifrino argued that such action could cause the Soviets to claim that the accord was breached and would have to be renegotiated. Furthermore, Cifrino argued that the annual review served as a mechanism to seek redress for violations, and that forum needed to be used in this case. Cifrino's logic won the day. Two weeks later, the American delegation was in Moscow to discuss the *Harlan County* and other incidents.[19]

The 1980 meeting, however, differed from previous annual reviews. Citing recent events that had led to a downturn in U.S.-Soviet relations, the Americans declined to participate in extravagant social activities outside the capital. As Rear Admiral Hilton recalled, "Their Vice Chief would host a dinner for our people, and our ambassador hosted a return reception."[20] One U.S. delegation member recalled that their Soviet Navy counterparts were miffed at this change in the U.S. posture. Reflecting the parochialism of their service, the Soviet delegates kept pointing out that it was not the Soviet Navy that invaded Afghanistan![21]

After the changeover to the Reagan administration, the bilateral INCSEA reviews continued using the "saltines and seltzer" format. In contrast to the 1979 talks at the National War College, the 1981 talks were held at the Navy and Marine Corps Reserve Center, Anacostia. Whereas in 1979 the visiting Soviets toured New York and Newport, the 1981 group visited the Smithsonian and Hechinger's Home and Garden Center in Tysons Corner, Virginia. In 1982 Secretary Caspar Weinberger's instructions to the delegation forbade overnight travel outside Moscow. Still, the talks held in 1981, 1982, and 1983 were cordial. Three weeks after the 1983 meeting, Secretary of the Navy John F. Lehman held a news conference, brought up the recent review, and gave the following assessment: "It's worked very well." He noted that when certain types of Soviet harassment began to appear as a pattern of operations, the issue would be brought up at the next annual meeting "and those practices stopped." Lehman added, "Similarly, they've expressed some concerns about the way we join up on their bombers that come out to run against our exercises and we've discussed them and changed procedures to accord with them." The secretary went on to emphasize that the Soviet Navy had grown to 1,700 ships and was steaming around the world, so the potential for problems had increased.[22]

Lehman did not mention that the potential for problems had also increased as a result of American deployments to areas closer to the Soviet Union. With the end of the Iranian hostage crisis and the change of administrations, advocates for a more aggressive maritime strategy found a friend in the new Secretary of the Navy. As the title of his memoir, *Command of the Seas: Building the 600-Ship Navy,* indicates, Lehman came into his job with an agenda that demanded overwhelming maritime superiority over the Soviet Navy. Lehman further believed that this maritime superiority could occur only if the Navy had at least 600 ships built around fifteen carrier battle groups. The number 600 originated with the Republican Party platform of 1980, which Lehman helped draft. Although many naval officers welcomed Lehman's support for the development of a maritime strategy, many questioned the 600-ship figure. Hayward focused on deploying a highly ready, adequately manned and trained fleet. Hayward's Vice CNO, Adm. William N. Small, was especially skeptical about the need for 600 ships, noting that there were far more effective measures to determine the adequacy of force levels to fulfill the maritime strategy. Still,

Lehman was determined. He understood that such a goal was lofty, even given the proclivity of the Reagan administration to spend on national defense.[23]

To sell his program, Lehman needed a written maritime strategy with stated objectives to articulate how this 600-ship force would be used in the national defense. Lehman claimed, to his dismay, that he found no formalized maritime strategy in place. Over the next few years, this situation would change as seeds planted by Hayward bore fruit during Adm. James D. Watkins's tenure as CNO. In May 1984 Watkins approved the final version of the document that became known as "The Maritime Strategy."

In a January 1986 Naval Institute supplement to its *Proceedings*, Admiral Watkins presented an unclassified version of "The Maritime Strategy."[24] Focusing on a potential superpower showdown in Central Europe, Watkins wrote, "Should war come, the Soviets would prefer to use their massive ground force advantage against Europe without having to concern themselves with a global conflict or actions on their flanks." The CNO then stated how maritime forces would be utilized in three phases to counter this Soviet strategy. In Phase I, a crisis analogous to the Cuban missile crisis occurred, so forces would be moved forward to deter potential aggression. The movement would position forces within striking range of the Soviet fleet and force the Soviets' attack submarines into defensive positions to defend their SSBNs. The movement included sending air forces and Marines to such allied countries as Turkey, Norway, and Japan. In Phase II, war had broken out. Soviet forces were to be destroyed in the Mediterranean, the Indian Ocean, and other forward areas. Then the Navy would begin to fight toward Soviet home waters. With Soviet SSBNs targeted for destruction, anti-submarine warfare would prove to be one of the more challenging aspects of this phase. Phase III continued Phase II operations, except that now U.S. sea power focused on the Soviet Union itself. Naval aviation would bomb Soviet bases and Soviet support structures, and the Marines would seize territory. With pressure on the flanks, the battle on the Central European front could be favorably influenced. Watkins expressed confidence that the strategy could be executed successfully, citing the fact that the Navy had participated in 106 exercises in 1984, of which 55 were with allied nations.[25]

By 1983 a continuing American presence in the Arabian Sea region to monitor the ongoing Iraq-Iran War, an increasing U.S. presence in the eastern Mediterranean to support the U.S. Marine peacekeeping contingent in Lebanon, a stepping-up of the FON program, and naval maneuvers near the Soviet periphery all placed American ships in the constant presence of Soviet naval and air forces. These exercises often caused Soviet reaction. In September 1982 Soviet aircraft, including Backfire bombers, made over 100 sorties against American task forces operating in the northern Pacific. The Soviets also reacted diplomatically the following April, when six carrier fighters flew over the Zeleny Islands in the Kuriles.[26]

The hard-won civility on the high seas established under the INCSEA regime showed further signs of deterioration. In May 1982 the frigate USS *Lockwood* performed a FON mission in the Sea of Japan close to Peter the Great Bay in waters that the Soviets claimed as internal waters. The United States did not recognize the claim, and the skipper of the *Lockwood* said so when challenged by a Soviet cruiser. Soviet ships and aircraft then proceeded to harass the American frigate. Admiral Hayward responded by sending a note to Admiral Gorshkov using the INCSEA navy-to-navy channel to defuse the situation.[27]

The potential for FON confrontations with the Soviet Union further increased in 1982 and 1983 with the Soviet passage of the "1982 Law on the State Border" and the implementation of the "1983 Navigation Rules." Under these new rules, the Soviets refused to recognize the right of innocent passage through Black Sea territorial waters as a shortcut to continue transit in international waters. If a foreign ship traveling along the Soviet coastline came to a peninsula, the Soviets insisted that the ship divert its course to stay outside the twelve-mile Soviet territorial limit. Meanwhile, in the president's Ocean Policy Statement issued on 10 March 1983, Reagan reaffirmed his commitment to maintaining navigation rights and to carrying on the Carter FON program. With the renewed American insistence on upholding freedom of navigation, American warships would challenge the new Soviet regulations, which ran counter to the 1982 Law of the Sea Convention.[28]

While Soviet implementation of the 1983 Navigation Rules merely created a potential for confrontation, KAL 007 caused an actual confrontation. Early in the morning of 1 September 1983 a Soviet Su-15 Flagon fighter shot down a Korean Airlines Boeing 747 jumbo jet as the aircraft was leaving Soviet airspace west of Sakhalin Island. When vessels from the

Japanese Maritime Self-Defense Forces arrived at the presumed crash site, they reported two Soviet ships and five aircraft already searching. U.S. Navy vessels soon arrived. The State Department quickly drafted documents to effect South Korean designation of the United States and Japan as the search and salvage agents. This action sought to make any Soviet salvage operations illegal, allowing the United States to use force to counter any Soviet retrieval attempts. Prevented from conducting salvage operations in international waters, the Soviets focused their search within their territorial waters and judiciously defended them from foreign intrusion. They also intruded on American salvage operations, making low passes with aircraft, forcing ship course changes by aggressive maneuvering, and running parallel to salvage ships to drown out sonar reception.[29] Rear Admiral Kurth recalled:

> It was a very severe challenge to the agreement and intrusion on the part of the Soviet Navy, which was apparently driven by directive from the government — perhaps it would be speculating with KGB influence — as it appeared that the Soviet Navy, after being initially cautious in terms of the agreement, overnight almost began to be intrusive as though they received orders just to do that.[30]

Using the method prescribed in the agreement, the United States protested the harassment. In Moscow newly arrived Naval Attaché Capt. Steve Kime immediately contacted Soviet Navy officials to discuss the incidents occurring in the Sea of Japan. Then CINCPACFLT Adm. Sylvester R. Foley, who had headed the U.S. INCSEA teams in 1980 and 1981, summed up what happened: "the Soviets gave us trouble and hassled us and we said, 'if the Incidents at Sea Agreement means anything, cut it out,' and they did."[31] Already suffering from a world public-affairs disaster, the Soviets apparently realized that harassment incidents only made matters worse and hurt their credibility on abiding by agreements.

Undesired interactions continued to plague the U.S.-Soviet naval relationship. At the end of October 1983 a Soviet Victor III–class sub's screw became entangled in a cable towed by USS *McCloy* off South Carolina. In November the USS *Fife* collided with the Krivak I–class frigate *Razyashchey* in the Arabian Sea. Before the collision, the Soviet frigate had been attempting to approach the USS *Ranger,* and the American *Spruance*-class destroyer had shouldered her away. The Soviets claimed that their ship had steering problems and had signaled this fact.

The uss *David R. Ray* received special attention while cruising the Black Sea in February 1984, as a Soviet helicopter hovered right over the deck and another aircraft fired a cannon into the destroyer's wake.[32] Following these incidents, a message was sent to commanders warning them not to provoke the Soviets but advising against timidity or indifference in the face of Soviet harassment. During March 1984 the aircraft carrier uss *Kitty Hawk* overran a Soviet Victor I–class submarine in the Sea of Japan, snapping the submarine's shaft and imbedding a fragment of a propeller in the carrier's hull. In another incident, the Soviet *Kiev*-class carrier *Minsk* fired flares at the frigate uss *Harold E. Holt*. Despite these incidents, the "Evil Empire" speech by President Reagan, the suspension of START and INF talks, the invasion of Grenada, the Marine barracks bombing in Lebanon, and a Soviet announcement of the deployment of more missile submarines off the U.S. coast, neither side attempted to cancel the 1984 INCSEA review.[33]

Vice Adm. James "Ace" Lyons, the DCNO for Plans and Policy (OP 06), led the American delegation traveling to Moscow. One of Secretary Lehman's favorite flag officers, Lyons shared the Navy secretary's desire for an aggressive maritime strategy. Previously, as Second Fleet commander, he had deployed carriers to the Barents Sea to stage mock raids on Soviet Northern Fleet ports. Lyons also had a reputation as "a tough cookie." "He ate junior officers for breakfast," recalled the American interpreter.[34]

With all of the incidents that had occurred during the previous twelve months, the 1984 INCSEA annual session promised to be confrontational. However, the American delegation head established a good rapport with Admiral Navoytsev, and that helped set the tone. Navoytsev confided to Lyons that whenever U.S. heads of delegation possessed fleet command experience, incidents were resolved in a professional, speedy, and discreet manner. He emphasized the benefits of keeping incidents out of the public limelight and expressed displeasure with U.S. media publicity surrounding the *Kitty Hawk*–Victor I collision. Lyons later responded that little could be done in the *Kitty Hawk* case, since there had been a pool of over twenty-five journalists on the carrier. He agreed that fleet commanders with INCSEA experience "were best qualified to resolve such incidents."[35] Rear Admiral Kurth, head of the American aviation working group, recalled:

In 1984, after KAL 007, the Soviet Navy went, by far, the extra mile. They knew that we came to Moscow, after their conduct in the Northern Sea of Japan, ready to dump the agreement, because within our own minds we were under the opinion that if it does not work under adversity then it's not worth the paper it's written on. We were at least ready to relegate the agreement to a much lower priority and maybe even dump it. The Soviets really, really did everything possible to preserve the agreement and reestablish confidence. They handled their conduct in the Sea of Japan very openly, and we did, indeed, reestablish confidence.[36]

The State Department representative on the delegation later confided that "he was utterly amazed at the frankness, professionalism, and objectivity of the exchanges during the sessions, in contrast to the normal diplomatic intercourse between the two countries."[37] While in Moscow the American delegation accepted a short day trip to Leningrad, where there was a wreath-laying ceremony at Piskarevsky Cemetery, a tour of the Hermitage, and a dinner with the Leningrad Naval Base commander. After a quick tour around the city, the group flew back to Moscow to sign the results paper drafted by Melanson and Serkov. The agreement was extended for another three years.

In a letter to former CNO Admiral Hayward, CNO Adm. James Watkins commented that the Soviets were "extremely upbeat and cordial" and that the conference was "one of the best in terms of agreement on problem areas." The Navy secretary also chose to be conciliatory. Regarding the *Harold E. Holt–Minsk* incident, in which the latter fired flares at the *Harold E. Holt,* Secretary Lehman said, "I don't see anything sinister in the incident with the *Minsk.* Let's say there are two plausible sides to that story. The *Minsk* skipper may not have all been on the wrong side." In analyzing why the Soviets were so cooperative in 1984, retired Captain Melanson observed:

> While we saw it as a technical agreement, the Soviets, particularly the Soviet Navy, saw it more in a political context of an agreement that kind of set their service apart from the rest — as they were dealing on a bilateral basis with the United States Navy whereas the Army and the Air Force did not have similar agreements. So I think in terms of the Soviet Ministry of Defense, there probably was a sense of one-upmanship on the part of the Navy, and they

didn't want to do anything to cause us to call into question the efficacy of that agreement and therefore diminish their own importance in terms of relations with their own counterparts back home.[38]

To reduce tensions between the two sides, the Soviets also proposed reciprocal port visits in 1985 to commemorate the fortieth anniversary of the end of World War II. On 12 July Vice Admiral Lyons sent a letter to the Soviets supporting the idea and followed up with a letter in November discussing specific details. On 21 February 1985 the United States extended an invitation for the Soviet INCSEA delegation to come to Washington between 10 and 17 June. Continuing to walk a path toward warmer relations, review planners decided that the time was right to restart the social regimen and scheduled a few extra days to allow for a trip outside the Washington area.[39]

The planners were premature. On 24 March Soviet soldiers confronted Army Maj. Arthur B. Nicholson, an observer in East Germany, and shot him. Secretary of Defense Caspar Weinberger felt deeply and personally about the murder of Major Nicholson. He expected Soviet reparations and directed that there be no social contacts.[40] However, with the invitation for the 1985 review, which included a full social agenda, having already been sent, perhaps the Secretary of Defense would make an exception to his policy? Captain Melanson, who worked in the Office of the Secretary of Defense at that time, recalled:

> There's a lot of stuff that comes up to the Secretary's desk and at one point he probably got that paper across his desk that said we were having our annual meeting with the Soviets and we will be doing these events in connection with that, and also, since it was the Secretary's funds, he was interested in seeing how they were spent. So that combination of things probably influenced him to make the decision that he did.[41]

In his instructions to the chairman of the U.S. delegation, Weinberger wrote, "There should be no representational activities of any sort, to include social activities or visits to installations in or outside of the Washington area. These activities would be most inappropriate while the Major Nicholson matter remains unresolved."[42] The Navy received this directive at the end of May.

Tipped off about the secretary's decision, Sen. John W. Warner of Virginia called the aviation working-group head, Rear Admiral Kurth. These two members of the first U.S. delegation of 1971 talked at length, with Warner seeking out Kurth's advice. Kurth recalled, "I was in a very delicate situation, because I was being asked by a senator to join him in opposing the policy of the Secretary of Defense, and at that time, I was a junior admiral in the Navy."[43] After consulting with Kurth, Warner called the Secretary of Defense to express his concern about the decision. Sharing the secretary's distress over the death of Major Nicholson and his compassion for the family, Warner emphasized the importance of the agreement as a significant confidence-building measure that had done much to create safer conditions for sailors and aviators on and over the high seas. He further stated that the social activities associated with the annual reviews had contributed substantially to an atmosphere that "has been of overall benefit during the review sessions." Weinberger held his ground; his directive stood.[44]

In Moscow Captain Kime broke the news of the change. Apparently, the ban on social activities held far greater significance to the Soviets than Kime could have imagined. Kime noted that "they were heartbroken when they found out." The naval attaché later speculated that the Soviet Navy had laid some equities with the Ministry of Foreign Affairs and the Ministry of Defense, since it could claim that it was making meaningful diplomatic inroads with the United States during a period of extremely sour relations. Although they never told Kime, he could sense in later meetings with his counterparts that "they lost face big time."[45]

Consequently, on 7 June, two days before the scheduled arrival, Soviet diplomats informed the United States that their delegation would not arrive, stating that they "needed more time to prepare." Kurth observed that the Soviet decision not to come "dealt with the Soviet Navy's feeling that the structure of the review was going to be discourteous in terms of what had been done in the past, and they didn't care to experience that discourtesy."[46]

A 19 June *New York Times* article exposed the internal dissent on the American side, stating that Weinberger had acted without discussing the matter with the Secretary of State or the National Security Advisor and was strongly opposed within the Navy and State Departments. On the same day,

Warner sent a letter to the president restating the arguments made to Weinberger and requesting that the Senior National Security Staff review the situation so that the annual review would be conducted in a manner "consistent with the protocol and traditions of past years."[47] The secretary's "no socializing" policy in regards to U.S.-U.S.S.R. military contacts proved to be a hindrance particularly to Rear Admiral Kurth, who was being posted in Moscow to serve as defense attaché. Socializing was an important part of his new job description. Retired Captain Manthorpe, who had a tour in Moscow in the 1970s, recalled:

> As assistant naval attaché, you had to corner the Soviet admirals at a reception — say Burma Day. The Soviet military would be invited and, depending on relations, Soviet admirals would appear. Usually the flag officers crowded around a big buffet that was off in a side room, while the junior officers socialized in a huge room. To talk to the admirals you had to get past their aides and buttonhole them. Your language had to be real good, and you had to have a real good subject that you knew they would bite on so you would get a response. Often we used to do it in pairs. For example, retired Capt. Steve Kime and I would think of a topic in advance and then we would go through this phalanx of aides separately, meeting up on the other side next to the targeted officer. One of us would ask the question and the other would listen for the answer. The questioner would hardly pay attention to the answer, as he was thinking of how to phrase the next question. You really had to work at it.[48]

Naval analyst George Fedoroff, a veteran of over a dozen U.S. INCSEA delegations, also stressed the importance of such contacts: "Reading a newspaper or a press release is one-way communication. By contacting these people directly, you can ask, 'But what do you mean by this?' Misinterpretations of policy can be minimized."[49]

Halfway through his defense attaché tour, the frustrated Kurth returned to Washington to meet with Weinberger to request that he be "unleashed." Kurth argued that he would, in contacts with the Soviets, express Weinberger's "views on their actions as well as the other interests of the Department of Defense in their language and get them first-hand, so they would have to deal with his ideas." Kurth explained that the nonsocializing policy actually made the Soviets comfortable, "because at Red Army Day, embassy receptions and so on, they don't have to deal with me on these issues." Kurth found Weinberger adamant and recalled his stating, "After the Nicholson incident, I think they are barbarians, and I will not allow you to have any contact with them." The defense attaché was quick to point out that representatives of three Cabinet or just-below-Cabinet-level departments were dealing with their U.S.S.R. counterparts while he sat on the sidelines. Weinberger told Kurth that if the Soviets apologized for the Nicholson episode and offered compensation to the widow, he would consider turning him loose.[50] Meanwhile, Navy staff officers prepared point papers for the secretary citing the agreement's benefits and recommending "curtailed" representational social functions. The papers also recommended that some time should pass before again approaching the Soviets.[51]

The 1985 INCSEA review was finally held in Washington in November with minimal social activities. The Navy had requested $30,799 to host the talks. Assistant Secretary of Defense Richard Perle directed the Navy to cut that number. Consequently, all lunches were held at the Washington Navy Yard Officers' Club, and there were no social events except for a reception at the Navy Museum and one at the Soviet Embassy. Ironically, the $15,600 spent to host the talks earned the Pentagon one of Sen. William Proxmire's "Golden Fleece" Awards.[52] As for the talks themselves, in his opening remarks Vice Adm. D. S. Jones gave an assessment that the recent period had been one of the best since the agreement had been signed. He noted only one alleged incident involving Soviet ships training guns or missiles at U.S. ships and only one alleged violation committed by a Soviet aircraft interfering with U.S. carrier flight operations. He did note an increase of hazardous maneuvers by Soviet AGIs in the vicinity of surfaced U.S. Navy SSBNs, and the Americans brought eleven alleged Soviet violations to their counterpart's attention. Meanwhile, the Soviets tabled five complaints about American misbehavior, a reduction of twelve from the previous annual review. Privately, Vice Admiral Navoytsev expressed his concern about the mandated curtailment of social activities. After hearing Jones's response to his concern, the Soviet delegation chair stated that he was "incredulous" that the United States had linked this historically successful agreement "with the actions of a simple soldier who made a mistake in Berlin."[53]

The declining incident figures reflected the more cordial relations between the superpowers that accelerated with Mikhail Gorbachev's accession to power. Still, this warming trend did not preclude the United States from taking military action in other parts of the world when President Reagan perceived American national security interests to be at stake. For example, throughout the 1980s, America challenged the regime of Muammar al-Gaddafi in Libya. American warships frequently steamed into the Gulf of Sidra on FON exercises to dispute Libya's territorial claims to those waters. With evidence that Gaddafi's regime harbored terrorists, the State Department made efforts to isolate it diplomatically. Finally, U.S. Air Force and Navy aircraft struck several targets within Libya in April 1986 after communications intercepts linked it with a terrorist bombing in West Berlin. Concerned about retribution from terrorists who might attack Navy ships in suicide boats or aircraft, the United States issued a Notice to Mariners warning ships and aircraft to remain clear of U.S. warships.

During this period, Second Fleet Commander Vice Adm. Henry C. Mustin, slated for the post of DCNO for Plans, Policy and Operations, was assigned to head the 1986 American INCSEA delegation. The veteran surface sailor met in Moscow with Admiral Navoytsev two months after the Libyan raid. Mustin recalled Navoytsev's opening prepared statement:

So Admiral Navoytsev started off by saying to this young admiral that (paraphrasing) "the Soviet Union views with great concern these illegal and immoral acts that you are taking in the Mediterranean and your attempts to disrupt the normal flow of commerce of the high seas, and I want to tell you that unless you cease and desist from these acts immediately, you are bringing the world to the brink of nuclear warfare!"

I didn't know what to do. Here I saw myself spending the rest of my life in a Soviet prison. So I said, "Just a minute, you're not talking to some Polish admiral here — you're speaking to a United States Navy Fleet Commander, and the actions we have taken in the Mediterranean to which you refer were taken entirely in accordance with international law, and you know that. The procedures we have followed in those cases have been entirely in accordance with international law, and you know that. The United States Navy is not going to put up with state-sponsored terrorism at sea. I'm here to tell you that we will continue these practices, and if it ever happens again, we will do the same Goddamn thing." And the interpreter went along, and when he got to Goddamn, said that in English and went right on. And Admiral Navoytsev said, "Thank you very much, Admiral, I understand your position." Well, he was making a paid political announcement for the record, and that was my answer. He said what he was paid to say, and that was all he was worried about. He didn't care how I responded.[54]

The Memorandum for the Record confirmed Mustin's recollection. It also noted that Navoytsev complained of simulated attacks by American aircraft on Soviet ships and of territorial sea violations committed by the USS *Yorktown* and USS *Caron* in the Black Sea and the USS *Francis Hammond* off the Kuriles. With both navies having been well behaved during the previous year, Navoytsev pressed Mustin on the territorial violations. The Soviet admiral explained that the Soviet territorial sea regulations should be disputed through negotiations and that the American FON penetrations eroded mutual confidence and threatened the whole INCSEA regime. After the second plenary session, Navoytsev repeated the Soviet concern, taking Mustin aside to deliver a personal message from Fleet Admiral Vladimir N. Chernavin to the new CNO, Adm. C. A. H. Trost, discussing the seriousness of the territorial violations and their potential for destroying INCSEA.[55] Mustin, in turn, passed on a personal message from Secretary Weinberger mentioning the secretary's displeasure that the Soviet Union had not responded to requests for remuneration for Major Nicholson or the KAL 007 airliner.[56]

While there were serious sidebar discussions between the two delegation heads, the discussions did not prevent the two men from getting along. Following Weinberger's instructions, Mustin declined any overnight trips outside Moscow. Some social events did occur. There was a short day trip to Zagorsk to view the Trinity–St. Sergius Monastery. The Soviets hosted a dinner at the Rossiya, and the Americans countered with a reception at Spaso House. Fleet Adm. Nikolai I. Smirnov hosted the Soviet reception. Citing the history and efficacious operation of the agreement, Smirnov stated that he was raising his glass of vodka, only to be stopped by Navoytsev, who reminded him that wine had been substituted. The impact of Gorbachev's antialcohol policies became painfully apparent to the visitors as the Soviets were allowed only one refill. Despite valiant attempts, American delegation members could not engage their Soviet counterparts in small talk.

A lively discussion involving Smirnov, Mustin, and Navoytsev proved the exception. The three men discussed a wide range of naval topics, opening with a discussion of whether it was better to serve on the Atlantic or the Pacific. Mustin initially chose the Atlantic; however, Navoytsev expressed envy of the location of the Pacific Fleet Headquarters in Hawaii, citing the beautiful women. Smirnov agreed, noting that "beautiful girls always followed handsome navymen." Mustin came around, admitting that "real sailors" always wanted to steam across the additional 4,000 miles from Hawaii to the Orient. Mustin then fascinated his hosts with a discussion of his combat experience in Vietnam. The three admirals then argued over the advantages of various ship classes, especially aircraft carriers. Mustin cited the recent raids on Libya as affirming the employment of big-deck carriers, noting that American pilots had to confront Soviet weapon systems. Smirnov countered that the Libyans were ill-trained and challenged Mustin to state how a carrier might perform in the Norwegian Sea facing well-trained sea- and land-based forces armed with antiship missiles. Deciding not to fight World War III in words, Mustin discussed his naval heritage and the development of carrier aviation since the 1920s. The conversation concluded with a discussion of fiscal and programmatic support for their respective fleets. Afterwards, Mustin recalled walking out onto the balcony at the Rossiya with Navoytsev after the Russian-hosted dinner and watching the sun set over St. Basil's. Mustin later observed that one reason why INCSEA worked so well was that sailors do tend to have a bond with each other. He remembered telling Navoytsev that he understood and communicated better with the Soviet naval officers than he did with officers of the other U.S. military services.[57]

The following year's talks in Washington proved to be the last for Admiral Navoytsev as head of the Soviet team. There were few incidents to discuss as the Americans brought to the Soviets' attention two alleged violations and the Soviets countered with one accusation. One outcome from this June review was that voice radio (channel 16, 156.9 MHz) was added as a means of communication for the ships of the two navies. But, despite warming relations between the two superpowers, the social restrictions remained in place.[58]

At the time of the 1987 talks, Soviet and U.S. naval forces were simultaneously cooperating with and challenging each other. In the Persian Gulf, the Iran-Iraq War threatened the shipping of neutral nations. On 7 March 1987 President Reagan agreed to reflag Kuwaiti tankers and decided to step up the U.S. Navy's commitment in the region. Experiencing a setback when the ss *Bridgeton* hit a mine on 24 July, the Americans scored a success on 21 September when a U.S. Army helicopter deployed from the uss *Jarrett* discovered the *Iran Ajr* laying mines, then attacked and sank the craft. A month later four U.S. Navy destroyers attacked Iranian oil platforms that had served as bases for speedboat attacks. As with the Americans, the Soviets also desired safe navigation in the gulf. On 4 May small craft attacked the *Ivan Koroteyev,* causing considerable damage. Two weeks later, the tanker *Marshal Chuykov* hit a mine. Shortly thereafter, unidentified small craft fired on the *Sovetskiye Profsoyuzy* and the *Ivan Shepetkov.* Soon, Soviet frigates and minesweepers entered the gulf to provide escort to their merchant comrades. Frequently meeting American warships performing the same mission, Capt. Second Rank P. Zhuravlev observed, "We had no threats or provocations from U.S. ships, rather the opposite. For example, they greeted our ship, thanked us for combined work, and expressed their friendliness. In short, they built relations as though we were acting together and solving the same task."[59]

While U.S. and Soviet warships acted amicably in the gulf, other U.S. naval forces continued to pursue the FON program and practice the Maritime Strategy. The year opened with Operation Kernal Potlatch 87/1, a late-January amphibious assault on Adak and Shemya Islands in the Aleutians. Supported by a battle group centered on the aircraft carrier uss *Carl Vinson,* the operation represented "the first winter amphibious operations in the Aleutians since World War II and the first-ever winter deployment of a carrier battle group to the Bering Sea." In a Navy press release, CINCPACFLT Adm. Ace Lyons stated, "No longer will we permit the Soviets to operate with impunity in this important area."[60] Three months later the nuclear cruiser uss *Arkansas* arrived off the Kamchatka Peninsula for a series of operations that included contesting Soviet territorial claims. The Soviet frigate *Rekiy* observed the *Arkansas* and acted to parry away the American ship. On 21 May the Soviets formally protested the nuclear cruiser's entry four days earlier into claimed territorial waters.[61] The year concluded with another major U.S. Navy exercise in the Northern Pacific. From 8 to 16 November, the uss *Enterprise* and her battle group operated in the Gulf of Alaska and near Adak.

While American naval combatant ships occasionally visited northern

Pacific regions near the Soviet periphery, American naval aviators maintained a constant presence throughout 1987. Authorized by Admiral Lyons, Navy F-14 fighters lifted off from Adak to intercept and escort away Soviet maritime patrol planes flying in the vicinity. Shortly after the F-14s were airborne, A-6E attack bombers lifted off and flew directly toward the Soviet Pacific Fleet base at Petropavlovsk to stage a mock attack. The Navy dubbed the F-14 flights Operation Coyote and the A-6E missions as Operation Shooting Star. On an estimated two dozen occasions, Soviet radar operators at Petropavlovsk detected oncoming American bombers, which finally turned away some 100 miles offshore. While the mock attacks received little media coverage in the United States, the Soviet press reported the aggressive American actions to the Soviet population in an effort to build public indignation toward the Americans.[62]

On one occasion, however, the Soviet Navy fell victim to public indignation. On 7 January 1988 the U.S. naval and assistant naval attachés slipped into the rear of an auditorium filled mostly with students and academicians to hear Rear Adm. Konstantin M. Khumbarov present a lecture on the history of the Soviet Navy. After the lecture, the Americans watched in fascination as the admiral attempted to respond to pointed questions directed at him from the crowd. In turn Khumbarov addressed why the Soviet Navy didn't have "real" aircraft carriers, why a Soviet submarine had sunk in the Atlantic, and why the Soviet Navy censored the media. Responding to a question asked by an elderly lady about U.S. Navy incursions into Soviet territorial waters, he said, "We have protested these actions. They are wrong and any foreign ships violating our sovereignty in the future should be destroyed." The Americans took note.[63]

On the morning of 12 February, in the Black Sea, the commanding officer of the Krivak-class patrolling frigate *Bezzaventny*, Vladimir I. Bogdashin, was ordered to intercept two American warships that had altered course and were expected to enter Soviet territorial waters within sixty to seventy minutes. Along with the Mirka-class patrol frigate SKR 6, Bogdashin soon met up with the cruiser USS *Yorktown* and the destroyer USS *Caron*. "I contacted the cruiser and warned it. They replied that they understood; however, they didn't change course or speed." Bogdashin placed his ship between the *Yorktown* and the coastline, and SKR 6's commander did likewise with his small ship alongside the *Caron*. As the ships entered Soviet territorial waters, Bogdashin repeatedly warned the *Yorktown*, "Your course is heading for danger." The *Yorktown* responded, "We are exercising our right of innocent passage." Bogdashin closed to 12 meters and again issued his warning, with no effect. The Soviet skipper then sent his crew to emergency quarters and ordered his helmsman to turn *Bezzaventny* toward the American cruiser. As Bogdashin's ship rubbed along the port side of the *Yorktown*, SKR 6 nudged into the port quarter of the *Caron*. Damage to all four ships was relatively minor, although broken Harpoon missile canisters on the *Yorktown* caused that ship's skipper, Capt. Philip A. Dur, some anxiety.[64]

The two American ships' attempt to cut across waters off the tip of the Crimean peninsula, near the Black Sea Fleet home port of Sevastopol, had been approved "at the highest level." Only hours after the collision, Undersecretary of State for Political Affairs Michael H. Armacost called in Ambassador Yuri Dubinin to deliver a strong protest. The Americans also used the navy-to-navy channel to register displeasure. The following day in Moscow, Deputy Foreign Minister Alexander Bessmerthykh summoned Ambassador Jack F. Matlock to protest the American violation of Soviet borders. Later that day, Soviet Foreign Ministry spokesman Gennadi Gerasimov held a press briefing to present the Soviet view of the collisions. "We cannot help but view this serious and dangerous incident as undermining recent improvements in relations." Noting an upcoming meeting planned later in February between Secretary of State George Schultz and Foreign Minister Eduard Shevardnadze, Gerasimov stated that Moscow considered the American action a "military provocation," similar to the U-2, aimed at undermining Soviet-American relations ten days prior to the Schultz-Shevardnadze meeting. With First Deputy Commander in Chief of the Soviet Navy Adm. Konstantin Makarov at his side, Gerasimov re-created the incident on a chart set up behind them.[65] At the end of February, the State Department responded to the 13 February protest note, directing the American ambassador to deliver a drafted text reiterating international statutes concerning innocent passage and reserving the right to seek appropriate compensation for any damage.[66] The State Department also had to react to a 19 February letter from Sen. Alan Cranston. The senator from California expressed concern that such incidents could have "dangerous repercussions" in view of ongoing negotiations to remove Intermediate Nuclear Forces (INF) from Europe.[67]

In retrospect, the incident merely caused a hiccup in the overall relationship between the two sides. The Schultz-Shevardnadze meeting went on as planned, as did a March meeting between Secretary of Defense Frank C. Carlucci and Defense Minister Dmitri T. Yazov. In early June Ronald Reagan and Mikhail Gorbachev happily embraced each other at a Moscow summit. However, arriving in Moscow a week after the summit, American INCSEA delegation head Vice Admiral Mustin would find out that the Soviets had not forgotten about the Black Sea incidents.

The Soviets placed the Black Sea incidents on the official agenda for review. Vice Admiral Kamarov explained the Soviet position that as a signatory of the 1982 UN Convention on the Law of the Sea the Soviet Union had canceled prior rules regarding foreign warships in territorial waters. He further stated that the Soviet law accepted the right of innocent passage only if the intruding warship didn't violate Soviet peace, goodwill, or security. From the Soviet perspective, the question was what constitutes a violation of peace, goodwill, or security? Echoing Navoytsev's argument of two years earlier, Kamorov proposed that these definitions were legal questions that could be negotiated separately from INCSEA. The bumping incidents were again discussed when Vice Admiral Mustin called on Admiral Makarov. Marakov spoke frankly to the American flag officer. Mustin recalled the forty-minute discussion:

> He said, "You are causing us a lot of problems. I'm getting calls from the commissars and politicians saying that we spend hundreds of millions of rubles on the Soviet Navy so that the Soviet Navy can protect us from the U.S. Navy and you can't protect us! What the hell's going on?" So he said they were going to cut his budget. You know it was just like talking to a U.S. Admiral. He said, "These things are unnecessarily provocative. We would very much appreciate it if you could stop." I came back and recommended that we back off, which we did.[68]

This understanding was formalized over a year later on 23 September 1989, at the Jackson Hole, Wyoming, meeting between Foreign Minister Shevardnadze and the new U.S. Secretary of State, James Baker. With the

Soviets signing a statement acknowledging international laws regarding the right of other nation's vessels to conduct innocent passage through Soviet territorial waters, the United States declared that there was no longer a need to conduct FON cruises through these waters to assert this right.[69]

While the Cold War at sea continued, dramatic changes occurring in the Soviet Union led to a reevaluation of U.S.-Soviet political relations. What struck Vice Admiral Mustin about the 1988 trip was the openness and frankness of his hosts. Touring around Moscow a week after the Reagan visit, the guide pointed out that only one side of the buildings along the president's motorcade route had been painted. In effect, the whole city had been turned into a potemkin village.[70]

With the departure of Secretary of Defense Weinberger and an apology from the Soviet Ministry of Defense for the Nicholson slaying, the "saltines and seltzer" regime and travel restrictions were lifted.[71] Thus the Soviets hosted the American delegation on a trip to Leningrad. Prior to departing Washington, the "intelligence guys" approached Mustin to sound out the Soviets on perestroika:

> So we arrived in Leningrad and spent a delightful day, with lunch and dinner with the president of their war college. The lunch started off, and this fellow turns to me and asks, "What do you think of perestroika?" So I said that we had a lot of interest in this for obvious reasons: "We have determined that you will need an enormous influx of Western capital and technology, which we don't see coming and we don't think that your military will stand for reductions in size and capability." He stated that the influx of capital had already begun and he stated that "we are counting on corresponding military reductions on your part."[72]

Events played out, leading to the end of Soviet domination in Eastern Europe and the eventual collapse of the Soviet Union itself. As symbolized by the Reagan visit to Moscow, the forty-year confrontational relationship between the United States and the Soviet Union was drawing to a close, bringing to an end the Cold War at sea. There would be hardly any incidents between the maritime surface and air forces of the two sides after 1988. However, the Cold War under the sea would continue for some time before tailing off, as illustrated by collisions occurring in the Barents Sea between American and Soviet submarines in 1992 and 1993.[73]

When reviewing the daily operations of the two navies, the 1980s proved to be one of the most confrontational decades on and over the high seas. Although there was no Cuban missile crisis or Middle East war to bring naval forces to the brink, events and initiatives affecting both sides placed ships and aircraft in constant contact. Fortunately, throughout most of the period, captains and commanders of ships and aircraft on both sides abided by the procedures spelled out in the agreement, limiting the possibility of incidents like the KAL 007 shootdown that could only have soured relations further.

Others outside of the two navies began to note the success of the INCSEA regimen as a "confidence-building measure." Consequently, there were lessons learned that would have applications after the end of the Cold War and the demise of the Soviet Union.

Epilogue

A POSITIVE
LEGACY

With the warming of Soviet-American relations, other military-to-military contacts began to occur. Starting at the top, the chairman of the U.S. Joint Chiefs of Staff, Adm. William J. Crowe, hosted his counterpart, Marshal Sergei F. Akhromeyev, to an extensive U.S. visit in July 1988. At this summit, the two top military men agreed to an exchange program that included ship visits.

A year later, the second visit of Soviet warships since the end of World War II took place at Norfolk, Virginia. On 21 July the new *Slava*-class cruiser *Marshal Ustinov*, the *Sovremennyy*-class destroyer *Otlichnny*, and the replenishment oiler *Genrikh Gasanov* coasted up Thimble Shoals Channel to call at the Naval Base, Norfolk. The Soviet commander, First Deputy Commander in Chief of the Soviet Northern Fleet Vice Adm. Igor V. Kasatonov, carried on the naval heritage established by his father, Vladimir. As with his father, this Kasatonov also led a group of Russians to the United States, except in this case the Russians were hundreds of officers and sailors from three Soviet warships.

Despite the 90-degree-plus heat, Soviet sailors participated in a range of activities including visiting a shopping mall, attending a pig roast, listening to several concerts, and traveling to Williamsburg to experience Busch Gardens. Many of the foreign sailors had opportunities to join area families for a home-cooked meal. Vice Admiral Kasatonov found the American effort at "citizens' diplomacy" impressive.

Kasatonov admitted that at first he felt reluctant to play the role of guest, in view of the past history of Soviet-American relations. While he experienced warm hospitality from his American hosts, at times he was reminded of the adversarial relationship. Kasatonov noticed an F-16 used for simulating an "enemy" aircraft had red stars painted on its fuselage, and during a tour of the Armed Forces Staff College Marine Gen. J. Dailey boasted how in a recent command-staff game, "we wiped the 'Reds.'" The Soviet vice admiral also noted the emblem of the Second Fleet as characteristic: "a nuclear trident pointing to the northeast."[1]

A week and a half after the departure of Vice Admiral Kasatonov and his three ships from Norfolk, the Deputy Commander, U.S. Naval Forces Europe, Vice Adm. Raymond P. Ilg, approached the Soviet Black Sea port of Sevastopol, riding the cruiser USS *Thomas S. Gates* escorted by the frigate USS *Kauffman*. On the pier, thousands of Soviet citizens jubilantly waited to greet the Americans, tossing up to the visitors souvenir pins, cigarettes, and rubles. To the crowd's delight, some American sailors reacted by flinging their "dixie cup" hats onto the pier. Over the next four days, more than 25,000 Soviets would tour the two vessels.

In contrast to the treatment given to two American warships offshore a year and a half previously, these sailors experienced a positive thrill. After the visit, one senior Soviet officer observed:

> Admirals Khronopulo [then Commander in Chief, Black Sea Fleet] and Ilg exchanged caps. The American ships left Soviet territory. What will our relations be like after the visit? After all, we are still rivals, and not only in the Mediterranean. But all the same, without exaggeration, this visit was historic. We have grown closer and closer to each other. Let us hope that it will not be the last. Isn't this natural and sensible?[2]

During the following year, Pacific fleet units from the two countries cruised to port calls in San Diego and Vladivostok. In 1991 Soviet Navy ships called at Mayport, Florida, and in 1992 American ships called on the home port of the Northern Fleet, Severomorsk. Visits continued throughout the 1990s.

The Prevention of Dangerous Military Activities Agreement, signed in Moscow on 12 June 1989 by the CJCS Admiral Crowe and Chief of the Soviet General Staff Marshal Sergei Moiseyev, established a second bilateral military-to-military contact program. The accord had its inception in a meeting between Soviet General Staff Chief Marshal Sergei Akhromeyev and Admiral Crowe in Washington in December 1987. The discussions initiated by the two military leaders to reduce dangerous military practices continued when U.S. Secretary of Defense Frank C. Carlucci met with Soviet Defense Minister Dmitri Yazov in Bern, Switzerland, in March 1988.[3] This spring meeting led to a military-to-military working group to work out the accord's provisions. Although the "PDMA" was a "military-to-military" versus "navy-to-navy" agreement, the document's provisions had substantial applications to the maritime environment when it went into effect on 1 January 1990.

Captain First Rank Serkov, a member of the Soviet delegation that negotiated this new agreement, discussed PDMA in an October 1990 article in the naval journal *Morskoy Sbornik*. The INCSEA veteran examined the agreement's four major provisions from a nautical standpoint. First, he noted that the agreement laid out procedures for forces operating near the territory of the other country when unforeseen circumstances caused an inadvertent penetration of the other's territory. A series of radio frequencies and signals and phrases were worked out to establish direct communications in such circumstances. Serkov noted that "tests of the communications channels between various points conducted in December 1989 showed the reliability of the developed measures."

Second, laser use had become a concern. In 1988 the issue was addressed at the annual INCSEA review after a series of incidents in which flashes of "directed energy" emanating from Soviet vessels had momentarily blinded American pilots. Both sides agreed that such laser use was a violation of the INCSEA provision that deterred weapons pointing. However, PDMA formalized this understanding in writing and expanded the concept to cover land-border regions.

The agreement's third major provision "envisions measures necessary for the facilitation of the action of personnel of armed forces of the other party in special jointly determined 'regions of special attention.'" With negotiations conducted during U.S. peacekeeping and convoy escort duties in the Persian Gulf, the United States asked for this provision to ensure that in future crises involving the forces of one party or both "Special Caution

Areas" could be mutually agreed on where both sides could utilize the established communications channels to prevent dangerous misunderstandings.

Finally, both sides agreed to work to prevent interference with each other's command and control networks. As in INCSEA, the two sides would use a military-to-military channel, with the defense attachés serving as the envoys. The accord established a joint military commission to review implementation of the agreement.[4] The first meeting took place in Tampa, Florida, in March 1990. While the downfall of the Soviet Union and the emergence of the Russian Federation made the accord almost superfluous, the framework is there for the two nations to use as relations fluctuate.

The demise of the Soviet Union, however, had little effect on the INCSEA regime. Even though there were no more incidents to discuss, the two sides continued to hold their annual talks. The 1992 talks in Moscow represented the twentieth anniversary of the accord. With retired Admiral Crowe serving as the honorary head of the U.S. delegation, the Moscow talks added a new wrinkle. For the first time, the two navies held staff talks to exchange information, coordinate activities, and discuss joint training opportunities. In the years following the twentieth-anniversary talks, staff talks held in conjunction with the annual INCSEA review assumed the greater portion of the annual get-together. With virtually no incidents occurring after 1991, the annual review was pared down to focus mostly on reviewing the use of communications and updating the accord to reflect political changes. The remaining schedule was dedicated to staff talks and orientation. In 1993 the U.S. side hosted the talks in San Diego, allowing the Russian delegation to tour training facilities and units of the U.S. Pacific Fleet. No review was held in 1994 because of Russian fiscal constraints. After the 1995 talks in Moscow, the U.S. Navy hosted the 1996 talks in Seattle to familiarize the Russians with Trident missile submarine and other facilities in and around Puget Sound. After another round in Moscow, the Americans held the 1998 review in Annapolis. During 1998 the two sides completed the exchange of diplomatic notes to change the language of the accord to reflect geopolitical changes on the Russian side and to extend the accord to cover commercial aviation. The 1999 session was scheduled for Moscow in November.[5]

The INCSEA regimen established by the Soviets and Americans in 1972 also found a continued existence in other parts of the globe. In the 1980s, America's allies, who had maintained an interest in the U.S.-Soviet accord since its negotiation, negotiated their own INCSEA accords with the Soviets. Throughout the 1971–72 INCSEA negotiations, the United States took steps to keep its allies informed. Twice, Undersecretary Warner traveled to Brussels to address the North Atlantic Council about negotiations. The British were singled out for special treatment because of their interest in the subject and because of the special maritime relationship between the two close allies. Acting on behalf of America's partners, as the May 1972 negotiating round came to a close, Secretary Warner broached to Admiral Kasatonov the subject of making the accord multilateral. Receptive to the idea, Kasatonov pointed out that if NATO was to be added, then all of the Warsaw Pact countries should be allowed to sign on. However, this reasonable-sounding counterproposal presented problems for the Americans, for it would allow the German Democratic Republic (G.D.R.) to participate in the process. The United States did not care to bestow any recognition on what it considered an illegitimate regime. Warner dropped the proposal.[6]

Prior to the 1973 review and protocol signing, NATO Ambassador Donald Rumsfeld inquired about the multilateral question. He noted that the East German question could be neatly handled if under an agreement accession clause Moscow and Washington would act as depository powers, holding open copies of the agreement for signatures by third countries.[7] With the G.D.R. signing in Moscow, the United States would be spared the necessity of bestowing recognition on the East Germans. However, the United States again decided to drop the issue.

An annual review participant many years later, Comdr. Howard Sidman observed:

> The success of this agreement has been bilateral. Trying to do this agreement during this same time period as a multilateral agreement would have made it just another piece of paper — a footnote in history. It wouldn't have worked. One reason is that the Soviets would never have been able to stand up and say "one of our C.O.s messed up," which has happened. The Soviet Union doesn't mind confiding with an equal that there was a mistake, but admitting that in front of the Danes or, God forbid, the Germans would have made this agreement a non-player.

No accession clause would be added. The INCSEA agreement would remain unique to U.S.-U.S.S.R. relations — until 1986.

In one of those "on the margin" discussions in 1986, the Soviets brought up the subject of negotiating incidents at sea agreements with other countries. Vice Admiral Mustin told Admiral Navoytsev that he had no objections to the Soviets having agreements with other countries if they were identical with the agreement they had with the United States. Mustin tactfully stated that if the Soviets attempted to incorporate in these new agreements provisions on submerged submarines, or fixed distances, the United States would seriously consider terminating the bilateral U.S.-U.S.S.R. agreement. Navoytsev assured Mustin that there would be no problems. The substance of this conversation was conveyed to each of America's maritime allies.[8]

Incidents had occurred over the years between the ships and aircraft of America's NATO allies and those of the Soviet Union and its Warsaw Pact allies. The collision between the HMS *Ark Royal* and a Soviet destroyer in early November 1970 may have even inspired the Soviets to accept the American long-standing offer to conduct bilateral negotiations. From time to time, the Soviet media had complained of "buzzings" from the maritime aircraft of a variety of NATO nations. However, harassment on and over the high seas could not have been the prime motivation for the series of "copycat" INCSEA accords that were signed starting in July 1986. The Soviet naval behavior toward the NATO allies reflected the improvement in their behavior toward the United States. Rear Admiral Kurth, defense attaché in Moscow during this period, remarked on this sudden Soviet urge to sign additional INCSEA agreements:

> It was very hard to figure out just why the Soviets wanted to extend the Agreement. The reflection of those of us who spent a lot of time in the Soviet Union springs all the way to the pursuit of legitimacy for the Soviet Navy for advantage in internal battles in the Ministry of Defense regarding the theoretical position of the navy in military science, down to the desire in the Soviet Navy to get some of their officers overseas experience.[9]

Commander Sidman later observed that an agreement signing gave Gorbachev an accomplishment to claim as he traveled to summit meetings throughout Western Europe.[10]

The Soviets did not initiate negotiations on all ten of the bilateral INCSEA agreements that they had entered into by the end of 1991. For example, the West Germans initiated discussions that would conclude with an agreement signed with the Soviets on 25 October 1988. In discussing the German initiative to negotiate INCSEA agreements with the Soviet Union in 1988 and later with Poland in 1990, German Navy Capt. Dieter Leonhard explained: "The value of these treaties rests primarily in the political sphere since they serve the further development and normalization of the bilateral relationships and reduction of tensions, thus having a confidence-building effect."[11] Some of the Western European motivations for negotiating with the Soviets to resolve a crisis that didn't exist might have been to "keep up with the Joneses." Once Great Britain inked the first copycat agreement with the Soviets in conjunction with a Gorbachev visit in July 1986, followed by the Soviet-German signing, could France be far behind?

Perhaps the Soviet (and now Russian) Naval Ministry came to regret signing so many agreements requiring annual preparations to host or send delegations to nearly a dozen countries to discuss incidents that were no longer occurring given the reduction in the operations of the former Soviet Navy. At the Conference on Security and Cooperation in Europe in 1990, the then–Soviet delegation tabled a proposal for a multilateral INCSEA agreement involving the CSCE participants. However, the proposal at that Vienna forum received a cold shoulder from the NATO participants, who preferred to maintain their bilateral relationships.[12]

Some support for this proposal came from some of the conference's traditionally neutral parties, such as Sweden and Finland. Sweden had long been in the forefront in advocating such an arrangement. In 1983, at Sweden's instigation, the UN General Assembly adopted a resolution calling for the Secretary General to assemble a panel of experts to conduct a comprehensive study of the global naval arms race. Both the United States and the Soviet Union declined to participate in this effort. In 1985 the panel presented a completed study to the General Assembly. One panel suggestion that was singled out for special consideration called for converting the bilateral U.S.-U.S.S.R. INCSEA Agreement to a multilateral format. This recommendation received a cold shoulder from the United States for the reasons cited by Commander Sidman. Other observers noted that such an accord could actually cause incidents, since lesser maritime powers might "provoke" incidents with one of the superpowers to attain a sense of prestige or enhance some strongman's image. Any annual UN conference to address INCSEA complaints could easily become politicized, focusing instead on limiting superpower naval activities. Understanding this concern, the United Nations Disarmament Commission, in its 1986 session, reviewed the panel's recommendation and recommended that a multilateral agreement coexist with the U.S.-U.S.S.R. agreement and not supersede it.

This proposal has been rehashed over the ensuing years but with little progress. Sweden has distributed several working papers with sample multilateral INCSEA agreement proposals.[13] However, when the consultation group that examined the issue for the 1990 Disarmament Commission reported on 25 May 1990, the feedback was mixed. Some members of the group favored pursuing the multilateral approach, while others favored continuing to seek additional bilateral accords. Sweden persisted in advocating the multilateral option. In 1990 the Swedish naval attaché to Washington, Capt. C. Hagg, wrote:

> U.S.S.R. proposed a similar agreement to the Swedish government in 1986, but the latter turned it down as a matter of principle, as Sweden does not sign any bilateral agreements of this kind but works towards general agreements issued by the UN. From a professional Swedish navy standpoint the U.S.-U.S.S.R. agreement is nothing more than the international rule of the way of the seas and did not offer any increased safety.[14]

Proponents of the more bilateral agreements option can point to the German-Polish agreement signed on 25 November 1990 as an ideal working model. This agreement became the first INCSEA to be signed that did not involve either the United States or the former Soviet Union. There had been incidents between the West German and former Warsaw Pact navies, most notably when the Bundesmarine ship *Neckar* was hit by Polish shells in 1987 during a Pact wargame, but, as Captain Leonhard has pointed out, the value of such agreements between two peoples who have had a history of mistrust and conflict is their long-term "confidence-building effect."[15]

Advocates for additional bilateral agreements based on the German-Polish model have cited Greece-Turkey, Iran-Iraq, India-Pakistan, Japan-China, and North Korea–South Korea as ideal candidates.[16] Meanwhile, the United States, long an opponent of multilateral arrangements, raised no objections to the concept of a Middle East multilateral regime. Vice Adm. Leighton W. Smith lectured on the successful aspects of the U.S.-U.S.S.R. agreement at a session of the Middle East Peace Conference held in Washington in May 1992, suggesting that the Arabs and Israelis could adapt mechanisms from the agreement to cover their unique situation. Smith discussed how the nearly nonexistent media exposure kept the talks out of the public spotlight during periods of superpower tension and thus spared the process of cancellation demands from hard-liners on both sides. He noted that the talks were held between naval professionals, freeing the process of the normal polemics associated with bilateral talk between diplomatic corps. He added that the requirement for an annual review forced the two sides to communicate.[17]

The Middle East peace process emerging from the October 1991 Madrid Conference had one track devoted to a series of bilateral negotiations between Israel and its neighbors. A second track consisted of multilateral working groups to address regional problems. A possible Middle East INCSEA fell under the Arms Control and Regional Security Working Group. Canada volunteered to serve as a mentor and subsequently hosted a workshop in Sydney, Nova Scotia, to explore with Middle East representatives the feasibility of regional INCSEA and search-and-rescue (SAR) understandings. At follow-up meetings in Turkey and in Jordan in March and November, respectively, the parties agreed to language for the multilateral INCSEA and SAR agreements. A problem arose because some of the parties did not have diplomatic relations with Israel and thus were confronted with the "East German" problem that the United States faced in 1972. However, in 1995, the Rumsfeld solution was applied. At a final meeting held in Turkey in March 1995, the parties agreed to call the negotiated documents "guidelines," and Canada agreed to serve as a repository for the document.[18]

Finally, on 19 January 1998, the United States signed an agreement with the People's Republic of China establishing a consultation mechanism for strengthening military maritime safety. The United States avoided using the title "Incidents at Sea" for this accord because the term had Cold War connotations inappropriate for the relationship it sought to maintain with China. Still, with growing Chinese maritime forces, and the long-term presence of the Seventh Fleet in the Western Pacific, both sides agreed that it would be mutually beneficial to establish a military-to-military communications mechanism. As such, the agreement represents the first permanent military-to-military relationship between the two countries. As with the U.S.-Russian accord, there will be annual consultations, to be hosted on a rotating basis. Between meetings, communications between the two military establishments are to be handled through each country's defense attaché.[19]

In summary, the lessons learned from the Cold War at sea will have applications for international relations well into the twenty-first century. During the first two decades of the Cold War, diplomats using conventional means of diplomacy attempted to address the problems created by the drive of both superpower navies to contest space on and over the high seas. Throughout much of the Cold War, much of this contested space was along the Soviet periphery. During the 1950s air incidents led to the death of over 100 Soviet and U.S. airmen. Conventional diplomatic practices by both sides scored some successes in restraining aggressive military activities, but the introduction of satellite reconnaissance may have made a greater contribution since air incidents virtually ceased after the launch of Discoverer XIV in August 1960.

Growing Soviet maritime activities placed ships bearing the hammer and sickle in daily contact with the West. In some cases, Soviet merchant ships berthed in Cuba and North Vietnam found themselves in harm's way. Others found themselves under constant surveillance. The Soviets lodged several protests. Of course, the Soviets designed or converted some of their ships to also perform a surveillance role. These ships, known as AGIs, often hindered Western navy operations. While AGI and Soviet merchant activities led to many American protests, it was a growing Soviet Navy that truly alarmed the Americans. Collisions involving the USS *Walker* in the Sea of Japan in May 1967, followed by close interactions between Sixth Fleet and Soviet warships in the Mediterranean a month later during the Six-Day War, moved OpNav to push for bilateral talks with the Soviets on safety at sea. Eventually, the State Department approached the Soviets in April 1968.

In November 1970 the Soviets accepted the American proposal, and negotiations led to the May 1972 INCSEA agreement. Mainly devised by naval personnel, the accord served to moderate the behavior of the naval surface and air forces of the two sides through the end of the Cold War. It did so despite the October 1973 Middle East War and the strains of the 1980s: a period of deteriorated superpower relations and reassertion of American maritime superiority. Seven fundamental reasons can be given for the accord's success and its use as a model confidence-building measure into the twenty-first century.

First, the agreement served both sides' best interests. Rear Admiral Hilton once wrote: "Neither country wants to have its valuable ships damaged by inadvertent or imprudent actions of its officers. Neither nation wants an incident to escalate into a governmental confrontation."[20] The Soviet Navy leaders had particular reason to be concerned, since the rapid buildup of the fleet had forced them to promote junior officers to command positions. With contacts on and over the high seas promising to increase as the Soviet Navy continued to expand, a maintenance of the status quo would only increase the odds that the actions of an inexperienced officer on either side would lead to an escalation of tensions or even an exchange of fire. Both sides found the prospects of inadvertent warfare undesirable. With the implementation of the agreement, the two sides established behavioral norms that provided reassurance for ship commanders. Naval operations are complex and nerve-wracking in times of peace. Tension is only multiplied in times of crisis. The naval buildup during the 1973 Arab-Israeli war illustrated why both superpowers benefited from adhering to the behavioral norms established by the accord.

Simplicity is the second reason for success. Over the long term, the American insistence on a simple formula calling for commanders to abide by the Rules of the Road and use prudent judgment probably served each side's best interests. As a result of this provision, the annual consultations process focused on serious transgressions only and did not become bogged down in minor disputes. Hours of arguments on whether ship *A* inadvertently entered the come-no-closer zone of ship *B* were avoided.

The professionalism exhibited by both sides also warrants recognition. Former ship operators and aviators served on the delegations. Each side could easily place itself in the other's shoes. Rooted in a shared environment, professional naval officers are often able to communicate better with officers from other navies than with those from sister services. Hence, if an aircraft or ship violated the agreement, the offending side acknowledged responsibility, and the two sides moved on to the next problem. And of course, when discussing professionalism, the conduct of those on both sides actually serving on the high seas also must be recognized.

Preparation was the fourth reason for success. If an incident occurred, the reported violation was passed through the other nation's naval attaché well in advance of the normal review, allowing the opportunity to investigate. Often one side acknowledged fault even before the review session. Six to eight weeks prior to the review, the host nation submitted a proposed agenda and delegation list through the other nation's naval attaché. Shortly thereafter, the guest nation proposed any additions or changes to the agenda and provided the visiting delegation list. Consequently, both sides entered the annual review with the benefit of a set agenda and confidence in knowing that there would be no unexpected surprises.

Atmospherics represents a fifth reason for success. During the October 1971 talks the Soviets set two precedents that later contributed to productive annual review sessions. At the first Moscow talks, the Soviet side took care of all expenses associated with the negotiations except for travel to and from the Soviet Union. The "host-pays-all" regime eased the burden of the visiting delegation and fostered good will. The second precedent involved the proposed touring or entertainment schedule. This was not transmitted by the host in advance but was agreed upon when the visiting delegation head made a courtesy call on the host delegation head shortly after arrival. By working together on a touring/entertainment itinerary, the two delegation heads had the opportunity to get a sense of each other's likes and dislikes. Agreement on an itinerary also established a spirit of cooperation that carried on when tougher issues were later tabled. In addition, the touring/entertainment regime fostered a better understanding of each other's culture and country.

The lack of publicity and visibility of the INCSEA accord is a sixth reason for success. Since INCSEA did not require Senate ratification, it avoided politicization from the start, a hurdle fatal to other accords. Also, INCSEA received little press attention at its signing as a result of concurrent events related to the Nixon summit trip to Moscow. A consistent effort to maintain this low profile led to there being no publicity about the annual reviews. Although the actions of the Secretary of Defense did postpone the

1985 annual review, the agreement survived far greater Cold War crises because of strong support within both naval leadership establishments.

Verification and accountability represent the final reason for success. The establishment of direct navy-to-navy communications mechanisms and the provision of annual consultations provided means for holding both parties accountable. Unlike arms-control agreements, such as those curtailing weapons that can be obfuscated by either side, a violation of INCSEA occurs only in the presence of the other party. Each side produced photographs, videotapes, charts, and deck logs at the annual reviews to demonstrate which party was at fault.

Although INCSEA did not end all U.S.-Soviet incidents at sea, it served as a confidence-building mechanism addressing the serious problem of growing harassment at sea that plagued both sides in the late 1960s and early 1970s. INCSEA also helped lay the groundwork for establishing closer military-to-military ties after the fall of the Berlin Wall. It is one of the positive legacies of the Cold War at sea. Those individuals involved in the INCSEA negotiation and implementation process can take great pride in what they accomplished.

Since the fall of the Berlin Wall and the subsequent breakup of the Soviet Union, the U.S. Navy once again reigns unchallenged on the high seas. However, it is a smaller navy, just half the size of the navy of a decade previous. While many of the ships and aircraft currently serving are of Cold War vintage, most of the ships and planes that defended the nation during those challenging times have been retired. At locations such as Philadelphia and Bremerton, the passing visitor can view dozens of mothballed frigates, destroyers, cruisers, aircraft carriers, and auxiliaries. At Davis-Monthan Air Force Base in Tucson, row upon row of fighter, attack, and ASW aircraft lie quietly in the desert sun. While some ships and aircraft are seeing service with other nations, most of these Cold War veterans have been or will soon be scrapped.

For the former ships of the Soviet Navy, the picture is more grim. Along inlets near such ports as Murmansk and Vladivostok, Kyndas, Krestas, and Kashins have been abandoned to rust. Of greater environmental concern is the fate of many of the nuclear-propelled submarines. Proper disposing of these ships has taken on greater urgency.

A few lucky ships and aircraft on both sides have survived as static displays and memorials. This is altogether fitting. These displays and memorials will serve as an important reminder to future generations on the importance of sea power and serve as part of the legacy of the Cold War at sea. Another part of the legacy is the memories of the participants and the documents they left behind. These memories need to be shared and documents made available so that we can fully understand the Cold War at sea in a proper context and that the sacrifices made by sailors and airmen of the two nations receive a most deserved recognition.

Chronology

The majority of the events listed below were extracted from documents found at the National Archives, the Naval Historical Center, or obtained from the Defense and State Departments through the Freedom of Information Act. A 20 August 1966 letter from U. Alexis Johnson to Cy Vance found at the National Archives provided a very detailed listing of incidents that occurred in the mid-1960s. Other sources include "Some Significant Air Incidents Involving the United States and Communist Nations, 1945–1964," an Aerospace Studies Institute report, and a folder labeled "Incidents Reported" (K168.1-21, Nov 51–Mar 63) both found at the Air Force Historical Research Center, Maxwell Air Force Base; and "Case Studies: Ten Unresolved Cold War Shootdowns," written in 1993 by Task Force Russia's Col. Stuart Herrington, USA. Secondary sources include Barry M. Blechman, William J. Durch, W. Philip Ellis, and Cathleen S. Fisher, "Appendix 3.1 Incidents at Sea Chronology," in *Naval Arms Control: A Strategic Assessment* (New York: St. Martin's Press, 1991), and Norman Polmar, Eric Wertheim, Andrew Bahjat, and Bruce Watson, *Chronology of the Cold War at Sea, 1945–1991* (Annapolis, Md: Naval Institute Press, 1998).

1945
2 Sept.	Japan formally surrendered, ending World War II.
15 Oct.	After a Navy PBM Mariner flying boat flew near Soviet-occupied Port Arthur, two Soviet fighters made firing passes at it over the Yellow Sea.

1946
20 Feb.	Two Soviet aircraft fired warning shots at another U.S. Navy seaplane flying near Port Arthur.

1949

25 Aug.   Soviets detonated atomic bomb.

1950

8 April   Soviet fighters shot down a Navy PB4Y-2 Privateer patrol craft over the Baltic. The crew of ten was never recovered.

25 June   The Korean War began.

4 Sept.   Navy fighter aircraft off the uss *Valley Forge* shot down a Soviet patrol bomber over the Yellow Sea.

8 Oct.   Two usaf F-80 fighters strafed a Soviet airfield near Vladivostok.

1951

6 Nov.   Soviet fighters shot down a Navy P2V-3 Neptune aircraft over the Sea of Japan, causing a loss of ten crewmen.

1952

23 Jan.   Soviet fighters fired on a Navy P4M Mercator reconnaissance aircraft flying over the Baltic.

13 June   An RB-29 and a crew of twelve were lost over the Sea of Japan. At the end of the Cold War, the Russians confirmed the aircraft had been shot down by a MiG-15.

7 Oct.   Soviet fighters shot down an Air Force RB-29 over Yuri Island north of Hokkaido. One body of a crew of eight has since been recovered.

18 Nov.   Soviet MiGs approached Task Force 77 off Vladivostok and were engaged by Navy F9F-5 Panther fighters. Two MiGs were shot down and one was damaged.

1953

15 Feb.   Two Soviet MiGs penetrated northern Japanese airspace and were intercepted by two Air Force F-86 Sabres. One MiG was fired on and damaged.

15 March   An RB-50 flying off Kamchatka was attacked by Soviet MiGs but escaped undamaged.

13 June   The Soviets shot down a Swedish Air Force DC-3 ferret aircraft near Gotland Island in the Baltic.

16 June   Soviet fighters shot down a Swedish Catalina flying boat over the Baltic.

27 July   Four American fighters ambushed a Soviet Il-12 passenger plane en route from Port Arthur to the Soviet Union; An armistice was signed ending the Korean War.

| 29 July | Soviet fighters shot down an Air Force RB-50 off the coast of Vladivostok. One of a crew of seventeen was recovered. |

1954

8 May	Soviet fighters fired shells into an RB-47 flying over the Kola Peninsula.
4 Sept.	A Soviet MiG-15 shot down a Navy P2V-5 Neptune off the east coast of Siberia. One crewmember drowned while trying to evacuate the ditched aircraft.
7 Nov.	Soviet fighters shot down another RB-29 near Yuri Island. A airman drowned after becoming entangled in his parachute.

1955

| 18 April | A USAF RB-47 was lost in the northern Pacific near Kamchatka with a crew of three. After the Cold War the Russians revealed two MiGs shot down the plane. |
| 22 June | One or two Soviet fighters ambushed a Navy P2V Neptune on patrol over the Bering Sea. The plane crash-landed on St. Lawrence Island in the Bering Sea. |

1956

| 4 July | First U-2 penetration of Soviet airspace. |
| 11 Dec. | An Air Force RB-57 aircraft detected over Siberia was chased by Soviet fighters. |

1958

10 July	An USAF RB-50 flying off Petropavlosk exchanged gunfire with Soviet fighters.
11–31 July	A Polish trawler collided with USS *Brownson* in the North Sea. (Poles paid $3,000.); Trawler *Kulkoba* harassed USS *Northampton* in Kattegat Strait between Sweden and Denmark; Four Soviet trawlers reportedly harassed USS *Elokomin* and USNS *Mascoma* during an unrep in the North Sea; Two Soviet trawlers harassed USS *Etemedor* off Norway.
7 Nov.	A Soviet fighter fired on an RB-47 over the Baltic Sea. An RB-47 over the Sea of Japan was subjected to mock attacks by other Soviet aircraft.

1959

| 26 Feb. | After five AT&T cables were severed in the North Atlantic, the USS *Roy O. Hale* stopped and boarded the Soviet trawler *Novorossisk*. |

1960

11 April — Soviet trawlers crossed ahead with close approach near USNS *Michelson*, USNS *Dutton*, and USNS *Bowditch* in the Norwegian Sea.

26 April — In crossing situation, the Soviet trawler *Vega* reportedly backed instead of maintaining course and speed in a situation with USS *Nipmuc* in the western Atlantic.

1 May — U-2 aircraft was shot down over Sverdlovsk.

9 May — Soviet press reported that an American carrier and destroyers surrounded the SS *Taras Shevchenko* near Genoa.

27 May– 28 Sept. — Over a dozen Soviet press reports alleged U.S. planes and ships harassed Soviet shipping at various locales during these months.

1 July — A Soviet MiG shot down an RB-47 over the Barents Sea. Two of the six crewmembers were recovered alive by the Soviets.

7 July — An American freighter was stopped by armed Soviet patrol vessel on high seas in the Pacific Ocean and asked to identify itself. In the Baltic the USS *Barry* turned in wrong direction, in violation of the Rules of the Road, to avoid collision with a Soviet ship.

20 July — USS *George Washington* demonstrated the capability to launch a ballistic missile.

18 Aug. — Soviet merchant *Vsl Uxeryink* maneuvered close to USS *Tallahatchie County* in the Caribbean Sea.

4 Nov. — U.S.S.R. charged that USS *Corry* made passes at the freighter *Faleshty* in the Mediterranean and almost caused a collision. U.S. rejected protest on 5 January 1961.

1961

13 Jan. — U.S.S.R. protested that an American patrol vessel and two other patrol vessels had attempted to halt the *Sverdlovsk* in the Caribbean. U.S. countered that the protest was groundless.

Jan. 61– mid-62 — The Soviets continued to allege that U.S. planes harassed Soviet shipping. It was noted that in many cases the ships under observation were equipped with intelligence-collection gear.

9 Oct. — *Novi Kov Triboi* (a fish factory trawler) maneuvered 360 degrees to port in a crossing situation with the USS *Kretchmer* in the Norwegian Sea. The Soviets alleged harassment.

21 Oct. — USS *John Willis* took improper action and maneuvered even though she was the stand-on vessel in a crossing situation with the merchant vessel *Narwick* in the western Atlantic. A U.S. Navy investigation of a Soviet complaint about harassment determined the American OOD had a faulty knowledge of the Rules of the Road.

30 Oct.   USS *Tioga County,* as an overtaken vessel, violated the Rules of the Road and sped up in a situation with a Soviet trawler in the Bering Sea. The Soviet trawler then maneuvered dangerously near *Tioga County.*

1962

25 Jan.   The merchant ship *Vlastni* maneuvered dangerously near USS *Arneb* in a crossing situation in the South Pacific.

1 April   The merchant ship *Metallurg Baykon* attempted a maneuver to turn into the USS *Claud Jones* at night.

3 April   Soviet tanker *Bugurusian* reportedly maneuvered dangerously near the USS *Shangri-La* in the Mediterranean.

7 May   The antisubmarine carrier USS *Wasp* and seven destroyers entered the Baltic Sea to perform operations.

28 July   The *Marcya Ulianavo* reportedly did not change course in a meeting situation with the USS *Warrington* in the Caribbean.

15 Sept. Reconnaissance aircraft photographed SS *Poltava* en route to Cuba.

30 Sept. The Soviet freighter *Unzha* passed dangerously near the USS *Rigel* in the Messina Straits.

22 Oct.   President Kennedy addressed the nation about Soviet missile facilities under construction in Cuba and the establishment of a quarantine.

24 Oct.   An American naval quarantine of Cuba was put into effect.

26 Oct.   A boarding party, mostly from the USS *Joseph P. Kennedy,* searched the SS *Marucla.*

30–31 Oct.   USS *Charles P. Cecil* flushed a Soviet Foxtrot submarine to the surface in conjunction with the Cuban Missile Crisis.

1963

Feb.–March   In February four Tu-95 Bears overflew USS *Forrestal* southeast of the Azores. Similar incidents occurred in March with USS *Constellation.*

4 March   USS *Hitchiti* was dead in the water when a Soviet trawler maneuvered, forcing it to take evasive action in the Pacific off Japan.

8 March   Soviets alleged two fishing vessels were endangered by the firing of rockets or flares by two U.S. Navy cruisers.

13 March U.S.S.R. charged that American warships had fired four nonexplosive shells near a Russian fishing vessel 70 miles off the Virginia Capes. The Russian charge was rejected.

17 March The Soviet cargo vessel *L'Gov* at Cuban port of Isabela La Sagua was attacked by a Cuban exile cutter. The State Department rejected the Soviet protest note on 3 April.

26–27 March	ss *Baku* at the Cuban port of Caibarien was fired on by a cutter as it prepared to depart with sugar. The Soviet protest note was rejected on 3 April.
31 March	Soviets alleged tanker *Balaklava* was buzzed by a U.S. plane.
5 May	uss *Luce* was dead in the water when a Soviet trawler maneuvered close by, causing the American warship to get under way in the western Atlantic.
6 May	The submarine uss *Croaker* was reportedly harassed by Soviet trawlers. The U.S. formally protested.
4 June	Aircraft from the uss *Ranger* intercepted six Tu-16 Badger aircraft as they approached the carrier steaming in the North Pacific east of Japan. Elsewhere in the Windward Passage, a Soviet tanker showing breakdown lights crossed the bow of uss *Caloosahatchee* and uss *Lindewald* during an unrep.
24 June	Trawler *Penhtep* harassed the uss *Fort Snelling* while *Trieste* searched for uss *Thresher* off Long Island. An informal protest was made by the U.S. military attaché.
27 June	The *Kuprin* (RT-401) allegedly passed close by *Fort Snelling* while *Trieste* searched for *Thresher*. An informal protest was made by the U.S. military attaché.
23 July	AGI *Repiter* maneuvered dangerously near the uss *Luce* in the western Atlantic.
24 Aug.	A Kotlin-class destroyer maneuvered dangerously around uss *Rehobeth* during hydrographic surveys in international waters off Kamchatka.
26 Sept.	A Soviet helicopter hovered dangerously close to the uss *Staten Island*.

1964

15 March	uss *William V. Pratt* expected the Soviet tanker *Budapest* to give way in an overtaking situation because the *Pratt* was in a formation in the Mediterranean. The Soviets alleged harassment and the Americans countered with an admission that the rules had been misinterpreted.
9 April	*Kronstadt* PC no. 193 reportedly maneuvered dangerously around uss *Chanticleer* in the Sea of Japan. Elsewhere the Soviet trawler *Polotsk*, after overtaking uss *Duxbury Bay*, passed close across her bow. The U.S. lodged a formal protest against U.S.S.R. In the Atlantic another Soviet trawler passed close to the uss *Lookout* in an overtaking situation.
10 April	A Riga-class frigate reportedly maneuvered dangerously around *Chanticleer*.
11 April	uss *Sioux*, while towing an Army crane in Gulf of Alaska, ran into a

Soviet fishing fleet and felt she had the right of way. In reality, the *Sioux* violated the Rules of the Road.

25 April U.S.S.R. alleged that a U.S. warship maneuvered dangerously near the merchant ship *Leonid Leonidev*.

28 May U.S.S.R. alleged that uss *Claud Jones* maneuvered dangerously and illuminated the bridge of the passenger ship *Turkmeniya*. The U.S. rejected the claim.

1 June U.S.S.R. alleged that uscg *Storis* maneuvered dangerously near the whaling ship *Dalni Vostok*.

18 June U.S.S.R. alleged that a U.S. Navy P-3 buzzed *Lena* in the Atlantic.

23–30 June U.S.S.R. alleged that U.S. aircraft buzzed *Pobeda* in the Atlantic.

27 June U.S.S.R. alleged that two U.S. aircraft buzzed the *Frunze* in the North Sea.

30 June uss *Daniel A. Joy* nearly collided with AGI *Randa* 450 miles east of New York. The U.S. formally protested.

8 July U.S.S.R. alleged that U.S. aircraft buzzed the steamer *Dubna*.

15 July ss *Sister Katingo* was fired on by Soviet patrol craft after departing Novorossisk without port clearance. The U.S. formally protested.

16 July U.S.S.R. alleged that U.S. aircraft buzzed the steamer *Dolinsk*.

18 July U.S.S.R. alleged that U.S. aircraft buzzed the *Kamenets-Podolsk* in the Sea of Japan.

18–21 July Soviet Cuba-bound passenger ship *Gruziy* was alleged to have been buzzed on 18–19 July and shouldered by uss *Kretchmer*. Additional Soviet notes protested other buzzings of ships on 18 June, 23–30 June in Atlantic, on 27 June and 16 July in the Mediterranean, and on 18 July in the Sea of Japan. The U.S. responded that it acted safely.

2 Aug. uss *Maddox* was attacked off the coast of North Vietnam.

8 Aug. The Soviet press claimed U.S. aircraft buzzed Soviet ships on more than 1,000 occasions and that its ships executed dangerous maneuvers in the presence of Soviet ships some twenty times.

10 Aug. An AGI reportedly passed dangerously close to ssbn uss *James Monroe* off Rota, Spain.

18 Aug. uss *Dash* hazarded the *Dubna* in the Windward Passage in the Caribbean. The Soviets alleged harassment. The *Dash* did violate the Rules of the Road. Meanwhile an AGI reportedly maneuvered dangerously around uss *John C. Calhoun* off Charleston, South Carolina.

6 Sept. uss *Burton Island* helicopter was harassed by Soviet helicopter from *Sibir*. The U.S. made a formal protest.

25–27 Sept. The U.S. alleged that three Soviet vessels, *Dzerzhinsky*, *Glazhyv*, and *Magomet*, maneuvered over this three-day period to hazard uss *Franklin*

D. Roosevelt flight operations in the Mediterranean. The U.S. protested on 24 February 1965.

1965

7 Jan. The U.S. claimed usns *Dutton*, operating in the eastern Atlantic, was harassed by *Vertikal*, which cut off a magnetometer cable. The Americans protested on 2 April.

10 Jan. U.S. claimed *Kotelnikov* interfered with unrep between *Saratoga* and *Neosho* in the Mediterranean. The Americans protested on 24 February.

14 Jan. The agi *Ampermetr* maneuvered dangerously by usns *Observation Island* to collect intelligence.

21–22 Jan. Tu-95 Bear passed dangerously over the uss *Coral Sea* in the Sea of Japan.

22 Jan. In the newspaper *Sovietskaya Rossiya* the Soviets claimed a U.S. plane simulated an attack on steamship *Nikolayev* near Cuba.

24 Jan. Soviets alleged uss *Joseph Strauss* harassed *Poronaysk* as the ship proceeded in the South China Sea to Haiphong. Soviets delivered the protest on 22 February.

26 Jan. Soviets alleged the destroyer uss *Ernest G. Small* maneuvered in dangerous proximity to tanker *Groky* in the South China Sea. Soviets protested on 22 February.

31 Jan. Soviets alleged *Poronaysk* harassed with weapons pointing by uss *Gurke*. Soviets protested on 22 February. U.S. would later refute the claim.

2 Feb. *Sovietskaya Rossiya* posted an article on buzzings, stating there had been an increase after a decrease following the 3 August 1964 note. The article said that hundreds of radiograms had been received from ships in January alone.

7 Feb. agi *Vertikal* reportedly harassed usns *Dutton*, which was conducting surveys to support the Polaris program in the North Atlantic.

16 Feb. U.S. alleged that *Zond*, operating with ssbn *Lafayette* west of Cadiz, crossed ahead six times and risked collision. The Americans protested on 2 April.

22 Feb. Soviets formally protested action of U.S. aircraft and ships in Atlantic, Pacific, and South China Sea. The charge appeared the next day in an upi article. The State Department received the Soviet note complaining of numerous buzzings and harassment by U.S. Navy ships. The U.S. would reject the note on 2 April.

24 Feb. Off the coast of California, *Arban* interfered with flight operations and underway replenishment of uss *Hornet* and uss *Ashtabula*. *Hornet*

	aborted approach to the oiler due to a risk of collision. The U.S. protested on 2 April.
2 March	Trawler *Sverdlovsy* alleged to maneuver dangerously amid uss *Courtney*, uss *Hartley*, and uss *Keywadin* exercises off Rhode Island. The U.S. protested on 2 April.
2 April	The U.S. submitted a follow-up protest note on *Dutton/Vertikal* incident, *Lafayette/Zond* incident, *Hornet/Arban* incident, *Courtney/Hartley Keywadin/Sverdlovsy* incident.
16 April	uss *Rigel* reported harassed by an AGI.
26 April	An unnamed USN SSBN was reportedly harassed by an AGI.
7 May	A Kotlin-class destroyer harassed destroyer uss *James E. Kyes* as the American warship tracked a Soviet submarine.
16 May	The Soviets alleged that a P-3 dropped sonobuoys dangerously close to a Kotlin-class destroyer.
4 June	The Soviets rejected the U.S. note of 2 April. Meanwhile a Tu-95 passed directly overhead of a task group transiting the Atlantic.
14–17 July	Two Tu-95s passed several times overhead in low altitude over the USNS *Vandenberg* while the American ship conducted oceanographic operations in Bering Sea.
7 Aug.	The Soviets protested the "piratical firing on the Soviet merchant ship *Polotsk*" by an USAF plane.
31 Aug.	A Soviet destroyer maneuvered dangerously near hydrographic ship *San Pablo*.
2 Sept.	Same Soviet DDGS again endangered the *San Pablo*. The next day (3 Sept.) this DDGS interfered with a boat transfer between the *San Pablo* and the uss *Papago*. ss *Karl Lynney* failed to yield to uss *Franklin D. Roosevelt* in the Mediterranean.
2 Sept.–26 Oct.	Tu-16 Badgers passed over uss *Staten Island* conducting oceanographic operations in the Arctic
6 Sept.	DLGM 239 maneuvered close to USCG *Northwind* in the Barents Sea. According to a protest dated 12 April 1966, the Soviets charged the *Northwind* with taking samplings from part of the continental shelf of the U.S.S.R., therefore violating sovereign rights of the nation.
7–8 Sept.	AGI *Deviator* exchanged searchlight illumination with *San Pablo*.
8 Sept.	Soviet DD 036 circled the USNS *Gibbs* in the Atlantic and raked the ship with searchlights for ten minutes.
13 Sept.	The AGS *Kompas* maneuvered dangerously near the *San Pablo*.
17 Sept.	Soviets protested a U.S. Navy helicopter penetrating Soviet airspace near Burton Island. The U.S. believed the penetration was inadvertent.
19 Sept.	The AGI *Lotsman* maneuvered close to uss *Corry* in the Black Sea.

20 Sept.	Two Tu-16s passed "low" overhead USS *Corry* and USS *Luce* conducting operations in the Black Sea.
29 Sept.	One Tu-16 buzzed the USS *Little Rock* in the Norwegian Sea.
24 Oct.	AGI *Protraktor* failed to yield to USS *Safeguard* at Yankee Station off Vietnam.
13 Nov.	USS *Banner* was circled three times by a Krupnyy-class DDGS claiming it had entered Soviet waters at the Peter the Great Bay. The Soviets went to General Quarters and manned the gun mounts.
14 Nov.	Soviets claimed *Dzhuzeppe Garibaldi* was buzzed.
16 Nov.	One Tu-16 passed dangerously overhead of the *Banner* in the Sea of Japan.
18 Nov.	U.S. submitted note protesting harassment of *Banner* and nonrecognition of Soviet territorial claim. Also the Soviets claimed helicopters and aircraft buzzed *Ostrogozhsk*.
22 Nov.	*Leninsky Pioner* off Yankee Station was allegedly buzzed for three hours and was again harassed on the following day.
5–6 Dec.	*Leninsky Pioner* reportedly harassed by a carrier and two destroyers. On the next day the buzzing was repeated. U.S. claimed the Soviet came close to USS *Bainbridge,* failed to give way to USS *Kitty Hawk*. Meanwhile, a Tu-16 passed overhead of USS *America* near the Azores.
8 Dec.	*Gidrofon* harassed the USS *Molala* on Yankee Station. The USS *Kitty Hawk* altered course to avoid AGI while conducting flight operations.
12 Dec.	The U.S. claimed the *Gidrofon* attempted to close on USS *Kitty Hawk*.
14 Dec.	RB-57 crashed in the Black Sea with a loss of two crewmen. In the South China Sea, the *Gidrofon* interfered with a U.S. Navy surface action group conducting an ASW exercise according to a U.S. protest note issued 18 January 1966. A Soviet note on 17 March 1966 rejected U.S. claims against *Gidrofon* and stated that the AGI was harassed.
15 Dec.	U.S.S.R. protested alleged buzzing of Soviet ships by U.S. aircraft off Vietnam.
16 Dec.	The Soviets submitted another protest note on buzzings, especially off Vietnam. The incidents allegedly occurred on 14, 18, and 19 November. The Americans rejected the note.
17 Dec.	Soviets rejected *Banner* protest. On 22 December U.S. again rejected Soviet territorial claim.
21 Dec.	AGI *Gidrofon* reportedly attempted to cross carrier's bow and jeopardized *Molala* on Yankee Station.

1966

4 Jan.   A Soviet trawler allegedly tried to cross between two U.S. ships in the South China Sea. Meanwhile, in the Liguran Sea, the ss *Uryupsky* failed to give way to uss *America* until the carrier sounded danger signal at 1200 yards.

7 Jan.   AGI *Gidrofon* maneuvered to hazard flight operations on uss *Enterprise*. U.S. protested on 18 January.

9 Jan.   uss *Hornet* was approached by Soviet DD 045, which interfered with her flight operations. uss *Fletcher* shouldered the Soviet warship away. The U.S. protested on 18 January. The Soviets protested two days later. The U.S. rejected this protest on 25 February.

17 Jan.   uss *Lafayette* had to give way to avoid hitting AGI *Lotsman* in the Atlantic.

18 Jan.   U. Alexis Johnson called Ambassador Dobrynin to protest Soviet harassment of U.S. vessels in South China Sea.

28 Jan.   AT&T complained to DoD of its cable loss in northeastern Pacific. They suspected the Soviet fishing flight, citing them as uncooperative in contrast with the Soviet fishing fleet in the northwestern Atlantic.

1 Feb.   Soviet fishing trawler reportedly passed close to uss *Yosemite* in the eastern Atlantic.

6 Feb.   uss *Edson* passed close by the ss *Grodekovo* in the Pacific.

20 Feb.   SSBN uss *John Marshall* was confronted by the AGI *Linza* in the Atlantic.

2 March   SSBN uss *John Adams* was confronted by the AGI *Linza* in the Atlantic.

26 March   The Soviets alleged that USAF fighters forced Il-14 passenger plane to dive over Bering Sea on this date. Soviets protested on 12 April.

3 April   AGI *Ekholot* passed closely by the uss *Ingraham* in the Atlantic.

12 April   The Soviets orally protested Il-14 case. The Americans responded on 4 May that the Soviets had no basis for the protest.

23 April   F/V *Kilchan* failed to give way to uss *Perseus* off the coast of Oregon.

10 May   F/V *Kapitan* failed to yield to uss *Hawkins* in the Atlantic.

11 May   uss *Banner* was shouldered by an AGI *Oka* in the Sea of Japan.

13 May   The ss *Makhachkala* failed to give way to uss *Terrell County* in the Pacific.

14 May   The *Groznyy* passed close to *Sea Robin* as the latter attempted torpedo retrieval in the Mediterranean.

23 May   Soviet DD 303 moved to force uss *Waccamaw* into the shoals during a meeting situation in the Dardanelles.

24 May   One Tu-95 passed directly overhead as uss *Randolph* conducted ASW operations in the North Sea. The next day a Tu-16 repeated the action.

26 May   AGI *Ekholot* anchored in Charleston channel with running lights on reportedly harassed uss *Betelgeuse*.

24 June	The USS *Banner-Anemometr* collision. On 25 June Ambassador Thompson briefed Ambassador Dobrynin. The U.S. sent a protest note. The Soviets responded two days later with a counterprotest note.
7 July	Soviets claimed that fragments landed near three ships moored near Haiphong and large metal objects fell around another ship anchored in Halong Bay.
13 July	SS *Sergy Yesenin* crowded USS *Furse* in Denmark channel.
25 July	Soviets alleged USS *Radford* and later USS *Walker* and Soviet DD 066 nearly collided in Sea of Japan. Meanwhile the Soviets claimed the freighter *Pankara* was subjected to photo runs.
30 July	USS *Guadalupe* allegedly twice approached *Izmeritel* in the Sea of Japan and created collision situations. The Soviets protested on 16 September.
1 Aug.	AGI GS-43 maintained a collision course with USS *William M. Wood* until a fishing boat interfered. Soviets alleged U.S. aircraft buzzed the merchant ship *Ingur* in the Gulf of Tonkin and four destroyers maneuvered and demanded her to stop. The Soviets protested on 5 August.
2 Aug.	Soviets stated that an air attack on Haiphong resulted in hits on the merchant ship *Medyn*. They protested on 5 August.
3–4 Aug.	Two U.S. aircraft buzzed the Soviet Black Sea fleet in the Eastern Mediterranean.
5 Aug.	*Gidrofon* allegedly conducted four harassing incidents with USS *Deliver* on Yankee Station while *Deliver* shouldered for a carrier.
21 Aug–9 Sept.	Tu-16 aircraft overflew USS *Atka* forty times. Sometimes there were up to fifteen passes. Twice the aircraft had the bomb bay open and once two red flares were dropped astern of the American oceanographic ship.
26 Aug.	USS *Conserver* forced *Gidrofon* away to avoid aircraft carrier.
30 Aug.	USS *Carpenter* allegedly maneuvered dangerously in the presence of Soviet hull no. 10 in the Pacific. The Soviets protested on 16 September.
1 Sept.	Soviets accused USS *McMorris* of failing to use running lights when approaching Soviet DD vessel hull No. 10. The Soviets protested on 16 September.
9–10 Sept.	A Tu-16 and an Il-28 passed nearby and circled USS *Corry* in the Black Sea.
17 Sept.	The merchant vessel *Kransnyy-Oktyabr* cut across the bows of USS *Neches* and USS *Beale* during an unrep.
20 Sept.	A Tu-16 passed directly overhead of the USNS *Vandenburg*.
8 Oct.	USS *Lynch* and USS *Sands* in the Norwegian Sea were approached by GN NC 7 which approached within twenty feet of *Lynch*'s stern. U.S. protested on 2 December.

27 Oct.	AGI *Ismeritel* reportedly harassed USS *Perch* near Guam.
10 Nov.	Kotlin-class destroyer no. 296 used a searchlight on each ship in TF-61 in the Mediterranean.
22–23 Nov.	*Kosmonaut Fedkistov* allegedly harassed the *Aeolus* while conducting underwater cable-repair operations.
6 Dec.	AGI *Teodolit* was accused of violating U.S. waters off Vieques Island and harassing USS *John W. Weeks*. U.S. protested on 10 January 1967.
10 Dec.	*Weeks* reportedly again suffered harassment from *Teodolit*.

1967

2 March	USCG *Storis* seized a Soviet fishing vessel off Alaska.
13 April	Soviets alleged five U.S. destroyers fired shells near the tanker *Dzhordano Bruno* in the Mediterranean Sea.
10 May	USS *Walker* and *Besslednyy* collided in the Sea of Japan.
11 May	USS *Walker* and Soviet destroyer DDGS 025 collided in the Sea of Japan.
30 May	Soviet Navy commissioned its first Yankee-class ballistic-missile submarine.
2 June	At the port of Cam Pha, the Soviet cargo ship *Turkestan* was hit by a bomb, killing a crewman. The U.S. later conceded possible responsibility.
6 June	War began in the Middle East, causing the two superpowers to increase naval forces in the region.
8 June	Soviet PC-160 forced USS *America* to turn in the Mediterranean. There was no indication that either ship was *in extremis*.
26 June	The Soviets claimed that U.S. aircraft hit the freighter *Frunze* at Haiphong. Again the U.S. conceded possible responsibility.
9 Aug.	Soviets alleged that USS *Davis* cut close to Soviet submarine 559 and tender while operating in the Mediterranean. The Soviets protested on 22 August and the U.S. eventually rejected the note.
17 Dec.	Collision between USS *Abnaki*/AGI *Gidrofon* at Yankee Station.

1968

4 Jan.	The Soviets claimed that a bomb nearly hit the *Pereyaslavi-Zalessky* and caused extensive damage during an American air attack on Haiphong.
23 Jan.	North Korea seized the USS *Pueblo*. The Soviet AGI *Gidrolog* blocked the path of the responding USS *Enterprise*.
31 Jan.	USS *Rowan*/*Kapitan Vislobokov* collision in the Sea of Japan. The Soviets protested the next day. The U.S. counterprotested on 4 February.
31 March	President Johnson ended the bombing campaign over North Vietnam.
16 April	The U.S. approached the U.S.S.R. on safety at sea talks.

25 May	A Tu-16 Badger aircraft crashed near USS *Essex* operating in the North Sea.
1 July	The Soviets forced down a chartered U.S. Seaboard DC-8 near the Kuriles.

1969

9–10 April	USS *Jack* met AGI *Lotlin* off Puerto Rico and was subjected to harassment.
14 April	North Korean fighters shot down a Navy EC-121M off the east coast of North Korea with a loss of a crew of thirty-one.
12 May	The Soviets complained in a note that U.S. planes buzzed Soviet aircraft in several instances during the month of April. The U.S. rejected this note on 9 June.
31 July	AGI *Girorulevoi* reportedly harassed SSBN USS *Sam Houston* in the Irish Sea.
25 Aug.	The Russian ship *Chuminkan* removed two U.S. research buoys in the North Pacific Ocean. U.S. protested on 27 October.
9 Sept.	AGI *Teodolit* reportedly crossed ahead of SSBN USS *Sam Rayburn* off Charleston. U.S. would protest on 27 October.
1 Dec.	On this date the Soviets responded to the buoy theft and *Teodolit* protests and claimed USS *Bronstein* maneuvered to hazard Soviet DD and that USS *Little Rock* maneuvered ahead of Soviet CG.
9 Dec.	U.S. protested to Soviets on Sea of Japan buzzings that occurred in the Sea of Japan in June and November.
12–13 Dec.	U.S. claimed *Kursograf* penetrated territorial waters off Guam. The U.S. protested on 11 February 1970.

1970

11 April	Soviet Navy units were deployed to conduct worldwide Okean naval exercises.
2–5 July	USS *Wasp* buzzed by Soviet aircraft during Norwegian Sea operations.
3 Aug.	AGI *Laptev* reportedly interfered with missile-recovery operations off Florida.
24 Aug.	AGI *Laptev* reportedly interfered with a U.S. submarine off Block Island.
15 Oct.	Aeroflot flight was hijacked to Turkey.
21 Oct.	U.S. Army Beechcraft carrying Army flag officers landed in Soviet Armenia.
9 Nov.	HMS *Ark Royal* collided with a Soviet destroyer.
10 Nov.	Soviets agreed to host safety at sea talks after releasing Army flag officers.
17 Nov.	SSBN USS *Sam Houston* was reportedly harassed by the AGI *Kurs* off the coast of Spain. The U.S. protested on 6 April 1971.
28 Nov.	U.S. ships and aircraft closely observed the Soviet ships and helicopters recover rocket nose cones in the northern Pacific. The Soviets subsequently protested the Americans' close maneuvering. The U.S. rejected the note.

1971

19 Feb.　Kissinger signed NSSM 119 to form a study to examine the U.S. positions with regards to incidents at sea.

13 April　The Soviets presented a note asking for adequate warning times for U.S. exercises having potential danger to shipping.

4 May　USAF planes allegedly staged mock attacks on Soviet warships in the Aegean.

6 May　Soviet tug *Diomid* rammed the USS *Hanson* in the Sea of Japan.

7 May　USN aircraft allegedly simulated an attack on a Soviet warship south of Crete.

10 May　Soviets charged a U.S. frigate conducted dangerous maneuvers in the vicinity of one of its ships in the Gulf of Tonkin on this date.

26 May　Kissinger signed NSDM 110, spelling out the U.S. positions for forthcoming incidents at sea talks.

14 June　*Izvestia* reported that Defense Minister Marshal Grechko was embarked on the *Dzerzhinsky* the previous weekend and was constantly followed and harassed by American warships.

9 Sept.　USS *Fox* entered the Sea of Okhotsk. The Soviets claimed the American ship penetrated territorial waters on 10 September.

12–22 Oct.　Incidents at Sea talks in Moscow.

11 Nov.　Kissinger signed NSSM 140 to reconvene a study group to examine the U.S. incidents at sea positions.

1972

11 Feb.　Kissinger signed NSDM 150, finalizing the U.S. positions on incidents at sea.

23 March　Merchant ship *Pioner Volkov* failed to yield to oncoming USS *Robert A. Owens* and USS *Seattle*, forcing an emergency breakaway in the Aegean Sea. U.S. protested on 29 April.

31 March　North Vietnam launched its spring offensive.

3–17 May　Second round of Incidents at Sea talks held in Washington.

8 May　U.S. conducted mining offensive against North Vietnam.

25 May　Secretary Warner and Admiral Gorshkov signed the INCSEA Agreement.

9–10 July　On two successive nights, Soviet warships anchored east of Crete illuminated overflying A-6C aircraft from the USS *Franklin D. Roosevelt*.

11 July　A USS *Butte* helicopter conducting surveillance of Soviet ships at the Kithira anchorage in the Mediterranean had two flares shot at it during its final pass. Meanwhile, USS *Stribling* reportedly had her bridge illuminated by the Soviet warships anchored east of Crete.

4–9 Oct.	U.S. Navy Silver Fox operations in the Black Sea.
18 Oct.	Soviet helicopter attempted to disrupt U.S. efforts to recover Soviet reentry vehicle parts.
13–18 Nov.	Follow-up INCSEA talks were conducted in Moscow.

1973

6 Feb.	Silver Fox Operations in the Black Sea.
8–14 May	USS *Josephus Daniels* and USS *Mitscher* conducted Silver Fox operations in the Black Sea and reported some interactions with Soviet naval units having some incident at sea significance.
14–22 May	First annual INCSEA review. The U.S. recorded twenty-four Soviet violations of the agreement over the previous year. The Soviets brought up three U.S. violations. At the conclusion of the first annual INCSEA review, a protocol was signed to expand the INCSEA accord to cover merchant ships.
23 June	U.S. Navy A-7 aircraft allegedly buzzed a Soviet destroyer in the Eastern Mediterranean. Admiral Sergeyev complained to the U.S. defense attaché on 3 July.
4 Oct.	An F-4 Phantom from USS *John F. Kennedy* nicked a Tu-16 Badger over the Norwegian Sea and an aircraft from USS *Midway* maneuvered closely to Soviet aircraft over the Pacific. A Soviet diplomatic note was received on 13 October.
6 Oct.	War broke out in the Middle East.
9 Oct.	USS *Guadalcanal* detected Soviet fire-control radar tracking her helicopters from nearby Soviet destroyers.
10 Oct.	USS *Little Rock* noted a Kashin-class destroyer no. 177 had trained a mount on her. The same destroyer locked on fire-control radars the next day.
11 Oct.	The patrol gunboat USS *Douglas* reported a *Sverdlov*-class cruiser and a Mod Kotlin-class destroyer trained their guns on her as she surveyed the Kithira anchorage.
18 Oct.	USS *Independence* observed a Kotlin-class destroyer train fore and aft guns at her. *Independence* notified the Soviet of its INCSEA violation by flashing light and the incident was brought to the attention of the Soviet naval attaché the next day.
24 Oct.	Eighty Soviet warships were in the Mediterranean.
25 Oct.	The U.S. raised its defensive posture to DEFCON Three.
31 Oct.	Soviet Mediterranean fleet rose to ninety-five vessels.
3 Nov.	Naval forces in the Mediterranean began to disperse.

4 Dec.	In the Gulf of Aden a Petya-class patrol frigate passed ahead of the oiler uss *Ashtabula* and then trained its gunmount on her. The Soviet naval attaché later rebuffed the complaint.
27 Dec.	Ambassador Dobrynin presented Kissinger with a note alleging 100 cases of U.S. aircraft near Aeroflot aircraft over the Mediterranean from 10 October to 19 November and a dangerous approach of uss *Kitty Hawk* F-4 fighters on Soviet aircraft near Wake Island.

1974

16 Jan.	While observing Soviet missile instrumentation ships, uss *Claud Jones* allegedly ignored a Soviet signal and passed through a Soviet ship formation in the Pacific.
17 Jan.	Silver Fox operations in the Black Sea.
22 Jan.	*Claud Jones* reported the *Chazma* maneuvered into an *in extremis* situation.
14–21 May	Second annual INCSEA review was held in Moscow. Americans claimed seven Soviet violations of the accord, and the Soviets claimed five U.S. violations, four of which were aircraft-related.
22 May	F-8s from uss *Oriskany* made threatening approaches on a Tu-95 Bear aircraft east of the Marianas.
31 May	Two Krivak-class frigates operating near Guantanamo, Cuba, trained their gunmounts on uss *Forrest Sherman*.
16 July	Both a Kotlin-class destroyer and the uss *Preserver* in the Mediterranean took turns illuminating the other with searchlights, both in violation of the INCSEA accord.
12 Sept.	Soviet warships cruised past Hawaii.
24 Sept.	Soviet naval force in Cuba represented the twelfth visit since 1969.
4–11 Oct.	U.S. Navy ships entered the Baltic on Freedom of Navigation patrol.
24 Nov.	The Soviet vessel *Sevan* executed a maneuver violating a multinational formation in the Arabian Sea.

1975

21 Feb.	A Petya-class frigate in the Arabian Sea trained its gunmount on the uss *Hewes* and its helicopter. The American investigation found that the *Hewes* failed to use INCSEA signals.
10 March	During another Silver Fox excursion into the Black Sea, both uss *Richmond K. Turner* and a Kashin-class destroyer took turns illuminating the other with searchlights, both in violation of the INCSEA accord.
16–23 May	Third annual INCSEA review was held in Washington, D.C. The U.S.

claimed five Soviet violations and the Soviets noted two American violations.

11 June   A P-3 Orion buzzed the *Professor Zubov,* prompting a Soviet protest.

26 Aug.   A helicopter from a Kresta-class cruiser reportedly interfered twice with flight operations from the USS *Nimitz* in the Mediterranean. The Soviets would counter that a helicopter was not aloft at the time indicated.

12 Sept.   Americans protested to the Soviets that a Kresta-class cruiser trained its missile launchers on USS *John F. Kennedy.*

14 Oct.   USS *Belknap* and USS *Sarsfield* entered the Black Sea for Silver Fox operations. A Kashin-class destroyer illuminated USS *Belknap*'s bridge. The U.S. protested.

2 Nov.   The Soviets protested USS *Dale* movements near the *Matsesta.* The U.S. Navy argued that *Dale* maneuvered correctly. Two days later the Soviets claimed USS *Turner Joy* maneuvered incorrectly in the presence of Soviet DD 221. Again the U.S. would find no fault with its ship.

10–20 Nov. NATO Ocean Safari exercise drew Soviet attention.

25 Nov.   The Soviets protested the movements of the USS *Edson* near the hydrographic vessel *Anadir.* U.S. Navy found no fault with *Edson*'s maneuvers.

1976

18 April   Silver Fox operations in the Black Sea.

23–31 May Fourth annual INCSEA review held in Moscow. The delegations reviewed three American and four Soviet protests along with several instances of violations of "the spirit of the agreement."

June–July Initial operations of *Kiev* drew close American surveillance and numerous charges of INCSEA violations by both sides.

3 June   The USS *McCandless* observed a *Sverdlov*-class cruiser training its aft mount at her. The Soviets would counter that the crew was watching a movie on the fantail.

8 June   The Soviets protested after an RF-8G off the USS *America* buzzed a Kara-class cruiser with Fleet Admiral Gorshkov embarked. The U.S. countered it was not an incident.

14 June   A helicopter from USS *Voge* reported being tracked by a gunmount on Kynda-class cruiser no. 847. On 16, 17, 20, 22, and 23 June, this ship tracked aircraft off the USS *America* and helicopters off the *Voge* and USS *Koelsch.*

15 June   A helicopter off *Koelsch* reported a gunmount tracking incident with Kashin-class destroyer no. 191.

19 June	An S-3A off *America* reportedly was tracked by a gunmount on a *Sverdlov*-class cruiser.
22 June	An A-7E off *America* reportedly was tracked by a gunmount on a Kashin-class destroyer.
14 July	An EA-6B off *America* reportedly was tracked by a gunmount on a Riga-class frigate.
19 July	A P-3 buzzed a Soviet ship in the Mediterranean. The U.S. Navy countered the Soviet complaint, stating the aircraft used care and prudence on each pass. The Soviets would also complain of the actions of the USS *Harry E. Yarnell*, which was observing the *Kiev*.
26 July	The USS *Josephus Daniels* reported she was shouldered by Krivak-class frigates no. 219 and 224 as she attempted to conduct a surveillance approach on the *Kiev*. Krivak no. 224 reportedly harassed the *Josephus Daniels* again on 29 and 30 July. The Soviets protested the movements of the American cruiser on 30 July.
14 Aug.	The USS *Ready* claimed that a Riga-class frigate anchored at Kithira aimed its guns at her.
28 Aug.	A partially submerged Echo II collided with the USS *Voge* in the Aegean Sea. At the Kithira anchorage, the helicopter off the *Koelsch* was reportedly tracked by a Kashin-class destroyer.
17 Sept.	A Petya II–class patrol frigate, moored at Hammamet, aimed its gunmount and fire-control radar at a passing P-3.
28 Sept.	The USS *Elmer Montgomery* reported gunmounts on a *Sverdlov*-class cruiser *Zhdanov* were trained at her while both ships were anchored at Kithira.
28 Sept.–12 Oct.	U.S. Navy conducted Freedom of Navigation exercises in the Baltic Sea.
19 Oct.	Silver Fox operations in the Black Sea.
3 Dec.	A Don-class submarine tender anchored at the Sollum anchorage, serving as a flagship for the Soviet Mediterranean fleet commander, reportedly trained a gunmount at the passing USS *Sarsfield*.
11 Dec.	Kashin-class destroyer no. 166 maneuvered in a hazardous manner amid the USS *Franklin D. Roosevelt* battle group.

1977

19 Jan.	In the Mediterranean, a P-3 reported a Kynda-class cruiser tracked it with her aft gunmounts.
7 March	Two U.S. Navy ships entered the Black Sea for five-day FON cruise.
9–17 May	Fifth annual INCSEA review held in Washington. The Americans brought

up twenty-four Soviet violations. The Soviets alleged two American violations.

22 May   Kashin-class destroyer no. 166 reportedly trained its gunmounts and fire-control radars on a P-3 aircraft during three photo-reconnaissance passes.

31 May   The U.S. reported that at the Kithira anchorage Riga-class frigate no. 684 tracked a P-3 aircraft with its forward gunmount. Meanwhile Kashin no. 166 tracked another P-3 aircraft with its gunmounts in the Eastern Mediterranean.

27 June   Two U.S. Navy ships entered the Black Sea for a five-day FON cruise.

2–23 July A Soviet task force operated in the Gulf of Mexico and called in Cuba.

10 July   An anchored Petya-class frigate at Hammamet reportedly tracked a P-3 aircraft with its gunmounts.

24 July   A Petya-class frigate tracked a P-3 aircraft with its gunmounts on two occasions.

26 July   Near the Kithira anchorage, a Mayak-class AGI maneuvered dangerously in the presence of USS *Wainwright,* forcing the American cruiser to reverse engines to avoid collision.

3 Aug.   A Mirka II–class frigate at Hammamet reportedly tracked a P-3 aircraft with its gunmounts.

6 Sept.   The U.S. claimed Krivak-class frigate no. 196 in the central Mediterranean tracked a helicopter from the USS *Connole* with its gunmounts and fire-control radar.

7 Sept.   Silver Fox operations in the Black Sea.

12 Sept. The same Krivak frigate (no. 196) reportedly tracked an A-7 from the USS *Saratoga* with its gunmounts and fire-control radars.

15–16   Don-class submarine tender no. 933 and Kotlin-class destroyer no. 375
Sept.   at the Kithira anchorage tracked P-3 aircraft with their gunmounts and fire-control radars.

17 Oct.   The U.S. reported Krivak-class frigate no. 245 in the Western Mediterranean tracked a P-3 aircraft with its gunmounts and fire-control radars.

31 Oct.– A Kildin-class destroyer reportedly tracked a P-3 aircraft with its
1 Nov.   gunmounts on three separate occasions. Meanwhile, the Soviets claimed that U.S. Navy patrol aircraft dropped sonobuoys near one of its ships on each of these days.

15 Nov.   Silver Fox operations in the Black Sea.

6 Dec.   In the Mediterranean, a Riga-class frigate maneuvered to hazard collision with the USS *Albany,* forcing the American cruiser to maneuver radically.

1978

25 Feb. U.S. reported a Mirka-class frigate in the Gulf of Hammamet tracked a P-3 with its gunmounts.

18 March Reportedly in the Straits of Florida, Kashin-class destroyer *Ognevoy* trained its gunmounts on uss *Harold J. Ellison* for periods of three and seven minutes.

20 March The U.S. Navy claimed a Kashin-class destroyer east of Kithira trained its forward surface-to-air missile launcher at uss *California* with missiles on the rails for a period of two minutes.

26 March The U.S. claimed the *Kiev* tracked a P-3 aircraft with its gunmounts off the coast of Algeria.

29 March Soviets stated that uss *South Carolina* performed dangerous maneuvers near two Soviet ships engaged in underway replenishment.

30 March A Mirka II–class frigate at the Hammamet anchorage reportedly tracked a P-3 aircraft with its gunmounts. Meanwhile the Soviets claim the uss *South Carolina* passed dangerously close to the *Moskva*.

2 April A Krivak-class frigate in the eastern Mediterranean tracked a P-3 aircraft with its gunmounts.

13 April A Krivak-class frigate near the Greek Kithira anchorage tracked a P-3 aircraft with its gunmounts.

29 May– Sixth annual incsea review was held in Moscow.
7 June

12 June The Soviets protested a P-3 dropped a sonobuoy 3,600 yards from a Soviet ship in the Mediterranean. The Americans countered that there was no hazard to shipping.

17 June A P-3 reported a Kashin-class destroyer no. 264 in the central Mediterranean trained its gunmounts on this day and the next.

18 June The Soviets complained of another P-3 sonobuoy drop. The Americans claimed no P-3 was in the vicinity.

18–25   uss *Stein*, uss *Fox*, and uss *Hassayampa* operated in the Sea of Okhotsk.
June

23 June Krivak-class frigate no. 602 reportedly maneuvered to hazard uss *Stein*.

24 June uss *Harry E. Yarnell* and uss *Charles F. Adams* entered the Black Sea.

27 June The *Yarnell* reported the agi *Bakan* performed antagonistic maneuvers and interfered with a small boat transfer on the following day.

30 June A S-2A reported a Mirka II–class frigate no. 691 in the Gulf of Hammamet area tracked it with her aft gunmount during its last three photo-reconnaissance passes.

11 July In the Mediterranean, the uss *Harry E. Yarnell* noted the Mirka II–class frigate no. 694 trained its gunmounts at her.

24 Aug.   Mirka II–class frigate no. 823 at Hammamet reportedly tracked a passing P-3 aircraft with her gunmounts.

29 Aug.   A P-3 aircraft reported a Kynda-class cruiser no. 120 at Hammamet tracked it with her upper aft gunmount.

4–19 Sept. NATO Northern Wedding Exercises involved over 200 ships.

21 Sept.   U.S. conducted FON operations in the Baltic Sea.

9–10 Oct. On successive days, Kashin-class destroyer no. 753 at Hammamet reportedly tracked a passing P-3 with her gunmounts.

28 Oct.   Over Hammamet, a P-3 reportedly was tracked by the aft gunmounts of Mirka II–class frigate no. 823.

31 Oct.   An S-3 off the USS *Saratoga* reported being tracked by a gunmount on a Petya I–class frigate at the Hammamet anchorage area.

8–10 Dec. On seven occasions in a three-day span, Soviet ships anchored at Hammamet aimed their gunmounts at passing P-3 aircraft.

1979

10 Jan.   Silver Fox operations in the Black Sea.

6–25   Soviet ships call on Da Nang and Cam Ranh Bay, Vietnam.
March

9 March   Kotlin-class destroyer no. 779 in the Arabian Sea reportedly trained her forward gunmount on the USS *Donald B. Beary*.

19 March   In the Gulf of Aden, the logistics ship *Boyevoy* reportedly maneuvered to risk collision with the USNS *Navasota*.

27 March   Kotlin no. 779 aimed its guns at the USS *Constellation* in the Arabian Sea.

18 April   The USS *Sumter* reportedly maneuvered to risk collision with a Soviet Charlie I–class submarine in the Barents Sea.

10 May   In the Barents Sea, the USS *Sumter* reported a Natya-class patrol frigate, no. 820, maneuvered to risk collision.

15 May   Two Il-38 May maritime patrol aircraft interfered with the flight pattern of U.S. Navy aircraft attempting to land on the USS *Midway* in the Arabian Sea.

21–29   Seventh annual INCSEA review was held in Washington.
May

23 May   A P-3 aircraft reported it was tracked by the forward and aft gunmounts of Mirka-class frigate no. 828 located at the Gulf of Hammamet. Two days later this frigate and a sister ship, no. 816, swung their forward mounts at a passing S-3 aircraft.

14 June   In the Indian Ocean, a P-3 aircraft reported it was tracked by a gunmount on the *Ivan Rogov*.

27 June	In the central Mediterranean, Mirka II–class frigate no. 816 reportedly fired a flare in front of a passing P-3 aircraft.
29 June	In the Gulf of Hammamet, Mirka II–class frigate no. 828 slew her forward gun in the direction of a passing S-3 off the uss *Dwight D. Eisenhower*.
13 July	Kara-class cruiser no. 736 reportedly fired two flares at a P-3 aircraft on patrol in the central Mediterranean.
30 July	In the eastern Mediterranean, Krivak-class frigate no. 801, while displaying the special signal for testing gun systems, slew both gunmounts at the uss *Caron*.
4 Sept.	Off Crete, Mirka I–class frigate no. 816, while displaying the special signal for testing gun systems, trained both gunmounts at uss *Independence*.
15–20 Sept.	A U.S. Navy ship entered the Sea of Okhotsk.
24 Sept.–5 Oct.	NATO Ocean Safari exercise involved 70 ships and 200 aircraft.
6 Oct.	Soviet destroyer no. 751 reported an S-3 from uss *Independence* flew out of the sun to conduct a simulated attack. The Americans could not identify a culpable aircraft.
10 Oct.	In the Mediterranean, the Soviets stated that Krivak-class frigate no. 809 was subjected to carrier-based aircraft conducting simulated attacks. The Americans countered that this frigate tracked passing aircraft with her gunmounts.
12 Oct.	Two U.S. Navy ships entered the Black Sea.
15 Oct.	One of those ships, the uss *Caron*, reported that a Mod Kildin-class destroyer slew her gunmount at *Caron*'s helicopter.
18 Nov.	In the Arabian Sea, Krivak-class frigate no. 809 reported she was shouldered by the uss *Julius A. Furer* after she had penetrated the *Midway* battle group formation.
19 Nov.	An Aeroflot aircraft reportedly was joined up by U.S. fighter aircraft on four occasions to as close as 37 meters over the Arabian Sea.
5 Dec.	The Soviets alleged that an F-14 from the uss *Kitty Hawk* flew under a Soviet aircraft at a distance of five meters. In a note passed in April 1980, an additional 112 close approaches were recorded by the Soviets from 12 December through 5 March 1980.

1980

| 6 Jan. | Two Hormone helicopters from *Moskva* passed over the starboard side of the uss *Forrestal* while the American aircraft carrier conducted flight-recovery operations in the Tyrrhenian Sea. |

22 Jan.	In the eastern Mediterranean, the AGI *Kildin* passed ahead of the USS *Concord*, USS *Savannah*, and USS *Forrestal* as the American ships prepared to conduct an unrep.
6 Feb.	Two U.S. Navy ships entered the Black Sea.
13 Feb.	In the Sea of Japan, the Krivak-class frigate *Razyashiy* reportedly tracked a passing P-3 aircraft with its aft gunmount.
17 Feb.	Off Georgia, AGI no. 514 reportedly maneuvered in the path of the SSBN USS *Daniel Boone*.
13 March	Over the Sea of Japan, an Il-38 May flew into a P-3 Orion forcing the U.S. plane to maneuver to avoid a midair collision. The P-3 was monitoring a sonobuoy pattern.
23 March	Off Georgia, SSBN USS *John C. Calhoun* maneuvered to avoid AGI no. 506.
29 March	A Soviet Yankee-class SSBN had to maneuver to avoid USS *Harlan County* in the Barents Sea. The Americans responded that there was no impropriety.
11–18 April	The USS *Harlan County* was harassed on six occasions during this period by Soviet ships and aircraft. The Soviets reprimanded the offending commanding officers.
18 April	In the Baltic, a Soviet frigate rammed a Danish minelayer monitoring a Warsaw Pact exercise.
20 April	*Kiev* reported that USS *Caron* maneuvered in a hazardous manner.
12–16 May	Eighth annual INCSEA review was held in Moscow.
2 June	Silver Fox operations in the Black Sea.
5 June	The U.S. claimed a Natya-class patrol frigate trained its gun on a P-3 Orion over the Tsushima Strait.
12 June	AGI stationed off Groton, Connecticut, to observe sea trials of USS *Ohio*.
29 July	The Soviets claimed repeated passes on *Chirikov* and *Rybachiy* by P-3 Orion aircraft. The Americans agreed that the P-3 overflights were excessive.
24 Aug.	Krivak-class frigate no. 678 reportedly fired a flare at a passing P-3 Orion aircraft over the East China Sea.
28–30 Aug.	In the Sea of Japan, the U.S. reported Krivak-class frigate no. 646 trained its guns each day on passing P-3 Orion aircraft. On 29 August, the *Minsk* was alleged to also have trained its guns.
2 Sept.	The *Minsk* fired a flare at a helicopter from the USS *Hewitt*.
10–24 Sept.	Soviets monitored NATO exercise Teamwork, which included 170 ships.
19 Sept.	The Soviets claimed an F-14 fighter conducted a simulated attack on a Coot patrol aircraft. The U.S. would counter this was a routine escort.

28 Oct.	The *Minsk* reported a P-3 Orion aircraft interfered with her flight operations.
9 Nov.	Two U.S. Navy ships entered the Black Sea for a short cruise.
14 Nov.	The *Minsk* claimed eight aircraft from USS *Midway* conducted a simulated attack. The Americans noted the Soviet account was fairly accurate. Six days later, two USAF B-52 aircraft overflew the Soviet ship. The U.S. considered it normal surveillance.

1981

7 Jan.	In the Arabian Sea Krivak-class frigate no. 678 reportedly maneuvered to hazard the USS *Independence* conducting unrep.
13 Jan.	In the Arabian Sea, Soviet Krivak-class frigate no. 789 reported an A-6 from the USS *Independence* dropped a bomb in its wake. The Americans admitted the aircraft had accidentally dropped a smoke device, having mistaken the Krivak for a U.S. Navy ship.
18 March	In the Indian Ocean, the USS *Independence* reported an Il-38 May aircraft hazarded flight operations.
25 March	Silver Fox operations in the Black Sea.
28 March	The U.S. claimed the AGI *Ekvator* maneuvered to hazard the SSBN USS *Henry L. Stimson* off the coast of Georgia.
1 April	Soviets protested an attempt by USS *Fairfax County* to retrieve a torpedo during a Soviet exercise in the Barents Sea.
3 April	Soviets claimed one of their submarines had an underwater collision with an unknown submarine. Also Krivak I–class frigate no. 903 allegedly maneuvered to hazard the USS *Fairfax County* in the Barents Sea.
10 April	The Soviets protested the USS *Conolly*'s entry into a Soviet ASW formation in the Atlantic.
11–12 April	A P-3 Orion aircraft reportedly buzzed Admiral Gorshkov's flagship in the Mediterranean.
24 April	In the Barents Sea, the USS *Fairfax County* reported Kashin-class destroyer no. 637 trained guns on her.
27 April	AGI no. 477 reportedly fired a flare at a passing EA-6B aircraft off the USS *Independence* steaming in the Arabian Sea.
1 May	A Royal Navy destroyer collided with a Soviet cruiser in the Barents Sea.
10 May	A Natya-class patrol frigate reportedly fired a flare at a passing P-3 Orion aircraft flying over the Indian Ocean.
12–14 May	A U.S. Navy ship was deployed to the Sea of Okhotsk to demonstrate FON.
31 May– 7 June	Ninth annual INCSEA review was held in Washington.

1 June	Silver Fox operations in the Black Sea.
4 June	A Soviet minesweeper collided with a Danish oiler in the Baltic Sea.
18 June	In the Northern Arabian Sea, two Soviet aircraft interfered with the flight operations on the uss *Kitty Hawk*. The Soviets countered that F-14s approached within five meters of these aircraft. The U.S. said they were no closer than 30 feet.
3 July	In the Indian Ocean, an *Ivan Rogov*–class LPD, no. 99, trained her guns on a passing P-3 Orion.
19 Aug.	Mod Kashin-class destroyer no. 709 reported being buzzed by an S-3 and an SH-2 helicopter while operating in the Mediterranean.
1–5 Sept.	Steaming in the Norwegian Sea, the uss *Forrestal* Battle Group reported maneuvering incidents with Krivak-class frigates no. 946 and 913. On 2 September no. 946 also interfered with a *Forrestal* helicopter hovering in a stationary position.
2 Sept.	Soviet naval task force positioned off the U.S. West Coast.
3 Sept.	Off Northern California, a Krivak II–class frigate tracked a P-3 with her gunmount and surface-to-air launcher.
2–9 Oct.	U.S. sent ships into the Baltic Sea to demonstrate FON.
10 Oct.	A Krivak-class frigate in the Indian Ocean reportedly pointed her guns at a passing P-3 Orion.
24 Oct.	In the Mediterranean, the Krivak-class frigate *Gromkyy* tangled with the uss *Texas,* forcing the latter ship to maneuver to avoid collision.
26 Oct.	*Gromkyy* maneuvered to hazard the uss *Coontz*. Both sides protested and accepted some blame.
5 Nov.	Two Il-38 May aircraft passed low over the uss *Coral Sea* while flight operations were in progress in the Arabian Sea.
20 Nov.	Silver Fox operations in the Black Sea.

1982

13 Jan.	In the Arabian Sea, the cruiser uss *Truxtun* reported being buzzed by two Il-38 May aircraft.
24 Feb.	The Soviets claimed an F-14 pulled to within two meters below an Il-38 flying over the Arabian Sea.
5 March	Krivak-class frigate *Bodryy* reportedly interfered with one of uss *Eisenhower*'s hovering helicopters that had extended its dipping sonar into the Mediterranean.
20 March	In the Norwegian Sea, Krivak II–class frigate no. 946 interfered with a formation of U.S. Navy ships led by the uss *Guadalcanal.*
27–28 April	uss *Lockwood* reportedly maneuvered dangerously in the presence of hydrographic ship *Lebedev*. The Soviets would also state *Lockwood*'s

	helicopter made frequent close approaches to their ships during this period.
3 May	*Stenka* allegedly harassed *Lockwood* in Peter the Great Bay. *Lockwood* reportedly made a hard starboard turn without signaling.
6 May	Kashin-class destroyer no. 544 fired three flares toward the uss *Lockwood*.
23–27 May	Tenth annual INCSEA review in Washington.
1–2 June	Petya II–class frigates no. 911 and 928 shot down weather balloons launched by uss *Barnstable County* operating in the Barents Sea.
8 June	In the Gulf of Thailand, the AGI *Aneroid* allegedly maneuvered to hazard the uss *Benjamin Stoddert*. Meanwhile, over in the Norwegian Sea, a Mod Kilden-class destroyer *Prozorlivy* tracked a passing P-3 gunmount with her gunmounts.
15 June	uss *Barnstable County* in the Barents Sea reported harassment from a Petya II–class patrol frigate.
17 June	Petya II reported the *Barnstable County* maneuvered in a hazardous manner.
12 July	The uss *Knox* reported her helicopter was tracked by fire-control radars on the cruiser *Tashkent*.
15 July	The U.S. protested after a Soviet aircraft flew over a hovering LAMPS helicopter.
30 July	The Krivak II–class frigate *Rezvyy* tracked a passing P-3 with its 100mm gunmount during operations in the Norwegian Sea.
31 July	The U.S. protested after a Krivak-class frigate interfered with an unrep involving the uss *Waccamaw*, uss *Manley*, and uss *Dupont* in the Mediterranean.
2 Aug.	A P-3 flying over the Norwegian Sea was tracked by a fire-control radar from the *Kiev*. On the next day nearby, the *Rezvyy* tracked another passing P-3.
6 Aug.	The AGI *Gavril Sarychev* reportedly disrupted a personnel transfer by crossing the bows of the uss *Conquest* and the uss *Gallant* off the U.S. West Coast.
11–12 Aug.	Near the Strait of Juan de Fuca, the uss *Oldendorf* reported *Gavril Sarychev* maneuvered in close proximity. Meanwhile, the Soviet ship reported that *Oldendorf* made three hazardous approaches. On 17 August the AGI reported *Oldendorf* maneuvered hazardously. The Soviet AGI was in place to monitor the initial transit of the SSBN uss *Ohio*.
23 Aug.	A Krivak-class frigate reportedly interfered with an unrep formation. On the same day there were five Soviet gun- or missile-pointing incidents.

25 Aug.	Soviets protested USS *Forrestal* aircraft dropping flares by one of their ships.
26 Aug.	A Tu-95 Bear aircraft interfered with flight operations on the USS *Peleliu* operating in the Sea of Okhotsk.
23 Sept.	USS *Harry E. Yarnell* took evasive action to avoid a Soviet exercise torpedo in the Baltic.
24 Sept.	A *Ropucha*-class LST interfered with USS *Rathburne* surveillance operations.
25 Sept.	In the northern Pacific, a Tu-95 disrupted flight operations on the carrier USS *Enterprise*. A similar violation was alleged to have occurred two days later with the USS *Midway*.
4 Oct.	In the Sea of Japan, a Tu-95 again reportedly interfered with flight operations on the USS *Enterprise*. Meanwhile, the Soviets alleged that F-4s from the USS *Midway* interfered with the flight of an Il-38 over the Sea of Japan.
31 Oct.	In the South China Sea, the USS *Goldsborough* reported that the *Minsk* turned toward her without warning, requiring evasive action. The *Minsk* reported that the American ship was the culprit.
24 Nov.	In the Black Sea the Soviets claimed the USS *William V. Pratt* and USS *Aylwin* interfered with shipboard gunnery exercises.

1983	
8 Feb.	Soviets claimed hazardous U.S. Navy air operations near their aircraft over the Arabian Sea. The USN evaluated it as a nonincident.
10–11 Feb.	In the Mediterranean, Soviet Krivak frigates no. 801 and no. 813 repeatedly crossed the bow of the USS *Edward McDonnell*.
18 Feb.	Soviets claimed hazardous U.S. Navy air operations near their aircraft over the Arabian Sea. The U.S. Navy evaluated it as a nonincident.
2 March	Two Tu-95 aircraft flying over the South China Sea interfered with flight operations on the USS *Enterprise*.
16 March	Soviets reported close maneuvers by USN aircraft to Il-18 aircraft over the Arabian Sea. The U.S. Navy considered it a nonincident.
22 March	Two Il-38 aircraft interfered with USS *America* flight operations in the Arabian Sea.
22 March –15 April	FLEETEX 83 involved three U.S. Navy carrier battle groups approaching the Kuriles from the Aleutians. It attracted 70 Soviet surveillance sorties. The Soviets alleged that on 8 April F-14 and A-7E aircraft from USS *Enterprise* endangered two Tu-95 aircraft monitoring the battle group.
16 April	In the Western Mediterranean, a Soviet auxiliary reported she was harassed by a helicopter off the USS *Connole*.

17–20 May	Eleventh annual INCSEA review was held in Washington. In addition to maneuvering incidents, the Americans reported twelve gun pointing and thirty-three instances of AGIS approaching surfaced submarines (in contrast to sixty-eight in 1981).
25 May	The Kotlin-class destroyer *Nakhodchivy* reportedly maneuvered to hazard the uss *Harlan County* in the Mediterranean.
5 June	An Alpha-class SSN reported that the uss *Sumter* interfered with its maneuvers in the Barents Sea. The USN defended the *Sumter's* performance.
13 June	The *Kirov* claimed that *Sumter* maneuvered to hazard her. Again the U.S. Navy considered it a nonincident.
22 Aug.	An Su-15 Flagon reportedly interfered with the flight of an SH-2 helicopter flying over the Sea of Japan.
1 Sept.	Soviet fighters shot down KAL 007 west of Sakhalin Island.
7 Sept.	The uss *Elliot* reported that her helicopter was harassed by Soviet aircraft during flight operations over the Sea of Japan.
15 Sept.	While conducting KAL 007 recovery operations, the USNS *Narragansett* reported hazardous maneuvering by the AGI *Alpinist* in the Sea of Japan.
16 Sept.	The AGS *Tajmyr* reported that the *Narragansett* maneuvered to hazard her.
17 Sept.	The Soviets claimed a U.S. Navy helicopter buzzed several of their ships in the Sea of Japan.
18 Sept.	The *Narragansett* was harassed by the AGOR *Pegas*.
19 Sept.	The USNS *Conserver* reported interference from the AGI *Gavril Sarychev* as did the uss *Sterett* with the *Pegas*.
23 Sept.	In the Sea of Japan, the uss *Callaghan* and the *Gavril Sarychev* came close to collision, and Kashin-class destroyer no. 660 interfered with the flight of a U.S. Navy helicopter. Over the next five days U.S. Navy ships reported several radar lock-ons made by the Kara-class cruiser *Petropavlovsk* and the Kashin-class destroyer *Odarennyy*.
28 Sept.	The *Petropavlovsk* reportedly trained her searchlights on the *Callaghan*.
2 Oct.	The Soviets claimed the uss *Brooke* interfered with one of its auxiliaries operating in the Sea of Japan. The U.S. Navy evaluated the claim as a nonincident.
16 Oct.	uss *Sterett* reportedly maneuvered dangerously among several Soviet ships. The U.S. Navy denied the claim.
25 Oct.	The *Revnostnyy* claimed the *Conserver* maneuvered to hazard her in the Sea of Japan. The U.S. Navy considered the encounter a nonincident.
26 Oct.	Two Soviet combatants crossed ahead of the *Conserver* and the uss *Towers* in the Sea of Japan in violation of COLREGS. The Soviets countered that the *Conserver* maneuvered to hazard the drill ship *Burovoye Sudno*.

31 Oct.   The ARS *Prut* reportedly trained a searchlight on the USS *Meyerkord* operating in the Sea of Japan. Over in the Atlantic off South Carolina, a Soviet Victor III–class submarine screw became entangled in a cable from the USS *McCloy*.

1–11 Nov.   In the Mediterranean, the Mod Kashin-class destroyer *Sderzhannyy* reported being buzzed by aircraft off USS *John F. Kennedy* and USS *Dwight D. Eisenhower*.

7 Nov.   The *Sderzhannyy* reported that the USS *New Jersey* trained its guns at her. Meanwhile, the Riga-class frigate *Kosmsomolets Gruziy* claimed the USS *Virginia* trained its missile launcher at her. The U.S. Navy disagreed with both reports.

18 Nov.   USS *Fife* and Soviet frigate *Razyashchey* collided in the Arabian Sea. Both sides protested.

1984

27 Jan.   An Aeroflot airliner over Cyprus reported being bracketed by three U.S. Navy fighters, with one 15–20 meters off each wing tip and one 20–30 meters above.

Feb.   U.S. alleged Soviets harassed USS *David R. Ray* in the Black Sea.

28 Feb.–
22 March   NATO Exercise Teamwork involved amphibious landings in Norway.

21 March   USS *Kitty Hawk* overran a Victor I–class submarine in the Sea of Japan.

23 March   An Aeroflot airliner reported being bracketed by USAF F-15s between Cypress and Greece.

28 March   Soviets conducted North Atlantic naval maneuvers.

2 April   The *Minsk* fired flares at the frigate USS *Harold E. Holt*.

21 May
–6 April   Soviets announced an increase of missile boats deployed off the U.S. coasts.

2 June   Twelfth INCSEA review concluded in Moscow.

30 June   The Soviets claimed that USS *Biddle* and USS *Truett* maneuvered to hazard a Mod Kashin-class destroyer and a Tango-class submarine in the Black Sea.

15 July   The AGI *Pelorus* reportedly maneuvered to hazard submarine USS *Simon Bolivar* near Kings Bay, Georgia.

29 Aug.   The AGI *Anteres,* off Oregon, reportedly fired a flare at a P-3 Orion.

21 Sept.   The Soviets claimed that USS *Aylwin*'s helicopter maneuvered to hazard a surfaced Victor I–class submarine and the *General Ryabikov* in the Mediterranean Sea.

23 Nov.   The USS *Coontz* and the USS *Spruance* ignored warning signals from

Kashin-class destroyer no. 707 and entered Soviet territorial waters in the Black Sea.

15 Dec.   Two U.S. Navy carriers 50 miles off Vladivostok drew repeated Soviet sorties.

1985

7 Jan.   The AGI *Nakhodka* reportedly maneuvered to hazard the SSBN USS *Stonewall Jackson* off Kings Bay.

28 Jan.   An Il-38 May patrol aircraft reported being bracketed by F-14s from the USS *Dwight D. Eisenhower* in the Mediterranean Sea.

28–29   Soviet soldiers in East Germany killed Major Arthur B. Nicholson.
March   During these two days a Don-class submarine tender in the Mediterranean Sea pointed its guns at a passing helicopter from USS *Trippe.*

4 June   A surfaced Tango-class submarine in the Barents Sea reported the USS *Mississippi* maneuvered to hazard her. A U.S. Navy review concluded the Soviet complaint was justified.

10 June   INCSEA talks were postponed until November.

14 June   The Soviet "Space Event Ship" *Marshal Nedelin* claimed the USS *Knox* maneuvered to hazard her while she conducted operations in the Western Pacific. A U.S. Navy review of *Knox*'s track concluded the American ship could have acted more seamanlike.

27 June   The USS *Midway* reported that her flight operations in the South China Sea were interfered with by passing Tu-16 Badger aircraft.

23–24   The USS *Texas* allegedly penetrated Soviet territorial waters off Siberia and
July   failed to respond to Soviet signals to depart.

25 July   The Soviets claimed USS *Texas* maneuvered to hazard the AGOR *Marshal Golovani* and the Krivak II–class frigate *Rezkiy*. U.S. Navy evaluation concluded that the *Texas* did act provocatively.

8 Aug.   In the Mediterranean, the AGI *Ladoga* reportedly maneuvered to hazard replenishment between the USS *Kalamazoo* and the USS *Iwo Jima.*

27 Aug.   In the western Atlantic, the replenishment ship USS *Milwaukee* reported the AGI *Balzam* maneuvered to hazard her.

29 Aug.   Off Holy Loch, the AGI *Nakhodka* impeded the path of the SSBN USS *Alexander Hamilton.*

4 Sept.   The Soviets claimed that aircraft from USS *Saratoga* simulated attacks on the nuclear battlecruiser *Frunze* off the Canary Islands. The U.S. Navy responded that its aircraft do not conduct simulated attacks on foreign vessels.

14 Sept.   Badger aircraft over the Norwegian Sea reported repeated close-ups by

aircraft off the USS *America*. The U.S. Navy responded that the Badgers were armed with air-to-surface missiles and warranted close surveillance.

15 Sept.   *America* aircraft reportedly simulated attacks on the frigate *Razviy*. Again the U.S. Navy rebuked the Soviet claim, stating its aircraft do not conduct simulated attacks.

28 Sept.–   NATO Ocean Safari exercise with 166 ships and 300 aircraft drew Soviet
20 Oct.   attention.

7–25 Oct. NATO Baltic operations included a U.S. Navy battleship.

31 Oct.   Soviet minesweeper collided with Swedish AGI in the Baltic Sea.

10–18   Twelfth annual INCSEA review was held in Washington.
Nov.

1 Dec.   In the western Atlantic, the *Solovat Ulayev* reported a helicopter hovered 25 meters overhead with a searchlight and followed her for fifteen minutes.

22 Dec.   A Soviet squadron reported low passes by a P-3 Orion in the Mediterranean.

1986

18 Jan.   USS *Kirk* off the Siberian coast reported the *Kapitan Kobets* maneuvered to place it *in extremis*. In the Mediterranean Sea, the cruiser *Slava* reported dangerous passes by an EA-6B off the USS *Saratoga* and that the USS *Caron* failed to signal a maneuver ahead of it. The U.S. Navy denied the dangerous pass claim but admitted fault for *Caron*'s failure to execute the correct signal.

10 Feb.   Off the U.S. West Coast, the Soviet vessel SSV-468 reported USS *Vandegrift* maneuvered on four occasions to force the captain to change course or back down.

16 March East of Kamchatka, a Su-15 Flagon passed within 150 feet of a patrolling P-3 Orion.

1 April   The Soviet alleged that F/A-18s off the USS *Coral Sea* closed up on Il-38 patrol aircraft flying over the Mediterranean.

16 April   In the central Mediterranean, a Kresta I–class cruiser reportedly failed to give way to the frigate USS *Jack Williams* in a crossing situation.

13 May   Off San Diego, the cruiser USS *Long Beach* and the frigate USS *Copeland* reported a *Balzam*-class AGI blocked their intended track.

27 May   The USS *Thach* reported that a Moma-class AGI repeatedly maneuvered in violation of COLREGS to risk a collision off Hawaii.

7–14 June Fourteenth annual INCSEA review was held in Moscow.

8 June	Soviets claimed USS *Francis Hammond* penetrated their territorial waters near the Kurile Islands. They issued their protest on 11 June.
24–27 Aug.	A U.S. Navy carrier entered Bering Sea, attracting Soviet observers.
27–31 Aug.	Four U.S. Navy ships cruised in the Sea of Okhotsk.
29 Aug.– 19 Sept.	NATO Northern Wedding exercise drew strong Soviet response.
11 Sept.	Off Florida, the AGI *Balzam* reportedly failed to give way to the SSBN USS *Will Rogers*.
3 Dec.	The U.S. claimed a Soviet Hind helicopter from *Minsk* maneuvered to endanger the flight of a helicopter off the USS *Kirk* in the Sea of Japan.

1987

7 March	President Reagan agreed to reflag Kuwaiti tankers and conduct escort operations.
2 April	Soviets accused the French of buzzing a Soviet ship.
15 April	A Tu-95 Bear aircraft reported a USAF RC-135 maneuvered to hazard it over the Barents Sea.
17 May	USS *Arkansas* operated in Soviet-claimed waters off the Kamchatka Peninsula.
9–16 June	Fifteenth INCSEA annual review was held in Washington.
9 July	An EP-3 reported that two separate MiG-23 Floggers closed to within inches while over the South China Sea.
12 July	A Su-15 Flagon reportedly made close passes on an EP-3 over the South China Sea.
17 July	A USAF RC-135 claimed an Su-15 made a high-speed pass over the Sea of Japan.
23 Sept.	Over the Barents Sea, the wing tip of an Su-27 Flanker came into contact with the outer starboard propeller of a British P-3 Orion, damaging the British aircraft.
28 Sept.	An Su-15 Flagon made close passes on another P-3 over the Sea of Japan.
30 Sept.	A P-3 Orion reported that a MiG-23 Flogger overlapped its wingtip while over the Sea of Japan. Near Hawaii, a USAF WC-135 was illuminated by a directed energy device of the Soviet ship *Sibir Age Chuotka*.
30 Oct.	In the Pacific Ocean, the USS *Chandler* and the USS *McClusky* reported close passes by a Hormone A helicopter.
15 Dec.	A USAF RC-135 reported close passes by a Su-15 Flagon over the Sea of Japan.

1988

12 Jan. An EP-3 reported that a MiG-23 overlapped its wingtip while over the Sea of Japan.

20 Jan. Il-38 May claimed an F/A-18 Hornet made a close approach over the Arabian Sea.

27 Jan. Another Il-38 reported two F/A-18s made close approaches over the Arabian Sea.

3 Feb. Another Il-38 claimed two other F/A-18s made close approaches over the Arabian Sea.

11 Feb. A MiG-25 Foxbat reportedly made high-speed approaches on a P-3 Orion over the Sea of Japan. The Soviets claimed a P-3 closed up on a Tu-95 over the Atlantic.

12 Feb. Soviet ships rammed USS *Yorktown* and USS *Caron* in the Black Sea.

15 Feb. The Soviets reported another P-3 closed up on a Tu-142 Bear over the Atlantic.

18 Feb. The Soviets reported three incidents of close U.S. aircraft approaches: a USAF F-106 approach on a Tu-142 Bear over the Atlantic, a USAF F-15 approach on a Tu-142 over the Atlantic, and a U.S. Navy F-14 approaches on a pair of Il-38s over the Arabian Sea.

31 March A Su-27 passed close to hazard a USAF RC-135 over the Barents Sea.

20 April A MiG-23 Flogger reportedly flew inside the wingspan of another RC-135 over the Sea of Japan.

5–10 June Sixteenth annual INCSEA review was held in Moscow.

21 July *Marshal Ustinov, Otlichnny,* and *Genrikh Gasanov* arrived in Norfolk.

4 Aug. USS *Thomas S. Gates* and USS *Kauffman* visited Sevastopol.

1989

22–27 May Seventeenth annual INCSEA review was conducted in Washington.

12 June Dangerous Military Activities Agreement signed to go into effect 1 January 1990. The agreement established a Joint Military Commission, which met in Tampa, Florida, on 9–12 March 1990.

Abbreviations

AGI	Auxiliary, General, Intelligence vessel
Amembassy	American Embassy
ASW	Antisubmarine warfare
CIA	Central Intelligence Agency
CINCPAC	Commander in Chief, Pacific
CINCPACFLT	Commander in Chief, U.S. Pacific Fleet
CINCUSNAVEUR	Commander in Chief, U.S. Naval Forces Europe
CJCS	Chairman of the Joint Chiefs of Staff
CNO	Chief of Naval Operations
CO	Commanding officer
COMASWFORSIXTHFLT	Commander, Antisubmarine Forces, Sixth Fleet
COMSIXTHFLT	Commander, Sixth Fleet
DCNO	Deputy Chief of Naval Operations
DEFCON	Defense Condition
DESRON	Destroyer Squadron
DoD	Department of Defense
ELINT	Electronic intercepts
FAST	Fast Automatic Shuttle Transfer system
FOIA	Freedom of Information Act
FON	Freedom of Navigation
HSTL	Harry S. Truman Library, Independence, Mo.
ICJ	International Court of Justice

INCSEA	Incidents at Sea Agreement
INF	Intermediate Nuclear Forces
ISA	International Security Affairs
JCS	Joint Chiefs of Staff
MEPEQ	Middle East Power Equation
MFA	Soviet Ministry of Foreign Affairs
MOU	Memorandum of understanding
NA	National Archives, College Park, Md.
NHC	Naval Historical Center, Washington, D.C.
NPIC	National Photographic Interpretation Center
NSA	National Security Agency
NSC	National Security Council
NSC/IG/EUR	National Security Council Interdepartmental Group/Europe
NSDM	National Security Decision Memorandum
NSSM	National Security Study Memorandum
OOD	Officer of the Deck
OpNav	Office of the Chief of Naval Operations
OSD	Office of the Secretary of Defense
Pol-Mil	Bureau of Political-Military Affairs, State Department
RG	Record Group
SAC	Strategic Air Command
SecDef	Secretary of Defense
SecNav	Secretary of the Navy
SecState	Secretary of State
sitrep	Situation report
State	Department of State
TG	Task Group
unrep	Underway replenishment
USAFHRC	United States Air Force Historical Research Center, Maxwell Air Force Base, Montgomery, Ala.
USDAO	U.S. Defense Attaché Office

Notes

Chapter 1. Playing with the Bear

1. Rear Adm. Robert P. Hilton Sr., USN (Ret.), interview by author, Arlington, Va., 29 Jan. 1997.

2. CTF-67 to CTF-60, 251008Z, March 1972, is a message report that a Soviet Foxtrot diesel boat was expected to arrive at the Soviet Hammamet anchorage for two to five days of rest alongside an anchored submarine tender. Hilton papers, Alexandria, Va.

3. CTU-67.5.0 to TU-67.5.0, 262100Z, March 1972, Subject: CTU 67.5.0 Letter of Instruction—Bystander/Ringside Ops, Hilton papers.

4. CTU-67.5.0 to AIG-348, 270524Z, March 1972, Subject: Bystander/Ringside Sitrep Nr 2, and 270700Z, March 1972, Subject: Bystander/Ringside Sitrep Nr 3, Hilton papers.

5. USS *William V. Pratt* to CTU-67.5.0, 270900Z, March 1972, Subject: Sitrep Feeder, Hilton papers.

6. CTU-67.5.0 to AIG 348, 271020Z, March 1972, Subject: Bystander/Ringside Sitrep Nr 4; 271610Z, March 1972, Subject: Bystander/Ringside Sitrep Nr 5; 272220Z, March 1972, Subject: Bystander/Ringside Sitrep Nr 6; USS *William V. Pratt* to CTU-67.5.0, 280844Z, March 1972, Subject: Feeder Report; CTU-67.5.0 to AIG 348, 281600Z, March 1972, Subject: Bystander/Ringside Sitrep Nr 9; 282222Z, March 1972, Subject: Bystander/Ringside Sitrep Nr 10, Hilton papers.

7. CTU-67.5.0 to AIG 348, 291250Z, Subject: Bystander/Ringside Sitrep Nr 13; 291334Z, March 1972, Subject: Bystander/Ringside Sitrep Nr 14; 291604Z, March 1972, Subject: Bystander/Ringside Sitrep Nr 16, Hilton papers.

8. CTU-67.5.0 to AIG 348, 302206Z, March 1972, Subject: Bystander/Ringside Sitrep Nr 23; USS *William V. Pratt* to CTU-67.5.0, 310240Z, March 1972, Subject: Feeder Report, Hilton papers.

9. USS *William V. Pratt* to CTU-67.5.0, 310816Z, March 1972, Subject: Feeder report; CTU-67.5.0 to CTF-67, 311030Z, March 1972, Subject: Personal for Rear Admiral Charbonnet, Hilton papers.

10. CTU-67.5.0 to AIG 348, 311952Z, March 1972, Subject: Bystander/Ringside Sitrep Nr 28, Hilton papers.

11. CTU-67.5.0 to AIG 348, 312106Z, March 1972, Subject: Bystander/Ringside Sitrep Nr 29, Hilton papers.

12. USS *William V. Pratt* to CTU-67.5.0, 010032Z, April 1972, Subject: Feeder Report, Hilton papers.

13. CTU-67.5.0 to AIG 348, 312220Z, March 1972, Subject: Bystander/Ringside Sitrep Nr 30, Hilton papers.

14. CTU-67.5.0 to AIG 348, 011040Z, April 1972, Subject: Bystander/Ringside Sitrep Nr 35, Hilton papers.

15. CTF-67 to CTU-67.5.0, 011219Z, April 1972, Subject: Bystander Ops, Hilton papers.

16. CTU-67.5.0 to AIG 348, 020406Z, April 1972, Subject: Bystander/Ringside Sitrep Nr 38, Hilton papers.

17. CTU-67.5.0 to AIG 348, 020610Z, April 1972, Subject: Bystander/Ringside Sitrep Nr 39, Hilton papers.

18. CTU-67.5.0 to AIG 348, 020912Z, April 1972, Subject: Bystander/Ringside Sitrep Nr 41, Hilton papers.

19. CTU-67.5.0 to AIG 348, 021120Z, April 1972, Subject: Bystander/Ringside Sitrep Nr 42, Hilton papers.

20. CTU-67.5.0 to AIG 348, 021330Z, April 1972, Subject: Bystander/Ringside Sitrep Nr 43; 021620Z, April 1972, Subject: Bystander/Ringside Sitrep Nr 44, Hilton papers.

21. CTU-67.5.0 to AIG 348, 031414Z, April 1972, Subject: Bystander/Ringside Sitrep Nr 54, Hilton papers.

22. COMSIXTHFLT to COMDESRON FOURTEEN, 050839Z, April 1972, Subject: Personal for COMDESRON FOURTEEN, Hilton papers.

23. COMSIXTHFLT to CINCUSNAVEUR, 071511Z, April 1972, Subject: Personal for Admiral Bringle, Hilton papers.

24. COMDESRON FOURTEEN to COMSIXTHFLT, 140116Z, April 1972, Subject: Personal for Admiral Miller; CINCUSNAVEUR to CNO, 151834Z, April 1972, Subject: Personal for Admiral Cousins, Hilton papers.

Chapter 2. Confrontation along the Periphery

1. Michael A. Palmer, *Origins of the Maritime Strategy: The Development of American Naval Strategy, 1945-1955* (Annapolis, Md.: Naval Institute Press, 1990), 38.

2. Palmer's work, originally published by the NHC in 1988 as *Origins of the Maritime Strategy: American Naval Strategy in the First Postwar Decade*, provides a detailed narrative of the development of a maritime strategy that advocated a balanced fleet designed to be deployed overseas. Palmer argues that the Navy's failure to promote this strategy publicly and Eisenhower's New Look led to the dismantling of the strategy. See Jeffrey G. Barlow, *Revolt of the Admirals: The Fight for Naval Aviation* (Washington, D.C.: NHC, 1994), for a detailed account of the DoD and budget battles of the late 1940s.

3. Robert W. Herrick, *Soviet Naval Strategy: Fifty Years of Theory and Practice* (Annapolis, Md.: Naval Institute Press, 1968), 9, 21–22.

4. Ibid., 59–61, 63–65.

5. Michael MccGwire, "The Evolution of Soviet Naval Policy: 1960-74," in *Soviet Naval Policy: Objectives and Constraints,* ed. Michael MccGwire, Ken Booth, and John McDonnell (New York: Praeger, 1975), 506; Sergei G. Gorshkov, "Razvitie Sovetskogo Voenno-morshogo iskusstva" ("Development of Soviet Naval Art"), *Morskoi Sbornik,* no. 2 (Feb. 1967): 19–20, quoted in Herrick, *Soviet Naval Strategy,* 68.

6. Commander Seventh Fleet, messages 180722 NCR 243 of 18 Nov. 1945 and 200510 NCR 602 of 20 Nov. 1945, Operational Archives, NHC; Alexander L. George, *RM-1349: Case Studies of Actual and Alleged Overflights, 1930-1953* (Santa Monica, Calif.: The Rand Corporation, 15 Aug. 1955), 27–29.

7. CNO, messages 281645 of 28 Nov. 1945 and 151535 of 15 Dec. 1945, Operational Archives, NHC. The American response, noting that this was the first time that any government had laid a twelve-mile territorial claim from an occupied territory, complained that the Soviet response still did not explain the attack occurring some forty miles out at sea. The Soviets ignored this subsequent query. George, *RM-1349,* 31–34.

8. Gen. Curtis E. LeMay, interview by John T. Bohn, March AFB, Calif., 9 March 1971, USAF Oral History Program, USAFHRC.

9. From tables provided in *The Development of the Strategic Air Command: 1946-1986* (Offutt Air Force Base, Neb.: Office of the Historian, Headquarters, Strategic Air Command, 1986).

10. R. Cargill Hall, "Strategic Reconnaissance in the Cold War: From Concept to National Policy," *Prologue* 29, no. 2 (Summer 1996): 111–12.

11. John T. Farquhar, "A Need to Know: The Role of Air Force Reconnaissance in War Planning, 1945-1953," M.A. thesis, Ohio State University, Columbus, 1991, 55;

Carrol L. Zimmerman, *Insider at SAC: Operations Analyst under General LeMay* (Manhattan, Kan.: Sunflower University Press, 1988), 53. The number of cities targeted for atomic leveling increased with the sequence of war plans reflecting the growth of the American nuclear arsenal. See Farquhar, "A Need to Know," 47–56; Gregg Herken, *The Winning Weapon: The Atomic Bomb in the Cold War, 1945–1950* (New York: Knopf, 1980), 219–21, 227, 228, 266; and Jeffrey Richelson, *American Espionage and the Soviet Target* (New York: Morrow, 1987), 100–105.

12. George, *RM-1349*, 40–41; Farquhar, "A Need to Know," 59.

13. Command History, 311th Air Division, Sept.–Dec. 1948, 5–6, USAFHRC; memorandum for SecDef: Subject Special Electronic Airborne Search Operations (SESP), Serial 6364, 5 May 1950, President's Secretaries files, HSTL.

14. Enclosure to letter from Commander, United States Atlantic Fleet Patrol Squadron 26, to Capt. Walter Karig, USN, Special Assistant to the CNO, 21 June 1950, Operational Archives, NHC.

15. "Secrets of the Cold War," *U.S. News and World Report*, 15 March 1993, 30, 32; "Soviet Decorates 4 Fliers," *New York Times*, 14 April 1950, 3; Text of protest note published in *New York Times*, 19 April 1950, 3; Alexander L. George, in a 1955 RAND Research Memorandum, speculated that the Soviets had decided to implement a severe air-defense policy at this time. George believed that the Yugoslavian incidents may have given the Soviets an incentive to act aggressively, noting that American aircraft stayed well clear of Yugoslav airspace in the wake of the 1946 downing of two U.S. transport planes. He conjectured that the Soviets learned from the Yugoslav experience of countering a harsh U.S. reaction. Unlike the Yugoslavs, the Soviets presented their case in terms that would undercut the U.S. position in international law, claiming that the planes crossed into Soviet airspace and fired on the intercepting aircraft. George, *RM-1349*, 54–57.

16. Memorandum for the SecDef: Subject: Special Electronic Airborne Search Operations (SESP), 5 May 1950.

17. Memorandum for the SecDef: Subject: Special Electronic Airborne Search Operations, 22 July 1950, President's Secretaries files, HSTL.

18. CTF-77, report to the CNO, late Sept. 1950, Subject: Attack and Destruction of an Unidentified Aircraft in the Yellow Sea on 4 Sept. 1950, Operational Archives, NHC.

19. Walter H. Waggoner, "Truman Sees Gain in War This Week," *New York Times*, 8 Sept. 1950, 1, 3; George, *RM-1349*, 112–17, in his review of the incident, considered the Soviet reaction rather mild. He speculated that the Soviets, who had denied complicity with the June 1950 North Korean attack, did not desire publicity that this flight may had been made to provide reconnaissance support to the North Koreans.

20. James D. Sanders, Mark A. Sauter, and R. Cort Kirkwood, *Soldiers of Mis-*

fortune: Washington's Secret Betrayal of American POWs in the Soviet Union (Washington, D.C.: National Press Books, 1992), 210–11; *Department of State Bulletin* (3 Dec. 1951): 909; *New York Times*, 25 Nov. 1951, 1, 4; George, *RM-1349*, 136, speculated that Soviets made the attack to counteract the impression of passivity of their air defenses in the wake of U.S. fighters accidentally strafing an airfield near Vladivostok a month earlier.

21. George, *RM-1349*, 141–43; Klaus, memorandum to English, Subject: 1955–1956 Work of Office, 5 Jan. 1956, RG 59, Lot 64D551, Box 97, National Archives and Records Administration Archives II, College Park, Md. (hereafter NA).

22. Klaus, memorandum to Paul, 6 Aug. 1942; and Klaus memorandum, 21 July 1950, both in Klaus files folder, RG 59, Lot 64551, Box 105, NA; "Samuel Klaus, 58, U.S. Legal Advisor," *New York Times*, 3 Aug. 1963, 17.

23. George, *RM-1349*, 144–45; Klaus, memorandum to English.

24. R. Cargill Hall, "The Truth about Overflights: Military Reconnaissance Missions over Russia before the U-2," *Quarterly Journal of Military History* (Spring 1997): 30–31.

25. History of the 91st Strategic Reconnaissance Squadron, 1 Oct. 1952–31 Oct. 1952, 5, 17, USAFHRC; "B-29 off Soviet Kuriles," *New York Times*, 9 Oct. 1952, 1, 3; Richelson, *American Espionage and the Soviet Target*, 122; Commanding General Far East Air Force, message to Chief of Staff, USAF, 100210Z, Oct. 1952, RG 59, Lot 64D551, Box 34, NA, contains the initial report of the incident.

26. *Department of State Bulletin* (27 Oct. 1952): 649–50, and (18 Oct. 1954): 580.

27. Klaus, memo to Thurston, 23 Aug. 1953, RG 59, Lot 64D551, Box 34, NA.

28. Hall, "Truth about Overflights," 31–32.

29. *Department of State Bulletin* (18 Oct. 1954): 579–86; Klaus, memo for the record, 27 April 1954, and memo to Phleger, 20 May 1954, RG 59, Lot 64D551, Box 34, NA.

30. Headquarters Far East Air Force, memorandum to Samuel Klaus, Subject: Transportation Request, 12 Oct. 1953, RG 59, Lot 64D551, Box 34, NA.

31. *Department of State Bulletin* (10 Aug. 1953): 179.

32. *Department of State Bulletin* (17 Aug. 1953): 207; George, *RM-1349*, 303–5.

33. Alvin Shuster, "Moscow Charges Plane Attack," *New York Times*, 1 Aug. 1953, 1, 3; Capt. John E. Roche, USAF, "Incident in the Sea of Japan," *Readers Digest* (Sept. 1957): 25–27. A controversy ensued over the question of survivors. Born the very day of the incident, Bruce Sanderson suspects that his father, 1st Lt. Warren Sanderson, and his fellow crewmembers were victims of a deliberate ambush to avenge the Il-12 shootdown and asserts that other crewmembers were picked up by Soviet patrol boats in the vicinity. Bruce Sanderson, phone interview by author, 2 April 1993.

34. RB-50 Case—Facts and Law, undated 1954 paper, RG 59, Lot 64D551, Box 55, NA; Klaus, memo to Thurston, 24 Aug. 1953, RG 59, Lot 64D551, Box 34, NA.

35. Hall, "Truth about Overflights," 33–36.

36. Commander Wayne's narrative is included in VP-19 letter, serial 0039, of 21 Sept. 1954, Operational Archives, NHC.

37. Transcript excerpts printed in the *New York Times,* 11 Sept. 1954.

38. George, *RM-1349,* 217–22, summarized reports of Soviet overflights of Alaska, northern Canada, and Greenland. The Baldwin claim was partially challenged by an Alaskan Air Command intelligence summary published in 1955 stating that there had been no known Soviet penetrations of Alaskan airspace: *Headquarters Alaskan Air Command Intelligence Review* 55, no. 1 (4 Feb. 1955): 8, K-484.608, USAFHRC.

39. Hanson W. Baldwin, "The Price of Survival—45 U.S. Airmen Have Died in Incidents with Soviet Planes Since April 1950," *New York Times,* 14 Sept. 1954.

40. William J. Jorden, "U.S. Photo Plane Downed in Japan by MiG Fighters," *New York Times,* 8 Nov. 1954, 1, 4; "U.S. Note Demands Payment for B-29," *New York Times,* 9 Nov. 1954, 1, 2; *Department of State Bulletin* (29 Nov. 1954): 811; *Department of State Bulletin* (27 July 1959): 122–24. As in previous cases, the Soviets would not accede to Court jurisdiction.

41. *Department of State Bulletin* (18 Oct. 1954): 579–86; SecDef, letter to Robert Murphy, 24 Feb. 1955, and instructions to Ambassador Freeman, 26 May 1955, RG 59, Lot 64D551, Box 34, NA.

42. CNO, report to the SecNav, 00103P33, 11 July 1955, and citation for AD2 Maziarz, Operational Archives, NHC; *San Francisco Chronicle* and *San Francisco Examiner* articles on the shootdown, 25 June 1955.

43. From *New York Times, San Francisco Chronicle, San Francisco Examiner* articles printed between 25 and 28 June 1955; *Department of State Bulletin* (11 July 1955): 52–53, (18 July 1955): 100–101, and (16 Jan. 1956): 94–95.

44. "Alleged Violations of Soviet Territory," *Department of State Bulletin* (30 July 1956): 191–92.

45. Hall, "The Truth about Overflights," 37–39; "Alleged Overflight of Soviet Area by American Planes," *Department of State Bulletin* (28 Jan. 1957): 135. In its response to the Soviet protest, the United States denied the RB-57D-0 flights had taken place. The CIA U-2 program would continue.

46. Incidents listing, 22 Oct. 1949–1 July 1960, K168.7017-46, and Report of Incidents, Nov. 1951–March 1963, K168.1-21, USAFHRC. See "Secrets of the Cold War," 46, 48–50, for updated interpretations concerning the loss of the C-118 and C-130 over Armenia. Apparently the C-118 served as a courier plane for the CIA. Richelson, *American Espionage and the Soviet Target,* 124–25.

47. Michael R. Beschloss, *Mayday: The U-2 Affair* (New York: Perennial Library, 1987), 162–63, provides an overview of the Berlin crisis.

48. Ibid., 177–78, 225–33.

49. Regarding the plane's mission, Command History of 55th Strategic Reconnaissance Wing: July–Aug. 1960, chap. 3, USAFHRC, stated that the aircraft had been on a Texas Star mission to conduct an electromagnetic survey of polar regions north of the Soviet landmass to obtain information for mapping purposes. Although this document was classified "SECRET," the Texas Star mission statement must be regarded with some skepticism because such a mission would not require the flight path later displayed by Ambassador Lodge at the United Nations. Furthermore, Klaus thought it was unrealistic to imagine that the Soviets believed the magnetic-field story when, in fact, the plane *was* on an ECM mission targeting Soviet radars. Klaus memo, call with Colonel Guild, RG 59, Lot 64D551, Box 79, NA.

50. Notes furnished by survivors Capt. Freeman B. Olmstead and Capt. John R. McKone at press conference, 3 March 1961, Appendix to Command History of the 55th Strategic Reconnaissance Wing, March–April 1961, USAFHRC.

51. *New York Times*, 13 July 1960, 1, 6–7. Transcript of Khrushchev news conference is on p. 6. Text of U.S. protest note is on p. 7.

52. Osgood Caruthers, "Moscow Bids U.N. Convene at Once on RB-47 Incident," *New York Times*, 14 July 1960, 1, 6.

53. *Kansas City Times*, 23 July 1960, 1, 7; *New York Times*, 23 July 1960, 1–3, excerpts on p. 2.

54. Excerpts from the *New York Times*, 26 July 1960, 4–5.

55. Lindesay Parrott, *New York Times*, 27 July 1960, 1, 5, excerpts p. 4.

56. Klaus, memo of McSweeney phone conservation, 27 Jan. 1961; Kohler memo, 27 Jan. 1961; Kohler, memo to Raymond, 8 Sept. 1960; appointment proposal letter from Herter to Gates, 14 Oct. 1960; Gates concurs letter, 27 Oct. 1960: all in RG 59, Lot 64D551, Box 79, NA.

57. Klaus, memo on Colonels Hall and Geary visit, 26 Sept. 1960, and memo of Colonel Gould conversation, 28 Sept. 1960, RG 59, Lot 64D551, Box 79, NA.

58. Draft note to Moscow Embassy, 28 Sept. 1961, Box 80, and Klaus, memo on Thacher phone conversations, 18 May 1961 and 27 July 1961, Box 79, RG 59, Lot 64D551, NA. Klaus eventually concluded that the plane went down between 1505 and 1508.

59. Draft of protest note and Klaus memo, 27 Dec. 1961, RG 59, Lot 64D551, Box 79, NA.

Chapter 3. Surface Contacts

1. Gary E. Weir, *Forged in War: The Naval-Industrial Complex and American Submarines Construction, 1940-1960* (Washington, D.C.: NHC, 1993), 246–48, 263.

2. Herrick, *Soviet Naval Strategy*, 71–73; MccGwire, "Evolution of Soviet Naval Policy," 507–8.

3. Robert E. Athay, "Perspectives on Soviet Merchant Shipping Policy," in *Soviet Naval Developments: Capability and Context*, ed. Michael MccGwire (New York: Praeger, 1973), 94–95.

4. "Soviets Press 'Buzzing' Charge," *New York Times*, 17 July 1960, 4. MFA notes 45/USA (3 Aug. 1964), 11/USA (22 Feb. 1965), 52/USA (15 Dec. 1965), 32/USA (5 Aug. 1966), and 30/USA (12 May 1969) are Soviet protests on numerous buzzing incidents that occurred worldwide. The United States rejected each complaint. RG 59, State Department Central Foreign Policy Files, Boxes 2552, 2873–74, NA.

5. Jack Raymond, "Soviet Trawler Called Spy Ship," *New York Times*, 14 July 1960, 9.

6. "Offshore Pickets," *Headquarters Alaskan Air Command Intelligence Review* 55, no. 5 (17 Oct. 1955): 3–9, K-484–608, USAFHRC.

7. The development of Soviet AGIS is discussed in G. Jacobs, "Soviet Navy AGIS," *Jane's Soviet Intelligence Review* (July 1989): 318–23.

8. 1972 Incidents Background paper, FOIA, NHC.

9. "U.S. Hits Actions by Soviet Ships," U.S. Naval Institute *Proceedings* 90, no. 12 (Dec. 1964): 150; John W. Finney, "U.S. Tells Soviet It Imperils Ships," *New York Times*, 4 April 1965, 1, 13.

10. Rear Adm. Robert P. Hilton Sr., USN (Ret.), interview by author, Alexandria, Va., 28 Nov. 1991.

11. Adm. Thomas B. Hayward, USN (Ret.), letter to author, 10 July 1992.

12. Adm. James L. Holloway III, USN (Ret.), interview by author, Washington, D.C., 21 May 1997; William Beecher, "French Join U.S. in Fleet Exercise," *New York Times*, 6 May 1967, quoted in Herrick, *Soviet Naval Strategy*, 93n.; U. Alexis Johnson, letter to Cy Vance, 20 Aug. 1966, RG 59 State Department Central Foreign Policy Files 1964–66, Box 2874, folder POL 33-6 U.S.-U.S.S.R. 1/1/66.

13. Adm. J. P. Weinel, USN (Ret.), interview by author, Bonsall, Calif., 17 May 1992 (hereafter Weinel interview).

14. Memorandum of conversation, Subject: Note to Soviet Embassy on Soviet Harassment of U.S. Naval Operations in South China Sea, 18 Jan. 1966, RG 59, Department of State Central Foreign Policy Files, 1964–66, Box 2874, Folder POL 33-6 U.S.-U.S.S.R. 1/1/66, NA; State, airgram to Amembassy Moscow, 2281, 26 Feb. 1965, RG 59, State Department Central Foreign Policy Files, Box 2873, Folder POL 33-4 U.S.-U.S.S.R. 1/1/65, NA.

15. Marvin O. Miller, John W. Hammett, and Terence P. Murphy, "Development of the U.S. Navy Underway Replenishment Fleet," in *Underway Replenishment of Naval Ships* (Port Hueneme, Calif.: Underway Replenishment Department, Port Hueneme Division, Naval Surface Warfare Center, 1992), 16–20. FAST proved to be too complex. During the 1970s the Navy adopted a simplified system called Standard Tensioned Replenishment Alongside Method (STREAM) that retained the tensioned highline feature of FAST.

16. Author had four years of experience assigned to replenishment ships in the U.S. Navy.

17. DCNO for Plans and Policy, memorandum to Assistant SecDef, International Security Affairs, 19 Sept. 1969, Pol-Mil Division 33, Box 555, USS *Sam Rayburn* Folder, Operational Archives, NHC. The memorandum also included reports of AGI harassment of USS *Jack* on 9–10 April 1969, and of USS *Sam Houston* on 31 July 1969. See also Memorandum of conversation, Subject: Protests on Incidents at Sea, 27 Oct. 1969, RG 59, Department of State Central Foreign Policy files, 1967–69, Box 2552, Folder POL 33-4 1/1/68, NA.

18. Capt. Robert Rawlins, USN (Ret.), interview by author, Healdsburg, Calif., 29 March 1992 (hereafter Rawlins interview).

19. Christopher Drew, Michael L. Millenson, and Robert Becker, "For U.S. and Soviets, an Intricate Undersea Minuet," *Chicago Tribune*, 8 Jan. 1991, 1, 8.

20. Weinel interview.

21. James Bamford, *The Puzzle Palace: A Report on America's Most Secret Agency* (Boston: Houghton Mifflin, 1982), 212–17. See also ship entries for USNS *Private Jose F. Valdez,* USNS *Sergeant Joseph E. Miller,* USS *Oxford,* USS *Georgetown,* USS *Jamestown,* USS *Belmont,* and USS *Liberty* in *Dictionary of American Naval Fighting Ships* (Washington, D.C.: NHC, n.d.): and Julie Alger, "A Review of the Technical Research Ship Program" (National Security Agency report, n.d.), 6–15, obtained through FOIA.

22. Edward J. Marolda, *By Sea, Air and Land: An Illustrated History of the U.S. Navy and the War in Southeast Asia* (Washington, D.C.: NHC, 1994), 51.

23. Bamford, *Puzzle Palace,* 229–33. State, telegram to Amembassy Moscow, 1298, 18 Nov. 1965, Subject: Banner Incident; State, telegram from Amembassy Moscow, 14873, 18 Dec. 1965, Subject: MFA Note No. 53/USA; State, telegram to Amembassy Moscow, 1549, 23 Dec. 1965, all in RG 59, Department of State Central Foreign Policy Files 1964–1966, Box 2873, Folder POL 33-4 U.S.-U.S.S.R. 1/11/65, NA.

24. Memorandum of conversation, Subject: Collision of Soviet vessel with the USS *Banner* between Llewellyn E. Thompson and Anatoly F. Dobrynin, 25 June 1966, RG 59, Department of State Central Foreign Policy Files 1964–1966, Box 2874, Folder POL 33-6 U.S.-U.S.S.R. 1/1/66, NA; State, telegram to Amembassy Moscow, 3045, 25

June 1966; and State, telegram from Amembassy Moscow, 4045, 28 June 1966, RG 59 Department of State Central Foreign Policy Files, 1964–1966, Box 2873, Folder POL 33-4 U.S.-U.S.S.R. 6/13/66, NA. The *Banner-Anemometr* incident was not publicized until May 1967. See John W. Finney, "A U.S. Destroyer in Far East Bumped by Soviet Warship," *New York Times*, 11 May 1967, 5.

25. *Dictionary of American Naval Fighting Ships*, 5:203.

26. Howard Blum, *I Pledge Allegiance. . .: The True Story of the Walkers: An American Spy Family* (New York: Simon and Schuster, 1987), 89–96, 153–55.

27. Alger, "Review of the Technical Research Ship Program," 130–33.

28. "Offshore Pickets," 8.

29. Background paper, Soviet Maritime Espionage activities, RG 59, Lot 64D551, NA; Jack Raymond, "U.S. Navy Board a Soviet Trawler in North Atlantic," *New York Times*, 27 Feb. 1959, 1; Jack Raymond, "U.S. Gives Soviet Report on Search of Fishing Vessel," *New York Times*, 28 Feb. 1959, 1.

30. "Moscow Sees Provocation by U.S. in Trawler Case," *New York Times*, 1 March 1959, 1, 12.

31. J. Stephen, AT&T, to William C. Harrington, Department of State, 28 Jan. 1966, RG 59, Department of State Central Foreign Policy Files, 1964–66, Box 2874, Folder POL 33-6 U.S.-U.S.S.R. 1/1/66, NA.

32. Norman Polmar, *Soviet Naval Power: Challenge for the 1970s*, rev. ed. (New York: Crane, Russak, 1974), 80–81.

33. Ibid., 83; *Understanding Soviet Naval Developments*, 3rd ed. (Washington, D.C.: Office of the CNO, Department of the Navy, 1978), 55–56; Legal Advisor memorandum for the SecState, 3636, 3 March 1967; and State, memorandum of conversation, Subject: Soviets Express Appreciation for Outcome of Trawler Incident, 7 March 1967, RG 59, State Central Foreign Policy Files 1967–69, Box 2552, Folder POL 23-10, 1/1/67, NA.

34. U.S. Coast Guard Investigation, F/V *Pierce*, 21 Sept. 1966, and Henry M. Jackson, letter to Dean Rusk, 21 Feb. 1967, RG 59, State Central Files 1967–1969, Box 2552, Folder POL 33-4 U.S.-U.S.S.R. PIERCE, NA.

35. *Understanding Soviet Naval Developments*, 56; Joseph Curran, letter to Dean Rusk, 9 Jan. 1968, RG 59, State Department Central Files 1967–69, Box 2552, Folder POL 33-4 1/1/68, NA.

36. Dino A. Brugioni, *Eyeball to Eyeball: The Inside Story of the Cuban Missile Crisis* (New York: Random House, 1990), 101–2, 149, 172.

37. Roger Hilsman, *To Move a Nation: The Politics of Foreign Policy in the Administration of John F. Kennedy* (Garden City, N.Y.: Doubleday, 1967), 207–11.

38. Ibid., 215–19; Brugioni, *Eyeball to Eyeball*, 419–20.

39. Brugioni, *Eyeball to Eyeball,* 434–36; Jerry McDonnell, "Incident in History: Intercept of *Marcula,*" *All Hands,* no. 551 (Dec. 1962); Joseph F. Bouchard, *Command in Crisis* (New York: Columbia University Press, 1991), 115–16.

40. Brugioni, *Eyeball to Eyeball,* 473–74.

41. Ibid., 514–23; Capt. Charles R. Calhoun, USN (Ret.), interview by Capt. Wilbur D. Jones Jr., USNR (Ret.), Wilmington, N.C., 12 June 1998, Naval Historical Foundation; Bouchard, *Command in Crisis,* 116–17.

42. Amembassy Moscow, telegram 2422, 27 March 1963, Subject: MFA Note No. 17/USA; and Amembassy Moscow, telegram 2435, 29 March 1963, Subject: MFA Note No. 19/USA, RG 59, State Department Central Foreign Policy Files, Box 3612, Folder Ships-Vessels-Equipment-U.S.S.R., NA; memorandum for Mr. McGeorge Bundy, Subject: Incident involving the United States Merchant Ship ss *Sister Katingo,* 17 July 1964, RG 59, State Department Central Foreign Policy File 1964–1966, Box 2873, Folder POL 33-6 U.S.-U.S.S.R. 4/1/64, NA.

43. Amembassy Moscow, telegram 609, 5 Aug. 1966; Johnson, letter to Vance, 12905, 20 Aug. 1966.

44. Neil Sheehan, *A Bright Shining Lie: John Paul Vann and America in Vietnam* (New York: Vintage Books, 1989), 679–70.

45. "Soviet Says Raid Periled Its Ships," *New York Times,* 10 July 1966, 1, 2. The United States responded to the protest on 23 July, stating that the Soviet note had contained inaccuracies and false allegations. Raymond H. Anderson, "U.S. Rejects Note by Soviets on Raids," *New York Times,* 6 Aug. 1966, 1, 3.

46. Amembassy Moscow, telegram 609, 5 Aug. 1966, RG 59, State Department Central Foreign Policy Files, Box 2874, Folder POL 33-6 U.S.-U.S.S.R. 1/1/66, NA.

47. Raymond H. Anderson, "Moscow Says U.S. Hit Ship in Vietnam Port," *New York Times,* 3 June 1967, 1; Hedrick Smith, "U.S. Denies Attack on Soviet Vessel in North Vietnam," *New York Times,* 4 June 1967, 1, 6.

48. Henry Kamm, "U.S. Sends Soviet 2d Note of Regret," *New York Times,* 16 July 1967, 10.

49. Raymond H. Anderson, "U.S. Raid Damaged Ship, Moscow Says," *New York Times,* 6 Jan. 1968, 1, 3.

50. Johnson, letter to Vance, 12905, 20 Aug. 1966.

51. Vance, letter to Kohler, 7702, 30 Nov. 1966, RG 59, State Department Central Foreign Policy Files, Box 2874, Folder POL 33-6 U.S.-U.S.S.R. 1/1/66, NA.

52. Kohler, letter to Vance, 17941, 12 Dec. 1966, RG 59, State Department Central Foreign Policy files, Box 2874, Folder POL 33-6 U.S.-U.S.S.R. 1/1/66, NA.

Chapter 4. The Rise of the Soviet Navy

1. John E. Lacouture, "The Confrontation at Sea between the U.S. and Soviet Navies," Litt. diss., University of Cambridge, 1979, 28-30.

2. Elmo R. Zumwalt Jr., *On Watch* (New York: Quadrangle Press, 1976), 391-93.

3. Hilsman, *To Move a Nation*, 214.

4. Bouchard, *Command in Crisis*, 120-21.

5. Ibid., 120-21, 123.

6. Brugioni, *Eyeball to Eyeball*, 509.

7. Bouchard, *Command in Crisis*, 126.

8. Ibid., 123-24.

9. Polmar, *Soviet Naval Power*, 40.

10. As told to then-SecNav John Warner by Gorshkov during the 1972 Moscow summit. John W. Warner, interview by Thomas B. Allen, 6 June 1989 (provided by Allen).

11. *Understanding Soviet Naval Developments*, 30-31.

12. Sergei Gorshkov, *The Seapower of the State* (Annapolis, Md.: Naval Institute Press, 1979), 119-23.

13. *Understanding Soviet Naval Developments*, 13-15. See also MccGwire, "Evolution of Soviet Naval Policy," 518-21; Lacouture, "Confrontation at Sea between the U.S. and Soviet Navies," 32.

14. USS *Walker*, *Dictionary of American Fighting Ships*, 8:61-64.

15. Amembassy Moscow, telegram 716, 10 Aug. 1966, with MFA Note no. 33/USA, RG 59, State Department Central Foreign Policy Files, Box 2874, Folder POL 33-6 U.S.-U.S.S.R. 1/1/66, NA. The note stated that on 25 July 1966 a Soviet destroyer (hull no. 66) had to stop twice to avoid collisions. The first incident occurred with the USS *Radford* and the second with the USS *Walker*.

16. Peterson enclosure, in OP-614C memo to OP-61B, Subject: Sea of Japan Collisions, 4 Oct. 1967, Pol-Mil Division 33, Box 555, *Walker* Folder, Operational Archives, NHC; Capt. Earl E. Buckwalter, USN, Investigation to Inquire Into the Circumstances Surrounding a Collision between USS *Walker* (DD 517) and Soviet DD 022 on 10 May 1967, and a Collision between USS *Walker* DD 517 and Soviet DDGS 025 on 11 May 1967 during the Sea of Japan Transit of Task Group 70.4, FOIA, Navy Judge Advocate General Corps (hereafter Buckwalter investigation).

17. Buckwalter investigation.

18. Finney, "U.S. Destroyer in Far East Bumped by Soviet Warship," 1, 5.

19. Buckwalter investigation.

20. Ibid.

21. John W. Finney, "A Soviet Warship Bumps U.S. Vessel, Second Time in 2 Days," *New York Times*, 12 May 1967, 1, 4.

22. *The Current Digest of the Soviet Press* 24, no. 20 (n.d.): 18–19. Article translated from *Izvestiya*, 18 May 1967, 5.

23. Bouchard, *Command in Crisis*, 143; Neil Sheehan, "A Larger Soviet Vessel Follows U.S. Carrier in Mediterranean," *New York Times*, 4 June 1967, p 4.

24. Bouchard, *Command in Crisis*, 144.

25. Ibid., 145; Memorandum Concerning Harassment uss *Lawe* and sov DLG-381, 7 June 1967, Pol-Mil Division 33, Box 555, Folder *Agile* 12 June 1967, Operational Archives, NHC.

26. Neil Sheehan, "Russians Continue to Harass 6th Fleet," *New York Times*, 9 June 1967, 1, 15; Memorandum Concerning Harassment, uss *America* and sov PCS-160, 8 June 1967, Pol-Mil 33, Box 555, Folder *Agile*, Operational Archives, NHC. Engen, quoted in Bouchard, *Command in Crisis*, 145.

27. Polmar, *Soviet Naval Power*, 66; Lacouture, "Confrontation at Sea between the U.S. and Soviet Navies," 36.

28. Leddy, letter to O'Grady, 3 July 1967, Pol-Mil Division 33, Box 555, *Walker* Folder, Operational Archives, NHC.

29. Draft reply to Amembassy Moscow, telegram 695, Pol-Mil Division 33, Box 555, *Davis* Folder, Operational Archives, NHC.

30. OP-614C, memorandum to OP-06, 15 Dec. 1967, Pol-Mil Division 33, Box 555, *Dealey*/sov DD 482 Folder, Operational Archives, NHC.

31. Ignatius, memorandum to Nitze, 02039P61, 11 Jan. 1968, Pol-Mil Division 33, Box 555, *Abnaki* Folder, Operational Archives, NHC.

32. Thomas J. Schoenbaum, *Waging Peace and War: Dean Rusk in the Truman, Kennedy, and Johnson Years* (New York, Simon and Schuster, 1988), 467.

33. State, airgram to Amembassy Moscow, A-203, 9 April 1968, RG 59, State Department Central Foreign Policy Files, Box 2552, Folder POL 23-10 1/1/67, NA.

34. DoD Press Release No. 120-68, in uss *Rowan* ship's history folder, Ships History Branch, NHC.

35. Nitze, letter to Katzenbach, 1 Feb. 1968; Katzenbach, letter to Nitze, 9 Feb. 1968, RG 59, State Department Central Foreign Policy Files, Box 2552, Folder POL 23-10 1/1/67, NA.

36. Draft Paper, Subject: Encounters between U.S. and Soviet Ships Near Japan, 12 March 1968, Pol-Mil Division 33, Box 555, *Rowan*/*Vislobokov* Folder, Operational Archives, NHC.

37. Memorandum of conversation between Igor D. Bubnov of U.S.S.R. Embassy and Herbert S. Okun and William T. Shinn at State of 27 Aug. 1970, FOIA, State.

38. Command History, USS *Essex*, 1968, Ships History Branch, NHC; Tu-16 data found in *Understanding Soviet Naval Developments*, 6th ed. (Washington, D.C.: Office of the Chief of Naval Operations, 1991), 170.

39. Capt. Russ Dickens, USN (Ret.), letter to author, 7 May 1992 (hereafter Dickens letter).

40. Command History, USS *Essex*; "Soviet Jet Falls Near U.S. Carrier," *New York Times*, 26 May 1968, 24.

41. Dickens letter.

42. State, memorandum of conversation, Subject: Crash of Soviet Tu-16 Aircraft and Proposed Lease of U.S. Navigational Equipment, 13 Aug. 1968, Pol-Mil Division 33, Box 555, Tu-16/*Essex* Folder, Operational Archives, NHC; Katzenbach, memorandum to Nitze, 16 Aug. 1968, RG 59, State Department Central Files 67–69, Box 2553, Folder 1/1/67, NA.

43. Capt. Robert N. Congdon, USN (Ret.), letter to author, 10 March 1992 (hereafter Congdon letter, 10 March 1992).

44. An official account of the shootdown is contained in Command History of Fleet Air Reconnaissance Squadron One, 1969, Operational Archives, NHC. Kissinger's account is found in Henry A. Kissinger, *The White House Years* (Boston: Little, Brown, 1979), 312–21.

45. Laird, letter to Rogers, 13026, 26 Aug. 1969, RG 59, State Department Central Foreign Policy Files 67–69, Box 2552, Folder POL 23-10 1/1/67, NA.

46. State, memorandum of conversation, Subject: Protests on Incidents at Sea, 27 Oct. 1969, RG 59, State Department Central Files 67–69, Box 2552, Folder 33-4 1/1/67, NA.

47. State, memorandum of conversation, Subject: Buzzing of U.S. Ships in the Sea of Japan, 9 Dec. 1969, RG 59, State Department Central Foreign Policy Files 67–69, Box 2552, Folder POL 33-4 1/1/67, NA.

48. John W. Warner, interview by author, Washington, D.C., 9 April 1992 (hereafter Warner interview); *Understanding Soviet Naval Developments*, 3rd ed., 21–22; Rear Adm. Peter K. Cullins, USN (Ret), interview by author, Washington, D.C., 19 Feb. 1998.

49. Zumwalt, *On Watch*, 83–84.

50. Ibid., 46–47.

51. Undated study conducted in early 1972 examining U.S.-U.S.S.R. Incidents at Sea, Operational Archives, NHC.

52. Memorandum of conversation between Bubnov, Okun, and Shinn of 27 Aug. 1970, FOIA, State.

53. Ibid., 600–607.

54. Ibid., 612–15; Zumwalt, *On Watch*, 298.

55. Zumwalt, *On Watch*, 300–301.

56. Kissinger, *White House Years*, 628; Zumwalt, *On Watch*, 299–300. Kissinger argues that American sea power contributed to a favorable resolution to the crisis on several levels: its presence held off European governments wanting to negotiate with the hijackers, pressured the hijackers to release hostages, emboldened King Hussein to act decisively, and might have deterred Hafez Assad from committing the Syrian Air Force to support the incursion into Jordan. Zumwalt argues that American sea power was sufficient but expressed concern that the Soviets were close to negating American supremacy in the eastern Mediterranean.

Chapter 5. The Road to Moscow

1. Bernard Gwertzman, "Soviet Passengers and Crew Describe Hijacking," *New York Times*, 18 Oct. 1970, A24; Richard Eder, "Turks Radio Says Courts Act to Free 2 Soviet Hijackers," *New York Times*, 18 Oct. 1970, A1.

2. Bernard Gwertzman, "Soviet Bars Immediate 2nd Visit to US Officers as Unneeded," *New York Times*, 29 Oct. 1970.

3. "Hostages for Hijackers?" *Newsweek*, 9 Nov. 1970, 37.

4. Chronology extracted from *New York Times* articles and Kissinger, *White House Years*, 795.

5. Amembassy Moscow, message to SecState, 101600Z, Nov. 1970, FOIA, State.

6. Adm. Elmo R. Zumwalt Jr., USN (Ret.), interview by author, Arlington, Va., 30 June 1992 (hereafter Zumwalt interview).

7. Rogers, letter to Laird, 3 Feb. 1972, FOIA, State. See also John Stevenson and George S. Springsteen, action memorandum to Rogers, 23 Jan. 1971, FOIA, State.

8. Laird, letter to Rogers, 7102558, 19 Feb. 1971, FOIA, OSD; Martin J. Hillenbrand, action memorandum to Rogers, 26 Feb. 1971, FOIA, State; Zumwalt interview; Warner interview; and Melvin Laird, letter to author, 1 May 1992.

9. Henry A. Kissinger, National Security Study Memorandum 119, 19 Feb. 1971, RG 273, NA. The document can also be found at the National Security Archive, Washington, D.C.

10. State, telegram to Amembassy Moscow, 032404, 25 Feb. 1972; Hillenbrand, action memorandum to Rogers, 26 Feb. 1971; invitation letter from Grover W. Penberthy, 26 Feb. 1971: all FOIA, State.

11. Amembassy Moscow, message to SecState, 270921Z, Feb. 1971, FOIA, State.

12. Capt. Robert D. Rawlins, USN (Ret.), letters to author, 13 March and 21 Aug. 1992.

13. "The Reminiscences of Vice Admiral Gerald E. Miller, U.S. Navy (Retired)," vol. 2, Oral History Program, U.S. Naval Institute, Annapolis, Md., 1984, 652–53.

14. Rawlins letter of 13 March 1992. See also D. D. Engen, OP-60 memo to OP-61, 5 March 1971, Pol-Mil Division 33, Box 558, Operational Archives, NHC.

15. Congdon letter (10 March 1992); Weinel interview. One way the Navy attempted to fulfill its intelligence collection activities was through a clandestine organization called Task Force 157. This intelligence organization used nonmilitary boats and helicopters to perform close surveillance of Soviet units. See Jeffrey T. Richelson, "Task Force 157: The US Navy's Secret Intelligence Service, 1966–1977," *Intelligence and National Security* 11 (Jan. 1996): 106–45.

16. Ambassador Herbert S. Okun, interview by author, New York City, 25 Feb. 1992 (hereafter Okun interview); CNO, message to USDAO Moscow, 051954Z, Oct. 1971, Accession 9670-18, Box 1, Book S616-036-92, Operational Archives, NHC.

17. Okun interview; Warner interview.

18. Theodore L. Eliot Jr., memorandum to Kissinger, 27 Feb. 1971, FOIA, State; Eliot, memorandum to Kissinger, 13 March 1971, FOIA, State.

19. Okun interview.

20. Congdon letter (10 March 1992); Congdon, interview by author, San Diego, 18 May 1992 (hereafter Congdon interview); Response to NSSM 119, RG 273, NSSM 119 Folder, NA.

21. Okun interview. Okun's observations are echoed in a point paper attached to the previously cited Rogers letter to Laird of 3 Feb. 1972.

22. Rear Adm. Walter L. Small, USN, memorandum to Vice CNO, 001762P61, 19 Feb. 1971; British Vice Chief of Naval Staff, letter to Adm. R. W. Cousins, USN, 15 March 1971, Operational Archives, NHC; Penberthy, memorandum to IG/EUR 1 April meeting participants, Subject: NSSM 119, 6 April 1971, FOIA, State.

23. Robert C. Brewster, memorandum to Kissinger, 16 April 1971, RG 273, NSSM 119 Folder, NA.

24. Plans and Policy Directorate (J-5) memorandum, Subject: National Security Council Interdepartmental Group/Europe (NSC/IG/EUR) Meeting, 1 April 1971, dated 3 April 1971, FOIA, Navy; Penberthy, memo to IG/EUR 1 April meeting participants, FOIA, State. State, CIA, OSD/ISA, NSA staff, OPNAV, and the JCS had representatives at the meeting.

25. Hillenbrand, memorandum to Eliot, 13 April 1971, FOIA, State; Robert C. Brewster, memorandum to Kissinger, 16 April 1971, RG 273, NSSM 119 Folder, NA; Sonnenfelt, memorandum to Kissinger, Subject: U.S.-Soviet Incidents at Sea, 21 April 1971, RG 273, NSSM 119 Folder, NA; Eliot, memorandum to Kissinger, 10 May 1971, FOIA, State.

26. Capt. Arthur L. Battson, USN, Investigation to inquire into the circumstances connected with the collision between USS *Hanson* (DD 832) and the U.S.S.R. tugboat *Diomid* which occurred at 061241I on 6 May 1971, 13 May 1971, FOIA, Navy Judge Advocate General.

27. Adm. Isaac Kidd, interview by Alex Kucherov, 8 July 1971. Records show that on 6 April 1971 the United States protested the 17 Nov. 1970 AGI harassment of the submarine USS *Sam Houston* off the coast of Spain. From memorandum of conversation between Vadim Kavalerov, Edward L. Killham, and Peter Semler, Subject: Protest to Soviets about Harassment of U.S. Submarine, 6 April 1971, FOIA, State.

28. Amembassy Moscow, messages to SecState, 101500Z and 111552Z, May 1971, FOIA, State.

29. Amembassy Moscow, message to SecState, 121400Z, May 1971, FOIA, State.

30. NSDM 110, RG 273, NSDM 110 Folder, NA.

31. State, telegrams 101568 and 101585, drafted 28 May 1971, FOIA, State.

32. Amembassy Moscow, message to SecState, 091600Z, June 1971, FOIA, State.

33. State, telegram 109972, drafted 18 June 1971, FOIA, State.

34. Bernard Gwertzman, "Soviet Says U.S. Fleet Harassed Grechko Ship," *New York Times*, 15 June 1971, 1, 4.

35. State, telegram 120407, drafted 29 June 1971, FOIA, State.

36. Okun interview.

37. CNO message to USDAO Moscow, 051954Z, Oct. 1971; Okun, Zumwalt, Rawlins, Congdon, interviews; *Walker* investigation; Dickens letter; Memorandum from Rear Admiral Small to Undersecretary Warner, Operational Archives, NHC; Rear Adm. Ronald J. Kurth, USN (Ret.), interviews by author, Murray, Ky., 18 Jan. and 5 Sept. 1991; Capt. William C. Lynch, JAGC, USN (Ret.), interview by author, San Diego, 18 May 1992.

38. Amembassy Moscow, messages to SecState, 051210Z and 071250Z, July 1971, FOIA, State; State, telegram 125524, drafted 9 July 1971, FOIA, State; Amembassy Moscow, message to SecState, 231234Z, July 1971, FOIA, State.

39. Memorandum for the SecDef, Subject: Report of July–August Seabeds Committee Meeting in Geneva, drafted 8 Aug. 1971, Warner papers.

40. Warner and Okun interviews.

41. Vice Adm. James H. Doyle, USN (Ret.), letters to author, 8 July and 20 July 1992 (hereafter Doyle letters); Vogt, memorandum to Moorer, Subject: U.S./Soviet Talks on Incidents at Sea, 8 Sept. 1971, FOIA, OSD; Warner, memorandum to Laird, Subject: Forthcoming "Incidents at Sea Discussions" with the Soviets, 9 Sept. 1971, Warner papers.

42. Memorandum for Vice Admiral Weinel, Subject: Incidents at Sea Delegation, 17 Sept. 1971, Warner papers.

43. Amembassy Moscow, message to SecState, 070955Z, Sept. 1971, FOIA, State; and State, telegram 164291, drafted 7 Sept. 1971, FOIA, State; Tad Szulc, "U.S. and Russians Will Open Parley on Incidents," *New York Times,* 9 Sept. 1971, 1, 14.

44. Memorandum for the SecDef, Subject: CINCPAC request for transit of the Sea of Okhotsk, Warner papers; Amembassy Moscow, 090945Z, Oct. 1971, FOIA, State.

45. Amembassy Moscow, message to SecState, 241437Z, Sept. 1971, FOIA, State; State, telegram 179317, drafted 29 Sept. 1971, FOIA, State. Other visitors included a delegation of governors, the undersecretary of Housing and Urban Development, a Social Security delegation, and Duke Ellington.

46. Capt. William H. J. Manthorpe, USN (Ret.), interview by author, Washington, D.C., 3 March 1992.

47. Kissinger, *White House Years,* 413.

48. John W. Warner, memorandum for the record, 7 Oct. 1971, Warner papers. The deep impression that Thompson left was reflected in interviews with Warner, Okun, Kurth, Rawlins, and Congdon.

49. Kissinger, *White House Years,* 755–60, 766, 838.

50. State Department telegrams 169183, drafted 14 Sept. 1971, and 183698, drafted 6 Oct. 1971, FOIA, State; State, airgram A-1153, 14 Oct. 1971, FOIA, State.

51. Doyle letters; Joint Chiefs Memorandum for the SecDef, JSCM-451-71, 9 Oct. 1971, FOIA, OSD.

Chapter 6. Negotiations

1. Robert W. Daly, "Soviet Naval Activities, 1970," U.S. Naval Institute *Proceedings* (May 1971): 286–92; *Great Soviet Encyclopedia,* vol. 3 (New York: Macmillan, 1975).

2. Cyril Muromcew, interview by author, Washington, D.C., 2 Dec. 1991 (hereafter Muromcew interview); Lynch interview.

3. Anthony F. Wolf, "Agreement at Sea: The United States-U.S.S.R. Agreement on Incidents at Sea," *Korean Journal of International Studies* 23, no. 3 (1978): 65.

4. Amembassy Moscow, messages to SecState, 081420Z and 122005Z, Oct. 1971, FOIA, State.

5. Amembassy Moscow, message to SecState, 122140Z, Oct. 1971, FOIA, State; Lynch interview.

6. Capt. Robert Congdon, USN (Ret.), letter to author, 11 Aug. 1992.

7. Amembassy Moscow, message to SecState, 122140Z, Oct. 1971, FOIA, State.

8. Lynch, Warner, and Okun interviews.

9. Amembassy Moscow, message to SecState, 130756Z, Oct. 1971, FOIA, State; also Warner and Okun interviews.

10. Rawlins interview; Doyle letter (8 July 1992); Moorer, memorandum for Laird, Subject: NSSM 119-U.S./Soviet Incidents at Sea, 9 Oct. 1971, FOIA, OSD.

11. Warner, memorandum to Nixon, Subject: U.S. Soviet Naval Talks on Preventing Incidents at Sea, 29 Oct. 1971, Warner papers (hereafter Warner memorandum).

12. Okun, Rawlins, Congdon, and Kurth interviews.

13. Wolf, "Agreement at Sea," 68.

14. Manthorpe interview.

15. Capt. R. D. Rawlins, Point Paper, Subject: Incidents at Sea (II) Issues, 8 Jan. 1972, FOIA, Navy.

16. Lynch interview.

17. Wolf, "Agreement at Sea," 68.

18. Warner interview.

19. Lynch, Congdon, Rawlins, and Okun interviews; John W. Warner, Report to the President, 1 Nov. 1971, Warner papers.

20. Kurth interview, 5 Sept. 1991.

21. Amembassy Moscow, message to SecState, 181650Z, Oct. 1971, FOIA, State; Lynch interview.

22. Warner interview; Amembassy Moscow, message to SecState, 181650Z, Oct. 1971, FOIA, State.

23. Congdon interview.

24. Rawlins, Position paper, 8 Jan. 1972; Warner memorandum.

25. Okun and Warner interviews; Amembassy Moscow, telegram to SecState, 211440Z, Oct. 1971, FOIA, State; "The Reminiscences of Capt. Herbert E. Hetu, U.S. Navy (Retired)" (Annapolis, Md.: Naval Institute Oral History Program, 1996), 470–71.

26. State, telegram 191947, 19 Oct. 1972, FOIA, State; Amembassy Moscow, message to SecState, 202150Z, Oct. 1971, FOIA, State; Amembassy Moscow, message to SecState, 211540Z, Oct. 1971, FOIA, State.

27. Warner memorandum.

28. Amembassy Moscow, message to SecState, 230935Z, Oct. 1971, FOIA, State.

29. Okun interview. Former CNO Adm. James L. Holloway III counted himself as one of those who had opposed reaching an understanding with the Soviets. Holloway interview.

30. NSSM 140, 11 Nov. 1971, RG 273, Folder NSSM 140, NA.

31. State Department Briefing Memorandum 7119478, drafted 16 Nov. 1971, FOIA, State.

32. Doyle letters; Henry Kissinger, NSDM 150, 11 Feb. 1972, RG 273, NA.

33. Rawlins, Point Paper.

34. Amembassy Moscow, message to SecState, 230832Z, Dec. 1971, FOIA, State; Hillenbrand, memorandum to Undersecretary, Subject: NSSM-140: U.S.-Soviet Talks on Preventing Incidents at Sea, 11 Jan. 1972, FOIA, State.

35. Kissinger, NSDM 150.

36. Amembassy Moscow, message to SecState, 240901Z, Feb. 1972, FOIA, State.

37. Amembassy Moscow, message to SecState, 071528Z, March 1972, FOIA, State.

38. State, telegram 058586, 5 April 1972, FOIA, State; Okun interview. Okun later noted that the Soviets hoped to press the United States to agree to a fixed-distance regime.

39. Kissinger, *White House Years,* 1115.

40. Amembassy Moscow, message to SecState, 071304Z, April 1972, FOIA, State.

41. Kissinger, *White House Years,* 1116, 1118.

42. State, telegram 061808, 11 April 1972, FOIA, State; Amembassy Moscow, message to SecState, 121338Z, April 1972, FOIA, State.

43. Amembassy Moscow, message to SecState, 271521Z, April 1972, FOIA, State; Memorandum for the CNO, 04411P61, dated 8 Dec. 1971, and SecNav, message to COMFIRSTFLT, 262304Z, April 1972, FOIA, DoD.

44. COMSIXTHFLT TO CINCUSNAVEUR, 071511Z, April 1972, Subject: Personal for Admiral Bringle, Hilton papers.

45. CINCUSNAVEUR to CNO, 151834Z, April 1972, Subject: Personal for Cousins, Hilton papers.

46. COMDESRON FOURTEEN to CINCUSNAVEUR/COMSIXTHFLT, 061020Z, May 1972, Subject: Personal for Admiral Bringle and Vice Admiral Miller, Hilton papers. Before he returned to the Mediterranean, Hilton also spoke with CJCS Admiral Moorer and formally briefed the CJCS staff.

47. Lynch interview.

48. Kissinger, *White House Years,* 1174-80; Marvin Kalb and Bernard Kalb, *Kissinger* (Boston: Little, Brown, 1974), 300-302; Walter Isaacson, *Kissinger* (New York: Simon and Schuster, 1992), 415-19; H. R. Haldeman, *The Haldeman Diaries* (New York: Putnam's Sons, 1994), 451-55; Stephen E. Ambrose, *Nixon: The Triumph of a Politician, 1962-1972* (New York: Simon and Schuster, 1989), 537.

49. Zumwalt, *On Watch,* 384-85; and Zumwalt interview.

50. Capt. Robert Rawlins and Mrs. Peggy Rawlins, interview by author, Healdsburg, Calif., 29 March 1992.

51. Warner, Okun, and Lynch interviews.

52. Okun interview; Capt. Mark Flanigan, USNR (Ret.), interview by author, Washington, D.C., 27 March 1997.

53. Kissinger, *White House Years,* 1184–86; Isaacson, *Kissinger,* 420–21.

54. Warner and Okun interviews; Laird, letters to author, 1 May and 9 July 1992. Laird verified Warner's account of their conversation.

55. Zumwalt, *On Watch,* 393–94; Zumwalt interview; Okun interview; Cyril Muromcew, interview by author, Washington, D.C., 2 Dec. 1991.

56. Ibid. Kasatonov spoke in Russian, and the English translation was provided by Okun and Muromcew. The Bubnov outburst was in English and was vividly recalled by Muromcew and Zumwalt. See also Kalb and Kalb, *Kissinger,* 306.

57. Kissinger, *White House Years,* 1193, 1196; Anatoly Dobrynin, *In Confidence: Moscow's Ambassador to America's Six Cold War Presidents* (New York: Random House, 1995), 246–47.

58. Hayward letter.

59. Talking points for 2 P.M. meeting, 11 May 1972, Warner papers.

60. Memorandum for Distribution List, Subject: Incidents at Sea Talks, 11 May 1972, Warner papers.

61. Memorandum for the SecDef, Subject: Incidents at Sea, 11 May 1972, Warner papers.

62. Article by Article Analysis of Draft Incidents at Sea Agreement—12 May 1972, and Warner, memorandum to Laird, Subject: Incident at Sea Talks, 12 May 1972, Warner papers.

63. Memorandum for the SecDef, Subject: Daily SitRep of Incidents at Sea Talks, 12 May 1972, Warner papers.

64. Doyle letter (20 July 1992).

65. COMFIRSTFLT, message to SecNav, 050150Z, May 1972, FOIA, DoD.

66. Talking Paper for Chairman, JCS, Subject: U.S.-Soviet Talks on Preventing Incidents at Sea, NSDM 150, 14 May 1972; Point Paper for the Secretary, Subject: Incidents at Sea: General Wording vs. Fixed Distance Formulations, n.d.; Laird, letter to Nixon, Subject: Incidents at Sea Talks: General Wording vs. Fixed Distance Formulations, n.d., Navy FOIA; Agreement between the Government of the United States of America and the Government of the Union of Soviet Socialist Republics on the Prevention of Incidents on and over the High Seas, FOIA, State. The Navy only provided the author the locator sheets for the first three documents listed.

67. Hillenbrand, action memorandum to Rogers, Subject: Request for Circular 175 Authority, 17 May 1972, FOIA, State.

68. For example, a tiny AGI could race ahead of an American carrier task force and

turn in front of it to cross from right to left, thereby obliging all ships in the American formation to turn right.

Chapter 7. Détente

1. Warner interview.

2. Laird memorandum, Subject: Incident at Sea Follow-on Measures, 22 May 1972, FOIA, DoD. Laird also notified the White House of his actions. Kissinger, memorandum to Laird, 19 June 1972, FOIA, DoD.

3. Day, memorandum to Pickering, Subject: U.S.-Soviet Incidents at Sea Talks, 31 May 1972, FOIA, State; Spiers, letter to Nutter, 2 June 1972, FOIA, DoD. Nutter responded by agreeing to State representation at the annual consultations. Nutter, letter to Spiers, I-7679/72, FOIA, Navy.

4. Laird, letter to Rogers, 9 June 1972, FOIA, DoD; SecState to Amembassy Moscow, 131502Z, June 1972, Subject: Incidents at Sea Consultations, FOIA, State; Amembassy Moscow to SecState, 301452Z, Aug. 1972, Subject: Incidents at Sea: Letter from Minister Grechko to Secretary Laird, FOIA, State. The three Navy captains were Wynn V. Whidden (OP-05), Robert D. Rawlins (OP-61), and William R. Martin (OSD/ISA).

5. Martin, memorandum for members of Incidents at Sea Group, Subject: Working Group Meeting, 3 July 1972, FOIA, Navy; Martin, memorandum for Incidents at Sea Working Group, Subject: U.S. Position Paper, 20 July 1972, FOIA, Navy; Martin, memorandum for record, Subject: Incidents at Sea Working Group, 24 July 1972, FOIA, Navy; Whidden memorandum to Rawlins, Subject: Paper for U.S.-U.S.S.R. Incidents at Sea Negotiations, 16 Aug. 1972, FOIA, Navy; Eagleburger, memorandum to Assistant SecDef, Subject: Incidents at Sea Position Paper, Serial I-12930/72, FOIA, Navy; Director Joint Staff LTG George M. Seignious II, memorandum to Assistant SecDef, Subject: Incidents at Sea Position Paper, 5 Oct. 1972, FOIA, Navy; Martin, memorandum to Weinel, Subject: U.S. Position for Incidents at Sea Meeting, Moscow, Nov. 1972, FOIA, Navy.

6. CTU-67.5.2 to AIG 348, 271640Z, May 1972, Subject: SAU Alfa Bystander Sitrep Supplement Eleven Alfa, Pol-Mil Division Series 33, Box 557, Folder IAS Bystander/May-June, Operational Archives, NHC.

7. John N. Irwin II, memorandum for the president, 28 July 1972, FOIA, State.

8. Amembassy Moscow, message to SecState, 110725Z, July 1972, FOIA, State.

9. Eagleburger, memorandum to Selden, Subject: Incidents at Sea Meeting—Moscow, 26 Oct. 1972, FOIA, Navy; Selden, memorandum to Warner, Subject: Incidents at Sea Meeting, 27 Oct. 1972, FOIA, Navy. Warner's concern did not reflect

a disagreement with the U.S. position but rather a concern that the White House not be surprised should the Soviets break off talks.

10. The instructions for the delegation were approved by Alexander Haig for Kissinger. From Report of Incidents at Sea Meetings, Moscow, 13–18 Nov. 1972, FOIA, DoD (hereafter Report of Incidents).

11. U.S. Naval Institute *Proceedings* 97, no. 5 (May 1971): 288.

12. Weinel interview; Capt. R. Y. Scott, USN (OP-61), memorandum for the CNO, Subject: Agreement between the U.S. and U.S.S.R. on the Prevention of Incidents On and Over the High Seas (INCSEA), 22 Nov. 1972, FOIA, Navy; Report of Incidents at Sea Meeting Moscow, 13–18 Nov. 1972, 29 Nov. 1972, FOIA, DoD; Amembassy Moscow, message to SecState, 181011Z, Nov. 1972, FOIA, State.

13. Weinel interview.

14. Report of Incidents.

15. Engen, letter to Zumwalt, 8 Dec. 1972, FOIA, DoD; Zumwalt, letter to Engen, 2 Jan. 1973, FOIA, DoD.

16. Eagleburger, memorandum to Laird, Subject: U.S.-U.S.S.R. Agreement on Prevention of Incidents on and over the High Sea, 20 Feb. 1973, FOIA, DoD.

17. The following messages detail social interactions with Soviet officials: Amembassy Moscow, to SecState, 081333Z, Feb. 1973, Subject: Incidents at Sea; USDAO Moscow, to SecNav, 260902Z, Feb. 1973, Subject: INCSEA; and USDAO Moscow, to DoD, 281351Z, Feb. 1973, Subject: INCSEA Talks, FOIA, Navy.

18. Deputy SecDef W. P. Clements, memorandum for Warner, Subject: Annual Review of the U.S.-U.S.S.R. Incidents at Sea Agreement, 7 March 1973, FOIA, Navy; SecState, 191635Z, March 1973, Subject: Incidents at Sea—Annual Review, FOIA, State; SecState to Amembassy Moscow, 062019Z, April 1973, Subject: Incidents at Sea Meeting, FOIA, State.

19. Assistant SecDef Robert C. Hill, memorandum for Laird, Subject: U.S.-U.S.S.R. Incidents at Sea Conference—Information Memorandum, 10 May 1973, FOIA, Navy; USDAO Moscow to CNO, 041347Z, May 1973, FOIA, DoD.

20. Briefing notes shared with author by Admiral Weinel.

21. Weinel interview; Spier, action memorandum to Acting Secretary, Subject: Request for Circular 175 Authority to Negotiate, Conclude, and Sign a Protocol to the Agreement Between the Government of the United States of America and the Government of the Union of Soviet Socialist Republics on the Prevention of Incidents On and Over the High Seas, 21 May 1973, FOIA, State.

22. *Protocol to the Agreement of May 25, 1972, between the United States of America and the Union of Soviet Socialist Republics,* signed at Washington, D.C., 22 May 1973.

23. Weinel interview.

24. Rear Admiral Robert J. Hanks, "Middle East Journal: U.S. Naval Diplomacy in the Middle East, 1972–75," 1989, 1993, 71–73.

Chapter 8. The 1970s

1. Malcolm Muir Jr., *Black Shoes and Blue Water: Surface Warfare in the United States Navy, 1945-1975* (Washington, D.C.: NHC, 1996), 202.

2. Adm. Harry D. Train II, USN (Ret.), interview by Paul Stillwell, U.S. Naval Institute, Annapolis, Md., 17 July 1996 (hereafter Train interview).

3. *Understanding Soviet Naval Developments,* 72, 74, 76.

4. Muir, *Black Shoes and Blue Water,* 199–200, 202.

5. Ibid., 202.

6. Train interview.

7. Exceptions included Portugal, Italy, Greece, and the Netherlands.

8. Muir, *Black Shoes and Blue Water,* 201–2; Bouchard, *Command in Crisis,* 142–45; Zumwalt, *On Watch,* 432–48.

9. Zumwalt, *On Watch,* 439–43.

10. Ibid.; Okun interview. At the time Okun was assigned as the political advisor to NATO's Southern Force Commander and was on loan to Warner to assist the secretary in meetings with local officials after a brawl between locals and American sailors.

11. Zumwalt, *On Watch,* 447.

12. Ibid., 446–47.

13. Weinel interview.

14. USDAO Moscow to JCS, 040924Z, May 1974, annotated by Rawlins, FOIA, DoD.

15. Train interview; Train, letter to author, 23 April 1994 (hereafter Train letter); Secretary's note to the JCS, JCS 1924/258, 29 April 1974, FOIA, DoD; 1974 Results of Consultation, n.d., Operational Archives, NHC.

16. Train letter.

17. Bouchard, *Command in Crisis,* 153–57; Assistant SecDef, memorandum to Director of Politico-Military Affairs, Subject: Implementation of Incidents at Sea Agreement, 14 Jan. 1974, FOIA, DoD; Draft Memorandum for the President, n.d., Operational Archives, NHC.

18. D. C. Hintze (USCG), letter to OP-616, 31 Dec. 1974, FOIA, DoD.

19. Amembassy Moscow, to SecDef/JCS, 211012Z, May 1974, FOIA, DoD.

20. Comdr. Richard Massey, USNR, served as an action officer within OP-616 from approximately 1991 through 1995.

21. 1974 U.S. Position Paper, Operational Archives, NHC.

22. 1978 U.S. Position Paper, Operational Archives, NHC.

23. 1974 U.S. Position Paper; 1978 U.S. Position Paper.

24. 1978 U.S. Position Paper; COMSIXTHFLT, 220711Z, Jan. 1977, to CINCUSNAVEUR London U.K., Subject: U.S.-U.S.S.R. Incidents at Sea (INCSEA) Agreement, Folder 1977 INCSEA Planning and Review, Operational Archives, NHC.

25. Train interview.

26. Assistant SecDef Eugene V. McAuliffe, letter to Director, Bureau of Political-Military Affairs George S. Vest, 2 Sept. 1976, Folder 1976 INCSEA Planning and Review, Operational Archives, NHC.

27. Brent Scowcroft, Memorandum for SecState and SecDef, 19 May 1976, Folder 1976 INCSEA Planning and Review; Zbigniew Brzezinski, Memorandum for Deputy SecDef, 3 June 1978, Subject: U.S.-U.S.S.R. Agreement on the Prevention of Incidents On and Over the High Seas, Folder 1978 Planning and Review, Operational Archives, NHC.

28. Captain Ellsworth, USN, interview by author, 2 March 1992, Washington, D.C. In a message to the U.S. defense attaché in Moscow after the May 1973 talks, it was reported that Captain Serkov possesses authority on INCSEA matters which surpasses his naval rank. CNO to USDAO Moscow, 252255Z, May 1973, Accession 9870-18, Box 4-6, Folder 1973 INCSEA Meeting, Operational Archives, NHC.

29. Kurth interview, 5 Sept. 1991. Kurth added that Weinel considered Serkov's complaint and decided not to extend an invitation.

30. Capt. William Manthorpe, USN (Ret.), interview by author, 3 March 1992, Washington, D.C.; Capt. Stephen Kime, USN (Ret.), interview by author, Washington, D.C., 12 March 1996.

31. Rear Adm. Robert P. Hilton Sr., USN (Ret.), interview by author, Alexandria, Va., 28 Nov. 1991. Melanson shared Hilton's and others' observations on Serkov's professionalism. Capt. Edward J. Melanson, USN (Ret.), interview by author, Washington, D.C., 4 Dec. 1991.

32. Melanson interview.

33. Weinel interview.

34. Ibid.

35. Capt. and Mrs. Rawlins interview.

36. Melanson, memorandum to Train, 1-3542/75, 2 April 1975, FOIA, DoD; Report of Incidents at Sea Meeting, undated, FOIA, DoD.

37. Melanson interview.

38. George Fedoroff, interview by author, Arlington, Va., 10 Jan. 1993; U.S./U.S.S.R. Seventh Review of Incidents at Sea Agreement, 20-29 May 1979, and William J. Crowe, letter to Malcolm S. Forbes, 29 May 1979, Folder INCSEA Planning 1979, Operational Archives, NHC.

39. Hilton and Fedoroff interviews.

40. Fedoroff interview.

41. Train interview.

42. Ibid.

43. Ibid.

44. Hilton interview.

45. Ibid.

46. Hilton and Fedoroff interviews.

47. Flanigan interview.

48. McDonald, letter to Middendorf, 26 June 1975, and Middendorf, letter to McDonald, 17 July 1975, FOIA, DoD.

49. Train interview.

50. Morgan, letter to Kissinger, 29 Oct. 1975, FOIA, State.

51. McCloskey, letter to Morgan, 24 Nov. 1975, FOIA, State; 1976 U.S. Position Paper, Operational Archives, NHC.

52. Derwinski, letter to Kissinger, 15 Dec. 1975, FOIA, State.

Chapter 9. The Age of the Evil Empire

1. John B. Hattendorf, "The Evolution of the Maritime Strategy: 1977 to 1987," *Naval War College Review* 41, no. 3/323 (Summer 1988): 8.

2. 1985 U.S. Position Paper, Operational Archives, NHC.

3. Roy A. Grossnick, *Dictionary of American Naval Aviation,* vol. 1 (Washington, D.C.: NHC, Department of the Navy, 1995), 531–32.

4. Lacouture, "Confrontation at Sea between the U.S. and Soviet Navies," III–8.

5. Zumwalt, *On Watch,* 360–63, 367–68.

6. *Understanding Soviet Naval Developments,* 15–16.

7. Lt. Comdr. John Rolph, USN, "Freedom of Navigation and the Black Sea Bumping: How 'Innocent' Must Innocent Passage Be?" *Military Law Review* 135 (Winter 1992): 146–47.

8. *The Commander's Handbook on the Law of Naval Operations: NWP 1-14M* (Washington, D.C.: Department of the Navy, Office of the Chief of Naval Operations, 1995), 2–12.

9. Operation Silver Fox briefing paper, 16 May 1973, Operational Archives, NHC.

10. Lt. Comdr. Charles Wallace, USNR, letter to author, 14 Feb. 1992.

11. Hattendorf, "Evolution of the Maritime Strategy," 9–10; Nathan Miller, *The U.S. Navy: A History* (New York: Quill, 1990), 272; John F. Lehman Jr., *Command of the Seas: Building the 600-Ship Navy* (New York: Scribner's, 1988), 117–18.

12. Hattendorf, "Evolution of the Maritime Strategy," 12–13, citing James M. McConnell, "Strategy and Missions of the Soviet Navy in the Year 2000," in *Problems of Sea Power as We Approach the Twenty-First Century,* ed. James L. George (Washington, D.C.: American Enterprise Institute for Public Policy Research, 1978), 61–62.

13. *Understanding Soviet Naval Developments,* 84–86, 88, 90.

14. Muir, *Black Shoes and Blue Water,* 200; Polmar, *Soviet Naval Power,* 45–46, cites these ships as having antiship missiles.

15. For a critique of the *Kiev,* emphasizing her role as an aircraft carrier, see Polmar, *Soviet Naval Power,* 53–54.

16. Hattendorf, "Evolution of the Maritime Strategy," 12–13.

17. Ibid., 10; Adm. William N. Small, USN (Ret.), interview by author, Naval Historical Foundation, Washington, D.C., 11 Oct. 1996 (hereafter Small interview).

18. Hattendorf, "Evolution in Maritime Strategy," 11.

19. Daniel J. Murphy, memorandum to Assistant SecDef, Subject: U.S.-U.S.S.R. Agreement on Prevention of Incidents On and Over the High Seas, 4 March 1980; Foley, letter to McGiffert, Subject: Soviet Violations of the Agreement between the United States of America and the Union of Soviet Socialist Republics for Prevention of Incidents On and Over the High Seas, 29 April 1980; Cifrino, memorandum to Melanson, Subject: Navy Proposal to Postpone the Conference Scheduled in Accordance with the Agreement on Prevention of Incidents On and Over the High Seas, 30 April 1980: all in Folder INCSEA Planning and Review—1980, Operational Archives, NHC.

20. Rear Adm. Robert P. Hilton Sr., USN (Ret.), interview by author, Arlington, Va., 28 Nov. 1991; Capt. Edward J. Melanson, USN (Ret.), interview by author, Washington, D.C., 4 Dec. 1991.

21. George Fedoroff, interview by author, Suitland, Md., 8 April 1992.

22. Program: Ninth Annual Review of U.S./U.S.S.R. Incidents at Sea, Folder 1981 Ninth Review; Caspar W. Weinberger, Memorandum for the Chairman, U.S. Delegation, 29 April 1982, Folder Tenth INCSEA Planning and Review, Operational Achives, NHC; news briefing transcript of Secretary Lehman, 10 June 1983, FOIA, DoD.

23. Lehman, *Command of the Seas,* 128–30; Hattendorf, "Evolution of the Maritime Strategy," 14; Small interview.

24. Lehman, *Command of the Seas,* 128–30; Hattendorf, "Evolution of the Maritime Strategy," 17–23.

25. Adm. James D. Watkins, USN, *The Maritime Strategy* (Annapolis, Md.: U.S. Naval Institute, Jan. 1986), 9–15; Joseph Metcalf, "The U.S. Maritime Strategy in Transition," in *East-West Relations in the 1990s: The Naval Dimension,* ed. John Pay and Geoffrey Till (New York: St. Martin's Press, 1990), 186–87.

26. Seymour M. Hersh, *The Target Is Destroyed: What Happened to Flight 007 and What America Knew about It* (New York: Random House, 1986), 18–19.

27. Rear Adm. Robert P. Hilton Sr., USN, "The U.S.-Soviet Incidents at Sea Treaty," *Naval Forces* 6, no. 1 (1985): 34. LCDR J. S. Nielson, Position Paper, Subject: USS *Lockwood* Alleged INCSEA Violations, 19 May 1982; CNO, message to USDAO Moscow, 081717Z, May 1982, Subject: Soviet Navy Response to Message on INCSEA Agreement, Folder 10th Review Planning and Review; OP-616 memorandum to OP-06, Subject: Incidents at Sea Review in Moscow, 26 July 1984, Folder 12th Annual Review, Operational Archives, NHC.

28. Rolph, "Freedom of Navigation and the Black Sea Bumping," 147, 157–58.

29. R. W. Johnson, *Shootdown: Flight 007 and the American Connection* (New York: Viking Press, 1986), 192–94.

30. Kurth interview, 18 Jan. 1991.

31. Kime interview; Sean Lynn-Jones, "The Incidents at Sea Agreement," in *U.S.-Soviet Security Cooperation: Achievements, Failures, Lessons,* ed. Alexander L. George, Philip J. Farley, and Alexander Dallin (New York: Oxford University Press, 1988), 488.

32. Joseph F. Bouchard, "Use of Naval Forces in Crisis: A Theory," Ph.D. diss., Stanford University, Stanford, Calif., 334, 370.

33. Lynn-Jones, "Incidents at Sea Agreement," 498–99; Rick Atkinson, "High Seas Diplomacy Continuing," *Washington Post,* 8 June 1984, A1, A15; Cyril Muromcew, notes on the May 1984 INCSEA Review Session in Moscow, Folder, 12th Annual Review, Operational Archives, NHC.

34. Muromcew interview, 2 Dec. 1992.

35. Cyril Muromcew, notes on the May 1984 INCSEA Review Session in Moscow, Folder 12th Annual Review, Operational Archives, NHC.

36. Kurth interview.

37. Hilton, "U.S.-Soviet Incidents at Sea Treaty," 37.

38. Watkins, letter to Hayward, 20 July 1984, Folder 1984 INCSEA General, Operational Archives, NHC; Lynn-Jones, "Incidents at Sea Agreement," 498; Melanson interview.

39. 1985 U.S. Position Paper, Operational Archives, NHC; SecState, message to Amembassy Moscow, 212217Z, Feb. 1985, FOIA, State.

40. Kurth interview.

41. Melanson interview.

42. Weinberger, memorandum for the Chairman, U.S. Delegation to U.S.-U.S.S.R. Review of the Incidents at Sea Agreement, Subject: Instructions to the U.S. Delegation, n.d., Operational Archives, NHC.

43. Kurth interview.

44. Warner interview.

45. Kime interview.

46. Kurth interview.

47. Senator Warner, letter to President Reagan, dated 19 June 1985, Warner papers.

48. Manthorpe interview.

49. Fedoroff interview.

50. Kurth interview.

51. Comdr. J. Bennett, memorandum to Admiral Crowe, 12 June 1985, Subject: INCSEA: Where Do We Go from Here?, and Craig Alderman, memorandum for Secretary Weinberger, Subject: Soviet Demarche on Incidents at Sea, Folder 13th INCSEA, Operational Archives, NHC.

52. Richard Perle, Memorandum for Major General Lary, Subject: Official Representation Funds/1985 U.S.-U.S.S.R. INCSEA Meeting, and D. S. Jones, memorandum for the CNO, Subject: Social Activity Associated with Annual Review of U.S.-U.S.S.R. Incidents at Sea Agreement, Folder 13th INCSEA, Operational Archives, NHC.

53. Welcoming Remarks by Vice Adm. D. S. Jones, USN, 11 Nov. 1985; Summary of Incidents Tables, 29 Oct. 1985; Lou Michael, memorandum to Dr. Ikle, Mr. Perle, n.d., Folder 13th INCSEA, Operational Archives, NHC.

54. Mustin interview. Mustin's reference to a Polish admiral alluded to an earlier briefing he had received discussing a recent Soviet Navy staff dressing down of a visiting admiral from the Polish Navy.

55. Memorandum for the record, Subject: 14th Annual INCSEA Review in Moscow, 18 June 1986; memorandum for the record, Subject: 14th Annual Incidents at Sea Review, 21 July 1986, Folder 14th Annual Review, Operational Archives, NHC.

56. Mustin interview; memorandum for the record, Subject: 14th Annual Incidents at Sea Review, 21 July 1986, Folder 14th Annual Review, Operational Archives, NHC.

57. Transcript, Folder 14th Annual Review, Operational Archives, NHC; Mustin interview.

58. 1987 U.S. Position Paper, Operational Archives, NHC; Mustin interview.

59. William H. J. Manthorpe Jr., "The Soviet Navy, 1987," U.S. Naval Institute Proceedings 5 (May 1988): 232–33. Ironically, Captain Zhuravlev's frigate Ladnyy had been assigned to intercept Yorktown and Caron in the Black Sea in March 1986.

60. Frank Elliot, "The Navy in 1987," U.S. Naval Institute Proceedings 5 (May 1987): 147.

61. Ibid., 147; Manthorpe, "The Soviet Navy, 1987," 231; USDAO Moscow to CNO, 211548Z, May 1987, Subject: Soviet Protest Violation of Their Territorial Waters by USN Ship, Folder INCSEA General 1987, Operational Archives, NHC.

62. Elliot, "The Navy in 1987," 147; Tom Burgess, "Armed U.S. Navy Bombers Fly Mock Raids at Soviet Base," *Washington Times,* 24 Nov. 1987, 1, 4.

63. USDAO Moscow, 291517Z, Jan. 1988, Subject: Soviet Gives Public Lecture, Folder INCSEA 87–88, Operational Archives, NHC.

64. "U.S., Soviet Naval Ships Collide Off Crimea," *The Current Digest of the Soviet Press* 7 (1986): 19–20.

65. John H. Cushman Jr., "2 Soviet Warships Reportedly Bump U.S. Navy Vessels," *New York Times,* 13 Feb. 1988, 1, 6; George C. Wilson, "Soviets Bump U.S. Ships in Black Sea," *Washington Post,* 13 Feb. 1988, A23; Philip Taubman, "Soviet Says It Hopes Provocation By U.S. at Sea Won't Hurt Talks," *New York Times,* 14 Feb. 1988, 1, 19; Gary Lee, "Soviets Protest Collision of Warships in Black Sea," *Washington Post,* 14 Feb. 1988, A46.

66. SecState to Amembassy Moscow, Subject: Protest Note on Black Sea Incident, 271949Z, Feb. 1988, FOIA, State; CNO to USDAO Moscow UR, Subject: Soviet INCSEA Violations, 122212Z, Feb. 1988, Folder Black Sea Ops, Operational Archives, NHC.

67. Action memorandum from Rozanne L. Ridgeway, H. Allen Holmes to Secretary, Subject: Responding to Senator Cranston's Concerns about Potential U.S.-Soviet Incidents, dated 16 March 1988, FOIA, State.

68. Memorandum for the record, Subject: 16th Annual Incidents at Sea (INCSEA) Review, 20 June 1988, Folder 1988 INCSEA Planning, Operational Archives, NHC; Mustin interview.

69. Robert P. Hilton, *A Workable Approach to Naval Arms Control: Development of Confidence-Building Measures at Sea* (Alexandria, Va.: Institute for Defense Analyses, 1990), 25–26, C-1, D-1–D-2.

70. Mustin interview.

71. Carlucci memorandum, Subject: Social Contacts with Soviet Officials, 1 July 1988, Folder 1988 INCSEA General, Operational Archives, NHC.

72. Mustin interview.

73. Sherry Sontag, Christopher Drew, and Annette Lawrence Drew, *Blind Man's Bluff: The Untold Story of American Submarine Espionage* (New York: Public Affairs, 1998), 266–69.

Epilogue

1. Vice Adm. I. Kasatonov, "Meetings Across the Sea," *Morskoy Sbornik* 11 (Nov. 1989): 34–37; Lt. Jeff Alderson, USN, "When the Russians Came to Town," *All Hands* (Nov. 1989): 19–20.

2. G. Ivanov, "When Stereotypes Are Broken," *Morskoy Sbornik* 11 (Nov. 1989): 37–39.

3. Lawrence J. Goodrich, *Christian Science Monitor,* 13 June 1989, 18.

4. Capt. 1st Rank V. Serkov, "From Confrontation to Cooperation," *Morskoy Sbornik* (Oct. 1990); Harry H. Almond Jr., "Dangerous Military Activities," U.S. Naval Institute *Proceedings* 115, no. 12 (Dec. 1989): 97–99.

5. During this period, Navy Staff Action Officers within N3/5 in the Pentagon included Captains Jim Byrant, James Voter, and Louis Hughes.

6. SecState, message to USMISSION NATO, 231500Z, May 1972, FOIA, State.

7. USMISSION NATO, message to SecState, 301105Z, April 1973, FOIA, State.

8. Vice Adm. Henry C. Mustin, USN (Ret.), interview by author, Arlington, Va., 9 April 1992.

9. Kurth interview, 18 Jan. 1991.

10. Comdr. Howard Sidman, USN, interview by author, Washington, D.C., 4 Dec. 1992.

11. Naval Attaché Capt. Dieter Leonhard, German Navy, letter to author, 19 March 1992 (hereafter Leonhard letter).

12. Hilton, *Workable Approach to Naval Arms Control,* 29.

13. Jan Prawitz, "A Multilateral Regime for Prevention of Incidents at Sea," in *Security at Sea,* ed. Richard Fieldhouse (New York: Oxford University Press, 1990), 220–25.

14. Capt. C. Hagg, RSwN, letter to author, 8 Jan. 1990.

15. Leonhard letter.

16. Sean M. Lynn-Jones, "Agreements to Prevent Incidents at Sea and Dangerous Military Activities: Potential Applications in the Asia-Pacific Region," Revision of paper for the ANU Peace Research Centre/ISIS Malaysia Workshop on Naval Confidence Building Regimes for the Asia-Pacific Region, Kuala Lumpur, Malaysia, 12 Aug. 1991. Lynn-Jones argues the feasibility and benefits of regional agreements in Northeast Asia and Southeast Asia. Since his presentation, Russia has signed INCSEA accords with Japan and Korea.

17. The author wrote the first draft, assisted with the final speech draft, and put together the accompanying visual presentation.

18. Peter Jones, "Maritime Confidence-Building Measures in the Middle East," in *Maritime Confidence-Building Measures in Regions of Tension,* ed. Jill Junnola (Washington: The Henry Stimson Center, 1996), 57–73. Since the March 1995 meeting, there has been little additional progress because of a lack of movement on the first track.

19. The author served as a consultant to the U.S. delegation.

20. Hilton, "U.S.-Soviet Incidents at Sea Treaty," 37.

Bibliography

Books

Athay, Robert E. "Perspectives on Soviet Merchant Shipping Policy." In *Soviet Naval Developments: Capability and Context*, ed. Michael MccGwire, 94–95. New York: Praeger, 1973.

Bamford, James. *The Puzzle Palace: A Report on America's Most Secret Agency.* Boston: Houghton Mifflin, 1982.

Barlow, Jeffrey G. *Revolt of the Admirals: The Fight for Naval Aviation.* Washington, D.C.: Naval Historical Center, 1994.

Beschloss, Michael R. *Mayday: The U-2 Affair.* New York: Perennial Library, 1987.

Blum, Howard. *I Pledge Allegiance. . .: The True Story of the Walkers: An American Spy Family.* New York: Simon and Schuster, 1987.

Bouchard, Joseph F. *Command in Crisis.* New York: Columbia University Press, 1991.

Brugioni, Dino A. *Eyeball to Eyeball: The Inside Story of the Cuban Missile Crisis.* New York: Random House, 1990.

Clancy, Tom. *The Hunt for Red October.* Annapolis, Md.: Naval Institute Press, 1984.

The Commander's Handbook on the Law of Naval Operations, NWP 1-14M. Washington, D.C.: Department of the Navy, Office of the Chief of Naval Operations, 1995.

The Development of the Strategic Air Command: 1946-1986. Offutt Air Force Base, Neb.: Office of the Historian, Headquarters, Strategic Air Command, 1986.

Franklin, H. Bruce. *M.I.A. or Mythmaking in America.* Brooklyn, N.Y.: Lawrence Hill Books, 1992.

George, Alexander. *RM-1349: Case Studies of Actual and Alleged Overflights, 1930–1953.* Santa Monica, Calif.: The Rand Corporation, 1955.

Gorshkov, Sergei. *The Seapower of the State.* Annapolis, Md.: Naval Institute Press, 1979.

Grossnick, Roy A. *Dictionary of American Naval Aviation.* Vol. 1. Washington, D.C.: Naval Historical Center, 1995.

Herken, Gregg. *The Winning Weapon: The Atomic Bomb in the Cold War, 1945–1950.* New York: Knopf, 1980.

Herrick, Robert W. *Soviet Naval Strategy: Fifty Years of Theory and Practice.* Annapolis, Md.: Naval Institute Press, 1968.

Hersh, Seymour M. *The Target Is Destroyed: What Happened to Flight 007 and What America Knew about It.* New York: Random House, 1986.

Hilsman, Roger. *To Move a Nation: The Politics of Foreign Policy in the Administration of John F. Kennedy.* Garden City, N.Y.: Doubleday, 1967.

Hilton, Robert P., Sr. *A Workable Approach to Naval Arms Control: Development of Confidence-Building Measures at Sea.* Alexandria, Va.: Institute for Defense Analyses, November 1990.

Isenberg, Michael T. *Shield of the Republic: The United States Navy in an Era of Cold War and Violent Peace, 1945–1962.* New York: St. Martin's Press, 1993.

Isaacson, Walter. *Kissinger.* New York: Simon and Schuster, 1992.

Johnson, R. W. *Shootdown: Flight 007 and the American Connection.* New York: Viking Press, 1986.

Jones, Peter. "Maritime Confidence Building Measures in the Middle East." In *Maritime Confidence Building Measures in Regions of Tension,* ed. Jill Junnola, 57–73. Washington, D.C.: The Henry Stimson Center, 1996.

Kalb, Marvin, and Bernard Kalb. *Kissinger.* Boston: Little, Brown, 1974.

Kissinger, Henry A. *The White House Years.* Boston: Little, Brown, 1979.

Lehman, John F., Jr. *Command of the Seas: Building the 600-Ship Navy.* New York: Scribner's, 1988.

Lynn-Jones, Sean M. "The Incidents at Sea Agreement." In *U.S.-Soviet Security Cooperation: Achievements, Failures, Lessons,* ed. Alexander L. George, Philip J. Farley, and Alexander Dallin, 482–509. New York: Oxford University Press, 1988.

Marolda, Edward J. *By Sea, Air and Land: An Illustrated History of the U.S. Navy and the War in Southeast Asia.* Washington, D.C.: Naval Historical Center, 1994.

MccGwire, Michael. "The Evolution of Soviet Naval Policy: 1960–74." In *Soviet Naval Policy: Objectives and Constraints,* ed. Michael MccGwire, Ken Booth, and John McDonnell, 506. New York: Praeger, 1975.

Meconis, Charles A., and Boris N. Makeev. *U.S.-Russian Naval Cooperation.* Westport, Conn.: Praeger, 1996.

Metcalf, Joseph. "The U.S. Maritime Strategy in Transition." In *East-West Relations in the 1990s: The Naval Dimension,* ed. John Pay and Geoffrey Till, 186–87. New York: St. Martin's Press, 1990.

Miller, Marvin O., John W. Hammett, and Terence P. Murphy. "Development of the U.S. Navy Underway Replenishment Fleet." In *Underway Replenishment of Naval Ships,* 45–59. Port Hueneme, Calif.: Underway Replenishment Department Port Hueneme Division, Naval Surface Warfare Center, 1992.

Miller, Nathan. *The U.S. Navy: A History.* New York: Morrow, 1990.

Muir, Malcolm, Jr. *Black Shoes and Blue Water: Surface Warfare in the United States Navy, 1945–1975.* Washington, D.C.: Naval Historical Center, 1996.

Oberg, James E. *Uncovering Soviet Disasters: Exploring the Limits of Glasnost.* New York: Random House, 1988.

Palmer, Michael A. *Origins of the Maritime Strategy: The Development of American Naval Strategy, 1945–1955.* Annapolis, Md.: Naval Institute Press, 1990.

Pay, John, and Geoffrey Till, eds. *East-West Relations in the 1990s: The Naval Dimension.* New York: St. Martin's Press, 1990.

Polmar, Norman. *Soviet Naval Power: Challenge for the 1970s.* Revised ed. New York: Crane, Russak, 1974.

Prawitz, Jan. "A Multilateral Regime for Prevention of Incidents at Sea." In *Security at Sea,* ed. Richard Fieldhouse, 220–25. New York: Oxford University Press, 1990.

Ranft, Bryan, and Geoffrey Till. *The Sea in Soviet Strategy.* 2nd ed. Annapolis, Md.: Naval Institute Press, 1989.

Richelson, Jeffrey. *American Espionage and the Soviet Target.* New York: Morrow, 1987.

Sanders, James D., Mark A. Sauter, and R. Cort Kirkwood. *Soldiers of Misfortune: Washington's Secret Betrayal of American POWs in the Soviet Union.* Washington, D.C.: National Press Books, 1992.

Schoenbaum, Thomas J. *Waging Peace and War: Dean Rusk in the Truman, Kennedy and Johnson Years.* New York: Simon and Schuster, 1988.

Sheehan, Neil. *A Bright Shining Lie: John Paul Vann and America in Vietnam.* New York: Vintage Books, 1989.

Sontag, Sherry, Christopher Drew, and Annette Lawrence Drew. *Blind Man's Bluff: The Untold Story of American Submarine Espionage.* New York: Public Affairs, 1998.

Understanding Soviet Naval Developments. 3rd ed. Washington D.C.: Office of the Chief of Naval Operations, Department of the Navy, 1978.

Watkins, James D. *The Maritime Strategy.* Annapolis, Md.: U.S. Naval Institute, 1986.

Weir, Gary E. *Forged in War: The Naval-Industrial Complex and American Submarine Construction, 1940–1960.* Washington D.C.: Naval Historical Center, 1993.

Wildenberg, Thomas. *Gray Steel and Black Oil: Fast Tankers and Replenishment at Sea in the U.S. Navy, 1912–1992.* Annapolis, Md.: Naval Institute Press, 1996.

Zimmerman, Carrol L. *Insider at SAC: Operations Analyst under General LeMay.* Manhattan, Kan.: Sunflower University Press, 1988.

Zumwalt, Elmo R., Jr. *On Watch.* New York: Quadrangle Press, 1976.

Dissertations and Papers

Alger, Julie. "A Review of the Technical Research Ship Program." Report, National Security Agency, Fort Meade, Md., n.d.

Bouchard, Joseph F. "Use of Naval Forces in Crisis: A Theory." Ph.D. diss., Stanford University, Stanford, Calif., 1989.

Farquhar, John T. "A Need to Know: The Role of Air Force Reconnaissance in War Planning, 1945–1953." M.A. thesis, Ohio State University, Columbus, 1991.

Hanks, Robert J., "Middle East Journal: U.S. Naval Diplomacy in the Middle East, 1972–75." 1989, rev. 1993.

Lacouture, John E. "The Confrontation at Sea between the U.S. and Soviet Navies." M. Litt. diss., University of Cambridge, Cambridge, 1979.

Lynn-Jones, Sean M. "Agreements to Prevent Incidents at Sea and Dangerous Military Activities: Potential Applications in the Asia-Pacific Region." Kuala Lumpur, Malaysia: ANU Peace Research Centre/ISIS Naval Confidence Building Regimes for the Asia-Pacific Region Workshop, 1991.

Tritten, James J., and Boris N. Makeev. "Strategic Antisubmarine Warfare and ASW-Free Zones: Good Ideas Today?" 1993. Photocopied.

Periodicals

Alderson, Jeff. "When the Russians Came to Town." *All Hands* (November 1989): 19.

Aleksin, V. "We Are Ready When You Are." U.S. Naval Institute *Proceedings* 119, no. 3 (March 1993): 54–57.

Almond, Harry H., Jr. "Dangerous Military Activities." U.S. Naval Institute *Proceedings* 115, no. 12 (December 1989): 97–99.

Chapman, Capt. William C., USN (Ret.). "Steve Brody and the *Banshee.*" *Foundation* (Spring 1993): 44.

Gorshkov, Sergei G. "Razvitie Sovetskogo Voenno-morshogo iskusstva" ("Development of Soviet Naval Art"). *Morskoy Sbornik,* no. 2 (February 1967): 19–20.

Hall, R. Cargill. "Strategic Reconnaissance in the Cold War: From Concept to National Policy." *Prologue* 29, no. 2 (Summer 1996): 107–25.

———. "The Truth about Overflights: Military Reconnaissance Missions over Russia before the U-2." *Quarterly Journal of Military History* (Spring 1997): 25–39.

Hattendorf, John B. "The Evolution of the Maritime Strategy: 1977 to 1987." *Naval War College Review* 41, no. 3 (Summer 1988): 17–23.

Hilton, Robert P., Sr. "The U.S.-Soviet Incidents at Sea Treaty." *Naval Forces* 6, no. 1 (1985): 30–37.

Ivanov, G. "When Stereotypes Are Broken." *Morskoy Sbornik* 11 (November 1989): 37–39.

Jacobs, G. "Soviet Navy AGIS." *Jane's Soviet Intelligence Review* (July 1989): 318–23.

Kasatonov, I. "Meetings Across the Sea." *Morskoy Sbornik* 11 (November 1989): 34–37.

McDonnell, Jerry. "Incident in History: Intercept of *Marcula*." *All Hands*, no. 551 (Dec. 1962).

McNeill, John H. "Military-to-Military Arrangements for the Prevention of U.S.-Russian Conflict." *Naval War College Review* 47, no. 2 (Spring 1994): 23–29.

Miasnikov, Eugene "Submarine Collision off Murmansk: A Look from Afar." *Breakthroughs* 2, no. 2 (Winter 1992/93): 19–23.

Richelson, Jeffrey T. "Task Force 157: The US Navy's Secret Intelligence Service, 1966–1977." *Intelligence and National Security* 11 (January 1996): 106–45.

Roche, John E. "Incident in the Sea of Japan." *Readers Digest* (September 1957): 25–27.

Rolph, John. "Freedom of Navigation and the Black Sea Bumping: How 'Innocent' Must Innocent Passage Be?" *Military Law Review* 135 (Winter 1992): 146–58.

"Secrets of the Cold War." *U.S. News and World Report*, 15 March 1993, 30, 32.

Serkov, V. "From Confrontation to Cooperation." *Morskoy Sbornik* (October 1990).

Trofimov, Vladimir, A. "When Putsch Came to Shove." U.S. Naval Institute *Proceedings* 118, no. 3 (March 1992): 55–58.

"U.S. Hits Actions by Soviet Ships." U.S. Naval Institute *Proceedings* (December 1964): 150.

"U.S., Soviet Naval Ships Collide Off Crimea." *The Current Digest of the Soviet Press* 7 (1986): 19–20.

Wolf, Anthony F. "Agreement at Sea: The United States-USSR Agreement on Incidents at Sea." *Korean Journal of International Studies* 9, no. 3 (1978): 57–80.

Government Documents

Command history files. U.S. Air Force Historical Research Agency, Maxwell Air Force Base, Montgomery, Ala.

Department of Defense, Washington, D.C.

Department of State, Washington, D.C.

Files of the Deputy Chief of Naval Operations for Policy and Planning. Operational Archives, Naval Historical Center, Washington, D.C.

President's Secretaries files. Harry S. Truman Library, Independence, Mo.

Record Group 59, Lot 64D551. National Archives, Washington, D.C.

Record Group 59, State Department Central Foreign Policy Files. National Archives, Washington, D.C.

Record Group 273, National Security Council Papers. National Archives, Washington, D.C.

Personal Papers

Hilton, Robert P., Sr. Alexandria, Virginia.

Warner, John W. Office of Senator John W. Warner, Washington, D.C.

Oral Interviews

Congdon, Capt. Robert N., USN (Ret.). Interview by author, San Diego, Calif., 18 May 1992.

Cullins, Rear Adm. Peter K., USN (Ret.). Interview by author, Washington, D.C., 19 February 1998.

Fedoroff, George. Interviews by author, Arlington, Va., 8 April 1992 and 10 January 1993.

Flanigan, Capt. Mark. USNR (Ret.). Interview by author, Washington, D.C., 27 March 1997.

Herrick, Comdr. Robert W. USN (Ret.). Interview by author, 3 October 1996. Transcript, Oral History Collection, Naval Historical Foundation, Washington, D.C.

Hetu, Capt. Herbert E. USN (Ret.). Interview by Paul Stillwell, 1996. Transcript. U.S. Naval Institute Oral History Program, Annapolis, Md.

Hilton, Rear Adm. Robert P., Sr., USN (Ret.). Interviews by author, Alexandria, Va., 28 November 1991 and 29 January 1997.

Holloway, Adm. James L., III, USN (Ret.). Interview by author, Washington, D.C., 21 May 1997.

Kidd, Adm. Isaac, USN. Interview by Alex Kucherov, 8 July 1971. Photocopied transcript provided by OpNav.

Kime, Capt. Steve, USN (Ret.). Interview by author, Washington, D.C., 12 March 1996.

Kurth, Rear Adm. Ronald J., USN (Ret.). Interviews by author, Murray, Ky., 18 January and 5 September 1991.

LeMay, Gen. Curtis E., USAF. Interview by John T. Bohn, March Air Force Base, Calif., 9 March 1971. USAF Oral History Program, U.S. Air Force Historical Research Center, Maxwell Air Force Base, Ala.

Lynch, Capt. William C., JAGC, USN (Ret.). Interview by author, San Diego, 18 May 1992.

Manthorpe, Capt. William H. J., USN (Ret.). Interview by author, Washington, D.C., 3 March 1992.

Melanson, Capt. Edward J., USN (Ret.). Interview by author, Washington, D.C., 4 December 1991.

Miller, Vice Adm. Gerald E. USN (Ret.). Interview by John T. Mason, 1984. Transcript. U.S. Naval Institute Oral History Program, Annapolis, Md.

Muromcew, Cyril. Interview by author, Washington, D.C., 2 December 1991.

Mustin, Vice Adm. Henry C., Jr., USN (Ret.). Interview by author, Arlington, Va., 9 April 1992.

Okun, Herbert S. Interview by author, New York, N.Y., 25 February 1992.

Rawlins, Capt. Robert, USN (Ret.). Interview by author, Healdsburg, Calif., 29 March 1992.

Sidman, Comdr. Howard, USN. Interview by author, Washington, D.C., 4 December 1991.

Small, Adm. William N., USN (Ret.). Interview by author, Naval Historical Foundation, Washington, D.C., 11 Oct. 1996.

Train, Adm. Harry D., II, USN (Ret.). Interview by Paul Stillwell, 17 July 1996. Transcript. U.S. Naval Institute Oral History Program, Annapolis, Md.

Warner, John W. Interview by author, Washington, D.C., 9 April 1992.

Weinel, Adm. J. P., USN (Ret.). Interview by author, Bonsall, Calif., 17 May 1992.

Zumwalt, Adm. Elmo R., Jr., USN (Ret.). Interview by author, Arlington, Va., 30 June 1992.

Correspondence

Congdon, Capt. Robert N., USN (Ret.), to author, 10 March and 11 August 1992.

Dickens, Capt. Russ, USN (Ret.), to author, 7 May 1992.

Doyle, Vice Adm. James H., USN (Ret.), to author, 8 and 20 July 1992.

Hagg, Capt. C., RSwN, to author, 8 January 1990.

Hayward, Adm. Thomas B., USN (Ret.), to author, 10 July 1992.

Laird, Melvin, to author, 1 May and 9 July 1992.

Leonhard, Capt. Dieter, German Navy, to author, 19 March 1992.

Rawlins, Capt. Robert D., USN (Ret.), to author, 13 March and 21 August 1992.

Train, Adm. Harry D., II, USN (Ret.), to author, 23 April 1992.

Wallace, Lt. Comdr. Charles, USNR, to author, 14 February 1992.

Index

agreement 7, 106–7; annual reviews (1970s), 111–17, 123–25; annual reviews (1980s), 143, 148–51, 153–56, 160–61; annual reviews (1990s), 166; delegations, 127–28; extended to commercial ships, 116; and FON, 140; and KAL 007 downing, 147, 149; and navy-to-navy communication, 135; publicity about, 134, 174; social activities during, 108–9, 113, 125, 129–34, 143, 150–53, 155, 161, 174; and dissolution of Soviet Union, 166; success of, 123–24, 173–75; talks with other nations, 167–71, 170n; violations of, 111, 123, 125–26, 137–38, 153, 156. *See also* safety-at-sea talks

Independence, 65, 120

Indian Ocean, 138

Ingur, 43

intelligence gathering. *See* reconnaissance

Intermediate Nuclear Forces, 160

International Court of Justice, 14, 17, 19, 25

International Rules of the Road: 30, 48, 54, 56, 173; INCSEA addresses, 106; and Memorandum of Understanding, 91; as basis of safety-at-sea talks, 86; and violations by Soviet commercial ships, 45

Iran Ajr, 157

Iranian revolution, 137–39

Iraq-Iran War, 145–46, 156

Ivan Koroteyev, 157

Ivan Polzunov, 42

Ivan Shepetkov, 157

James Madison, 64

Jarrett, 157

John F. Kennedy, 65, 135

Johnson, Louis, 13

Johnson, Lyndon B. (administration of), 43–44, 55, 57–58, 61–62

Johnson, U. Alexis, 32, 45, 75, 113

Jones, D. S., 153

Jordanian Crisis, 65–66

Joseph P. Kennedy Jr., 41

Josephus Daniels, 140

Juliett-class submarine, 1

KAL (Korean Airlines) 007, 146–47

Kapitan Vislobokov, 59

Kara-class ships, 141–42

Kasatonov, Igor V., 163–64

Kasatonov, Vladimir A.: career history of, 84; and fixed distances, 91, 103–4, 106; and INCSEA, 106, 123–24, 126, 133, 167; meets with U.S. navy representatives, 113; and Memorandum of Understanding, 92; and Nixon, 87, 100–102; and safety-at-sea talks, 85–86, 94–96; and John Warner, 89, 109

Kashin-class ships, 5–6, 51, 141–42

Kasimov, 40

Katzenbach, Nicholas deB., 59, 61

Kaufmann, 164

Kennedy, John F. (administration of), 24, 40, 49

Keywadin, 30

Khariton Laptev, 64

Khrushchev, Nikita: and Cuban Missile Crisis, 49; and RB-47 downing, 22–24; and Soviet Navy, 27–28, 50

Khumbarov, Konstantin M., 158

About the Author

David F. Winkler, a resident of Alexandria, Virginia, is the historian and director of Programs and Development with the Naval Historical Foundation, located in Washington, D.C. With a special interest in the Cold War, he has published several historical context studies for the Department of Defense examining the U.S. military infrastructure and has contributed articles to *Sea Power, Proceedings, Sea History,* and *The Naval Review.* He holds a bachelor's degree in political science from Penn State, a master's degree in international affairs from Washington University, and a Ph.D. in history from American University. A surface warfare officer and Naval War College graduate, he served on active duty for ten years and is currently a commander in the Naval Reserve.

The Naval Institute Press is the book-publishing arm of the U.S. Naval Institute, a private, nonprofit, membership society for sea service professionals and others who share an interest in naval and maritime affairs. Established in 1873 at the U.S. Naval Academy in Annapolis, Maryland, where its offices remain today, the Naval Institute has members worldwide.

Members of the Naval Institute support the education programs of the society and receive the influential monthly magazine *Proceedings* and discounts on fine nautical prints and on ship and aircraft photos. They also have access to the transcripts of the Institute's Oral History Program and get discounted admission to any of the Institute-sponsored seminars offered around the country.

The Naval Institute also publishes *Naval History* magazine. This colorful bi-monthly is filled with entertaining and thought-provoking articles, first-person reminiscences, and dramatic art and photography. Members receive a discount on *Naval History* subscriptions.

The Naval Institute's book-publishing program, begun in 1898 with basic guides to naval practices, has broadened its scope in recent years to include books of more general interest. Now the Naval Institute Press publishes about one hundred titles each year, ranging from how-to books on boating and navigation to battle histories, biographies, ship and aircraft guides, and novels. Institute members receive discounts of 20 to 50 percent on the Press's more than eight hundred books in print.

Full-time students are eligible for special half-price membership rates. Life memberships are also available.

For a free catalog describing Naval Institute Press books currently available, and for further information about subscribing to *Naval History* magazine or about joining the U.S. Naval Institute, please write to:

Membership Department
U.S. Naval Institute
291 Wood Road
Annapolis, MD 21402-5034
Telephone: (800) 233-8764
Fax: (410) 269-7940
Web address: www.usni.org